THE EVERYTHING HEALTHY PRESSURE COOKER COOKBOOK

Dear Reader,

When it came time to write this book, I knew that I wanted to include recipes that could not only be cooked in any kind of pressure cooker, but also did not require processed ingredients like canned beans, packaged soups, bullion cubes, and flavor packets. This, after all, is how I cook for my family anyway, so it was a pleasure to share my secrets with you.

You can thank my second child, who cried for almost the entire first two years of her life—except for two 20 minute naps every 24 hours—for giving me the perfect reason to start using a pressure cooker: I needed to cook more nutritious meals in less time (or for however long I could hold a writhing, screaming child in one arm while cooking dinner with the other!).

When I was invited to a friend's house for dinner, I watched her prepare a complete, delicious meal with her pressure cooker in about 15 minutes. I knew at that moment that I *had* to have this wondrous, amazing, noisy thing that could feed an entire family in no time! After she patiently showed me how to use it, I could not tear myself away from the pressure cooker and started to pressure cook everything in sight.

I hope that once you discover the time, flavor, energy, and vitamin-saving wonders of pressure cooking, you will do the same! I especially hope you'll find this cookbook to be helpful as you explore the world of healthier eating with pressure cooking.

For more recipes, tips, and pressure cooker reviews, please visit my website: www.hippressurecooking.com.

Laura D. A. Pazzaglia

Welcome to the EVERYTHING® Series!

These handy, accessible books give you all you need to tackle a difficult project, gain a new hobby, comprehend a fascinating topic, prepare for an exam, or even brush up on something you learned back in school but have since forgotten.

You can choose to read an Everything® book from cover to cover or just pick out the information you want from our four useful boxes: e-questions, e-facts, e-alerts, and e-ssentials.

We give you everything you need to know on the subject, but throw in a lot of fun stuff along the way, too.

We now have more than 400 Everything® books in print, spanning such wide-ranging categories as weddings, pregnancy, cooking, music instruction, foreign language, crafts, pets, New Age, and so much more. When you're done reading them all, you can finally say you know Everything®!

QUESTION

Answers to common questions

FACT

Important snippets of information

ALERT

Urgent warnings

ESSENTIAL

Quick handy tips

PUBLISHER Karen Cooper

MANAGING EDITOR, EVERYTHING® SERIES Lisa Laing

COPY CHIEF Casey Ebert

ASSISTANT PRODUCTION EDITOR Melanie Cordova

ACQUISITIONS EDITOR Lisa Laing

DEVELOPMENT EDITOR Eileen Mullan

EDITORIAL ASSISTANT Matthew Kane

EVERYTHING® SERIES COVER DESIGNER Erin Alexander

LAYOUT DESIGNERS Erin Dawson, Michelle Roy Kelly, Elisabeth Lariviere

Visit the entire Everything® series at *www.everything.com*

THE EVERYTHING®

Healthy
Pressure Cooker
Cookbook

Laura D. A. Pazzaglia

Founder of hippressurecooking.com

Avon, Massachusetts

To my brave husband, Roberto, who begrudgingly eats my pressure cooker experiments and enthusiastically praises the successes.

An Everything® Series Book.
Everything® and everything.com® are registered trademarks of F+W Media, Inc.

Published by Adams Media, a division of F+W Media, Inc.
57 Littlefield Street, Avon, MA 02322 U.S.A.
www.adamsmedia.com

ISBN 10: 1-4405-4186-8
ISBN 13: 978-1-4405-4186-5
eISBN 10: 1-4405-4187-6
eISBN 13: 978-1-4405-4187-2

Printed in the United States of America.

10 9 8 7 6 5 4 3 2 1

The Everything® Healthy Pressure Cooker Cookbook contains material adapted and abridged from *The Everything® Pressure Cooker Cookbook* by Pamela Rice Hahn, copyright © 2009 by F+W Media, Inc., ISBN 10: 1-4405-0017-7, ISBN-13: 978-1-4405-0017-6; *The Everything® Vegetarian Pressure Cooker Cookbook* by Amy Snyder and Justin Snyder, copyright © 2010 by F+W Media, Inc., ISBN 10: 1-4405-0672-8, ISBN-13: 978-1-4405-0672-7; and *The Everything® Healthy Slow Cooker Cookbook* by Rachel Rappaport with B. E. Horton, MS, RD, copyright © 2010 by F+W Media, Inc., ISBN 10: 1-4405-0231-5, ISBN-13: 978-1-4405-0231-6; *The $7 a Meal Pressure Cooker Cookbook* by Susan Irby, copyright © 2010 by F+W Media, Inc., ISBN 10: 1-4405-0654-X, ISBN 13: 978-1-4405-0654-3.

Always follow safety and commonsense cooking protocol while using kitchen utensils, operating ovens and stoves, and handling uncooked food. If children are assisting in the preparation of any recipe, they should always be supervised by an adult.

Many of the designations used by manufacturers and sellers to distinguish their products are claimed as trademarks. Where those designations appear in this book and Adams Media was aware of a trademark claim, the designations have been printed with initial capital letters.

Nutritional statistics by Nicole Cormier, RD.
Photos courtesy of *www.hippressurecooking.com.*

This book is available at quantity discounts for bulk purchases.
For information, please call 1-800-289-0963.

Contents

Introduction 9

1   Pressure Cooking Basics 11

The Benefits of Pressure Cooking 12

What Is Pressure Cooking, Anyway? 12

Types of Pressure Cookers 13

Pressure Cooker Dos and Don'ts 14

Heat Sources for Pressure Cooking 15

Pressure Cooking in Five Easy Steps 16

Opening Methods 17

High and Low Pressure 17

Pressure Cooker Accessories 18

About the Recipes in This Book 18

2   Appetizers 19

3   Vegetables and Sides 31

4   Stocks, Soups, and Chowders 69

5   Legumes 93

6 Chicken and Turkey. 113

7 Beef and Veal 129

8 Pork, Lamb, and Game. 143

9 Fish and Seafood 158

10 One-Pot Meals 172

11 Pasta Sauces. 195

12 Pasta, Rice, and Grains 202

13 Condiments and Preserves. 234

14 Fruits and Desserts. 255

Appendix A: Pressure Cooker Buying Tips 282
Appendix B: Pressure Cooking Times 286
Standard U.S./Metric Measurement Conversions 293

Index. 294

Acknowledgments

A big thanks to pressure cooker manufacturers Fagor, Kuhn Rikon, Magefesa, and Instant Pot for supplying the equipment to develop and test these recipes, to the readers of *www.hippressurecooking.com* for leaving your recipe feedback and critique, and especially to my readers JL Fields and Jen Smith for agreeing to share their recipes with you in this book. Thank you!

Introduction

THE FIRST PRESSURE COOKER was invented by the French physicist and mathematician Denis Papin in 1689. While the popularity of using the pressure cooker to prepare meals has waxed and waned over the years since, it has most recently become an essential tool for busy moms, environmentally conscious cooks, and even molecular gastronomists.

The pressure cooker has come a long way since Papin's initial invention, which was nicknamed the "bone digester" because of its ability to soften bones and extract nutrients; the high-pressure environment renders them brittle enough to be easily ground into bone meal. But it is important to note that the transformation from Papin's "bone digester" to the pressure cooker we know today really began in 1920. It was at this time that a large, industrial model was first produced and sold in France.

A short time later, at the 1926 Home Exhibition in Paris, the first pressure cooker model for home use was introduced, and thirteen years after that, in 1939, the National Pressure Cooker Company, now known as National Presto Industries, Inc., launched the first U.S. model at the New York Fair.

It didn't take long for aluminum pressure cookers to become a popular cooking tool in the United States, and for many companies to begin producing them regularly. By the start of World War II, pressure cookers were well used and loved in American homes, especially for pressure canning, but also directly for cooking. Then the war effort halted the production of pressure cookers. According to the Oregon State Archives, in 1943, the State Nutrition Committee, which was formed by The Oregon State Defense Council in 1941, released a bulletin that encouraged homemakers to start forming "canning circles" to better utilize resources. It even suggested that six or more families share each cooker and the preparation of the fruits and vegetables for canning and cooking.

In 1943, the National Pressure Cooker Company published this statement in *Life* magazine:

The manufacturing facilities of the makers of Presto Cookers
are now devoted to war production. Once victory is won—
there will be Presto Cookers for everybody. Until then, if you
own one, share it, won't you? It's a good neighbor policy.

The National Pressure Cooker Company kept its promise. By the end of the war, it was back to making pressure cookers, and many other factories that had originally produced weapons tried their hand at making pressure cookers as well. However, many of these factories produced poor-quality cookers. The market was flooded with subpar pressure cookers lacking basic safety controls (which is why you should never buy or put a vintage cooker into use, unless it has the required safety controls).

At the same time, the opposite was happening in Europe. German, French, and Spanish manufacturers were creating innovative two-pressure systems, redundant safety mechanisms, quiet, spring-valve operations, and new designs and features. These high-quality cookers helped the European companies to steadily increase and maintain market share.

Then, in the 1990s, European-manufactured pressure cookers began appearing in American stores. In 1991, Yong-Guang Wang, a Chinese scientist, filed what is believed to be the first electric pressure cooker patent. Though electric pressure cookers are a technological improvement over stovetop—removing the need to carefully watch and regulate the heat—the less durable materials and lower operating pressure (resulting in longer cooking times) of electric models has yet to convince owners of stovetop pressure cookers to make the switch.

Fortunately for the pressure cooker, today's interest in reducing carbon footprints and consuming more whole grains and legumes, not to mention the limited time available for cooking healthy meals, has produced the perfect opportunity to bring this tool back into U.S. homes as a trusted kitchen helper.

CHAPTER 1

Pressure Cooking Basics

The pressure cooker's time- and energy-saving properties make it a perfect partner for a healthier lifestyle. It opens up the possibilities of eating more whole grains (which take just minutes to prepare in a pressure cooker instead of hours with other methods), using dried beans instead of canned (to control the amount of sugar and preservatives), making preserves and conserves in minutes (you decide how much sugar to add), and steaming vegetables in a flash—preserving their taste, color, and most importantly . . . vitamins!

The Benefits of Pressure Cooking

The pressure cooker is a miracle appliance that can save you time and money, help your food retain its health-promoting vitamins, and make your cooking process greener by cutting down on the amount of energy you use.

Pressure Cooking Saves Time and Money

With a pressure cooker, cooking time can be reduced 60–90 percent (depending on the food). For instance, a vegetable stock can be ready in 5 minutes. Roasts can be ready in 30 minutes, legumes in 15 minutes, and desserts in just 20 minutes, instead of an hour in the oven! Using a pressure cooker also means that you can save money by cooking legumes alongside dry, tough cuts of meat.

ESSENTIAL

Don't ever throw away your produce again! With a pressure cooker, you can make quick use of veggies and fruits that might be past their prime and would otherwise go to waste.

Pressure Cooking Saves Vitamins and Energy

Pressure cooking can save 90–95 percent of the vitamins in your food. This is compared to steaming without pressure, which only saves 75–90 percent of vitamins, and boiling, which saves 40–65 percent. Since food cooks faster in a pressure cooker and you are using less heat than regular cooking, you will also see a significant decrease in the amount of energy you use when preparing a meal. With a pressure cooker, you will need approximately 30 percent less fuel than conventional cooking. It is also worth noting that since pressure cooking generates very little heat, using the pressure cooker in the summer will not put any additional strain on your air conditioning by heating up the house.

What Is Pressure Cooking, Anyway?

When cooking regularly, you put a lid on the pot and slow down evaporation. When pressure cooking, the lid locks shut and the evaporating liquid has nowhere to go, so it raises the internal pressure of the cooker. This rise in pressure directly corresponds to a rise in temperature, which in turn raises the maximum temperature at which food can cook by boiling liquid from 212°F to 250°F.

Types of Pressure Cookers

There are three main types of pressure cookers: first generation cookers, second generation cookers, and third generation cookers. Each generation is identified by the heat source (electric versus stovetop) and the way the cooker maintains pressure.

First Generation Weight-Modified or Jiggling Pressure Cookers

The first pressure cookers were weight-modified cookers.

In weight-modified pressure cookers, the sound is more of a "Shhhhhck!" but this is also referred to as a "whistle."

For the weight-modified cooker, the pressure valve goes up and down to maintain pressure and release excess. For Jiggling pressure cookers, when pressure is reached, the metal weight wiggles and jiggles to slowly let out small amounts of excess pressure. Generally, these cookers are very noisy, and most only have one pressure and require a very high amount of heat to operate (usually medium heat).

Second Generation Pressure Cookers

Spring-valve pressure cookers have a valve that is either a visible spring or a spring encased in a pressure-regulating mechanism. This spring holds the valve closed until the internal pressure is exceeded, and then it releases excess pressure. These pressure cookers boast a very quiet operation and need very little heat to maintain pressure (low or very low heat).

Third Generation Pressure Cookers

Electric pressure cookers, like second generation cookers, also operate very quietly. These pressure cookers use a floating valve similar to a weight-modified valve that does not need to raise and vent in order to release excess pressure. Instead, these cookers regulate pressure based on the internal temperature (i.e. using the temperature to regulate pressure versus an actual spring that resists pressure). Many have scheduling features that can delay pressure cooking until a certain time, as well as a keep-warm setting. However, these models can be less efficient when compared to a stovetop pressure cooker on a gas cooktop.

ALERT

Don't fear the pressure cooker! Today's modern pressure cookers are equipped with safety features to prevent mishaps.

Pressure Cooker Dos and Don'ts

While modern pressure cookers have multiple safety mechanisms in place to avoid cooking accidents, it is still important be cautious when using them. To ensure your safety, here are a few things you should do before and during pressure cooking.

DO:
- Read the instruction manual carefully.
- Follow minimum and maximum liquid and fill requirements.
- Tilt the lid away from you when opening the pressure cooker.
- Follow recommended cooking times.
- Check that the valves are free and the rubber or silicone gasket is undamaged prior to pressure cooking.
- Turn the long handle of stovetop pressure cookers away from the edge of the cooktop .
- Keep cords of electric pressure cookers out of reach from a curious child or pet who may want to pull them down.

Additionally, there are a few things you should avoid doing while using your pressure cooker.

DO NOT:
- Operate the pressure cooker near or around children.
- Fill the cooker more than half full of beans, grains, and rice, or ⅔ full for other foods. These will expand and could block the safety systems.
- Peek inside as you open the cooker. The super heated vapor could burn your face.
- Pressure cook with liquor or milk. They will foam, scorch, and (in the case of liquor) possibly ignite a fire in the pressure cooker.
- Use the pressure cooker for pressure frying or "broasting." The safety mechanisms are not designed to work with super-heated cooking oil and may fail. This could result in hot oil spraying from the cooker, which can ignite or seriously injure nearby persons.
- Force the pressure cooker open. The contents are under pressure and could cause injury.

Heat Sources for Pressure Cooking

When using a stovetop pressure cooker, there are several things you should keep in mind. First, since electric or halogen cooktops do not change temperature quickly, food could become scorched. To avoid scorching, start the pressure cooker on a high-heat burner while preheating a low-heat burner. When the cooker reaches pressure, turn off the high-heat burner and carefully move the cooker to the low-heat burner for cooking under pressure.

Secondly, pressure cookers heated on induction cooktops reach pressure quickly (60 percent faster than gas or electric) and could result in undercooked food. To avoid undercooking, you will need to add 2–3 minutes to your cooking time under pressure to compensate for the time the food would usually cook while the cooker is reaching pressure.

Lastly, when using a gas cooktop, follow the directions and cooking times as given for "standard" pressure cookers.

Pressure Cooking in Five Easy Steps

Pressure cooking is not as complicated as you would think considering all the technical features and mechanisms involved in the pressure cooking process. Luckily, you don't need to know the science behind your pressure cooker in order to make a quick, delicious meal. Here's how to do it!

1. Add food and 1 cup of liquid, or the minimum required by your pressure cooker model, into the pressure cooker. Don't fill the cooker more than ⅔ full with food and liquid (or ½ full for foods that expand like beans, grains, and dried vegetables).
2. Close and lock the lid. Turn the heat up to high (or push start) and heat up the cooker and its contents until it signals it has reached pressure. To signal that a cooker has reached pressure it could beep, lift up a rod, let out its first puff of steam, or begin jiggling. Check the manual to see how your cooker signals it has reached pressure.
3. Lower the heat to the lowest it will go without losing pressure. Got an electric? You can skip this step.
4. Start the timer for the recommended cooking time. If you have an electric pressure cooker, you can skip this step.
5. Open the cooker using the recommended method.

Most stainless steel pressure cooker bottoms can be placed directly in the dishwasher for cleaning, but you should always check the manufacturer's instructions first. If your pressure cooker must be cleaned by hand, avoid using a steel or metal wool scrubbing pad, as these can scratch the pressure cooker's finish. Instead, opt for a mild dish soap and a sponge or cloth when washing. Manufacturers recommend checking the parts for wear and tear before each use.

ESSENTIAL

While the major release methods are normal, natural, and cold-water quick release, some pressure cooker manufacturers offer additional methods of releasing pressure as an extra feature. Read your pressure cooker manual well to understand all of the options and precautions.

Opening Methods

The recipes in this book only use the normal or natural pressure release method; however, there is a third option for cooks with stovetop pressure cookers called cold-water quick release. Here is each method described in detail:

- **Natural Pressure Release:** This release method is the most energy-efficient opening method because when the cooking time is up, the heat source is turned off and the food continues to cook in the residual heat of the cooker. Stovetop pressure cookers release pressure naturally in 10–15 minutes, while electrics can take up to 20–30 minutes. This is because the heat coil needs to cool down first before the cooker begins to cool.
- **Normal Pressure Release (also called Automatic, Quick, or Valve Release):** This method usually takes 2–3 minutes. You push a button, flip a lever, or remove the valve to release pressure. Follow your instruction manual for detailed guidance.
- **Cold-Water Quick Release:** This method usually takes only 20 seconds, but it is for stovetop pressure cookers only. To release pressure with the cold-water quick release method, carefully place the cooker in an empty sink and run cold water over the lid. Be sure not to get the pressure signals or valves wet (this could mean tilting the cooker slightly). Remove the lid, tilting it away from your face.

High and Low Pressure

Most modern pressure cookers have two or more pressure settings. High pressure is 12–15 pounds per square inch (PSI), while low pressure is 6–9 PSI. Be aware that some manufacturers (especially those of electric pressure cookers) may differ in their definitions of high and low pressure. Check the manual or contact the manufacturer to be certain. It is important to know this information because pressure correlates directly to temperature. The higher the pressure, the higher the cooking temperature and the faster foods will be cooked. The lower the pressure, the lower the cooking temperature and the less quickly foods will cook, though it will always be faster than without pressure at all! See the Pressure Cooking Time Table (Appendix B) for more information.

Pressure Cooker Accessories

Some of the recipes in this book recommend using accessories. Here is an explanation of what these accessories are and how you should use them:

Trivet: This accessory is sometimes supplied by the manufacturer. Its purpose is to keep heatproof dishes or steamer baskets off the bottom of the pressure cooker and out of the steaming liquid. If your steamer basket has feet, it can be used as a substitute. A large jar lid can also do the same job in a pinch.

Steamer Basket: This accessory is sometimes supplied by the manufacturer. If you do not have one, you can purchase an adjustable steamer basket (one that opens and closes like a flower). For electric pressure cookers with nonstick coating, it is recommended that you use a silicone steamer basket to avoid scratching the liner.

Heatproof Dish: This accessory can be any dish that is small enough to fit in the pressure cooker, but must be ovensafe (the heat in the pressure cooker will be lower). The most recommended dishes include stainless steel containers or mixing bowls, but the container can be made of aluminum, ceramic, Pyrex, or silicone. **Never** use melamine (microwave-safe containers), plastic, wood, bamboo, or nontempered glass in the pressure cooker.

About the Recipes in This Book

This book is written for both stovetop and electric pressure cookers; however, electric models vary widely in the pressure they reach (8, 11, 13, and 15 PSI) versus stovetop which are almost all 13–15 PSI. See the Cooking Time Table (Appendix B) to see if you need to adapt cooking times to your pressure cooker and how to do so. In instances where a recipe recommends cooking at low pressure, the equivalent high pressure cooking time is also included.

Read your pressure cooker manual carefully before following recipes from this book. If your pressure cooker manual cautions against pressure cooking certain foods, follow your manual's advice.

CHAPTER 2

Appetizers

Baba Ganoush
20

Cipolline Agrodolce
(Sweet and Sour Pearl Onions)
21

Asparagus with Yogurt Crème
22

Hummus
23

Lemon and Rosemary Cannellini
Cream
24

Spicy Black Bean Dip
25

Steamed Artichokes
26

Steamy Carrot Coins
27

Boiled Peanuts
27

Tomatillo Salsa
28

Steamed Spring Rolls
29

Mini Cabbage Rolls
30

Baba Ganoush

*This Middle Eastern spread, also called eggplant caviar,
can be served with pitas, tortillas, or even crostini!*

INGREDIENTS | SERVES 6

1 tablespoon vegetable oil
2 pounds eggplant, roughly chopped
3 whole cloves garlic, with the skin on
1 teaspoon salt
¾ cup water
1 tablespoon tahini
Juice of 2 lemons (about ¼ cup of juice)
1 clove garlic, peeled and crushed
1 bunch thyme, chopped
¼ cup whole black olives
2 tablespoons fresh extra-virgin olive oil

1. In the preheated pressure cooker, on medium heat without the lid, add the vegetable oil and just enough eggplant to cover the bottom.
2. Sauté the eggplant until golden (about 10 minutes).
3. Add the whole garlic cloves, the rest of the eggplant, salt, and water. Close and lock the lid.
4. Turn the heat to high. When the cooker reaches pressure, lower the heat to the minimum needed to maintain pressure. Cook for 5–7 minutes at high pressure.
5. When time is up, open the pressure cooker by releasing pressure.
6. Carefully remove the garlic cloves from the pressure cooker, peel them, and return them to the cooker. Add the tahini, lemon juice, and crushed garlic. Mash everything with a fork or blend using an immersion blender.
7. Pour mashed ingredients into a serving dish and sprinkle with fresh thyme, olives, and olive oil before serving.

PER SERVING | Calories: 123 | Fat: 10 g | Protein: 2 g | Sodium: 450 mg | Fiber: 6 g | Carbohydrates: 11 g

Cipolline Agrodolce (Sweet and Sour Pearl Onions)

You can also make this recipe with regular onions that have been quartered, but they will not keep their shape as well as pearl onions.

INGREDIENTS | SERVES 6

1 pound Cipolline (pearl onions), outer layer removed

½ cup water

⅛ teaspoon salt

1 bay leaf

4 tablespoons balsamic vinegar

1 tablespoon honey

1 tablespoon flour

Impostors!

Pearl onions are actually more closely related to leeks than onions.

1. Place the onions in the pressure cooker with water, salt, and the bay leaf. Close and lock the lid.
2. Turn the heat up to high. When the cooker reaches pressure, lower to the minimum heat needed to maintain pressure. Cook for 5–6 minutes at low pressure (3 minutes at high pressure).
3. While the onions are cooking, combine the balsamic vinegar, honey, and flour in a small saucepan. Stir over low heat until well combined (about 30 seconds).
4. When time is up for the onions, open the pressure cooker by releasing pressure.
5. Pour the balsamic vinegar mixture over the onions and mix well.
6. Transfer to serving dish and serve hot, or let sit overnight in refrigerator prior to serving.

PER SERVING | Calories: 110 | Fat: 1 g | Protein: 1 g | Sodium: 55 mg | Fiber: 1 g | Carbohydrates: 12 g

Asparagus with Yogurt Crème

This steaming liquid will contain delicious asparagus juice. Reserve the liquid to use in another recipe!

INGREDIENTS | SERVES 4

2 cups plain whole yogurt
1 cup water
1 pound asparagus, trimmed
1¼ teaspoon salt

Yogurt Crème vs. Sour Cream

A crème made of plain whole yogurt contains about 75 percent less fat than sour cream, but is equally as tangy and refreshing.

1. To make the yogurt crème, put the yogurt in a fine mesh strainer over a bowl and refrigerate for about 4 hours, or until the yogurt in the strainer has reached the consistency of sour cream.
2. Place water in the pressure cooker and add the steamer basket.
3. Lay asparagus flat in steamer basket. If it does not fit in one layer, make a second layer perpendicular to the first. Sprinkle with salt. Close and lock the lid.
4. Turn the heat up to high. When the cooker reaches pressure, lower to the minimum heat needed to maintain pressure. Cook for 2–3 minutes at high pressure.
5. When time is up, open the pressure cooker by releasing pressure.
6. Serve with yogurt crème.

PER SERVING | Calories: 97 | Fat: 4 g | Protein: 7 g | Sodium: 797 mg | Fiber: 2 g | Carbohydrates: 10 g

Hummus

Hummus is a perfect snack—and a lower-fat option than peanut butter—to spread on raw veggies or wheat crackers.

INGREDIENTS | SERVES 6

1½ cups dried chickpeas

4 cups cold water

1 bay leaf

2 tablespoons vegetable oil

3 crushed garlic cloves, divided

2½ heaping tablespoons tahini

Juice of 1 lemon

¼ teaspoon cumin

1 teaspoon salt

1 tablespoon extra-virgin olive oil

½ bunch parsley, chopped

⅛ teaspoon paprika

Beans Under Pressure

Don't omit the vegetable oil while pressure cooking beans. It keeps them from foaming inside the pressure cooker while the valve is emitting vapor. If your pressure cooker has a spring pressure valve (i.e. does not emit vapor while cooking), you can omit the oil. If you're not sure what kind of pressure cooker you have, add the oil to be safe.

1. Rinse the chickpeas well and put them in your pressure cooker. Cover with water and add bay leaf, vegetable oil, and two crushed garlic cloves. Close and lock the lid.
2. Turn the heat up to high. When the cooker reaches pressure, lower to the minimum heat needed to maintain pressure. Cook 30–40 minutes at high pressure.
3. Open with the natural release method (see Chapter 1).
4. Drain the chickpeas, reserving 2 cups of the cooking liquid.
5. Pour cooled chickpeas into a food processor. Add ½ cup of your reserved cooking liquid along with tahini, lemon juice, cumin, and the remaining garlic clove. Purée, slowly adding the remaining reserved liquid, until the mixture has reached a creamy consistency. Add salt and purée again to mix well.
6. Pour into serving dish and garnish by making a deep groove with a spatula and pouring olive oil into the groove. Sprinkle with parsley and paprika.

PER SERVING | Calories: 174 | Fat: 11 g | Protein: 4 g | Sodium: 584 mg | Fiber: 5 g | Carbohydrates: 16 g

Lemon and Rosemary Cannellini Cream

You can use either Italian cannellini beans or navy beans for this recipe.

INGREDIENTS | SERVES 6

2 tablespoons vegetable oil

1 scallion, chopped

1½ cups dried cannellini beans, rinsed

3 cups water

Juice and zest of 1 lemon

½ teaspoon white pepper

2 sprigs rosemary (1 sprig finely chopped and 1 whole sprig)

1 tablespoon extra-virgin olive oil

1. Heat vegetable oil in an uncovered pressure cooker over medium heat. Add the scallion and sauté until softened (about 3 minutes). Add cannellini beans and water. Close and lock the lid.
2. Turn the heat up to high. When the cooker reaches pressure, lower to the minimum heat needed to maintain pressure. Cook 25–30 minutes at high pressure.
3. Open with the natural release method (see Chapter 1).
4. Drain the beans, let them cool, and pour them into a food processor. Add lemon juice, lemon zest, pepper, chopped rosemary, and olive oil. Purée until smooth.
5. Pour into serving dish and garnish with fresh rosemary sprig.

PER SERVING | Calories: 114 | Fat: 7 g | Protein: 3 g | Sodium: 169 mg | Fiber: 3.5 g | Carbohydrates: 10 g

Spicy Black Bean Dip

If you choose to omit the bacon, be sure to add 1 tablespoon of vegetable oil to keep the beans from foaming.

INGREDIENTS | SERVES 8

1 slice bacon, finely diced
1 small onion, peeled and diced
3 cloves garlic, peeled and minced
1 cup dried black beans
2 green bell peppers, finely chopped
½ teaspoon chili powder
½ teaspoon dried oregano
¼ teaspoon baking soda
2 cups water
2 tablespoons tomato paste
½ cup fresh lemon or lime juice
½ teaspoon salt
¼ cup finely chopped fresh cilantro
½ cup crumbled queso fresco or feta cheese

Hot!

Hot pepper intensifies in the pressure cooker. Start with just a little bit, as indicated in the recipe, and then increase only after you've tasted it!

1. Add the bacon to the pressure cooker. Fry over medium-high heat until the bacon has rendered its fat and is almost crispy. Add the onion and sauté in the bacon fat for 3 minutes or until the onion is soft. Add the garlic and sauté for 30 seconds.
2. Add beans, peppers, chili powder, oregano, baking soda, and water. Stir well, scraping up any bacon bits clinging to the bottom of the cooker. Close and lock the lid.
3. Turn the heat up to high. When the cooker reaches pressure, lower to the minimum heat needed to maintain pressure. Cook 25–30 minutes at high pressure.
4. Open with the natural release method (see Chapter 1).
5. Stir in the tomato paste, lemon or lime juice, and salt. Purée using an immersion blender or food processor until smooth.
6. Pour into serving bowl and garnish with cilantro and crumbled cheese before serving.

PER SERVING | Calories: 114 | Fat: 2 g | Protein: 6 g | Sodium: 248 mg | Fiber: 5 g | Carbohydrates: 20 g

Steamed Artichokes

These artichokes are particularly delicious with Lemon and Rosemary Cannellini Cream (see recipe in this chapter).

INGREDIENTS | SERVES 6

6 artichokes
1 cup water
Juice of 1 lemon

Artichoke Stems are Edible!

If you are lucky enough to buy fresh artichokes with the stems attached, be sure to use them in this recipe. You can cut them off so the artichokes will stand straight. Peel off the exterior with a potato peeler. Slice the stems into 2-inch pieces and boil them in the water below, while the artichokes steam above. They are as delicious as the artichoke heart!

1. Clean the artichokes by cutting off the top ⅓ and removing the tough exterior leaves.
2. Place artichokes upright in the steamer basket. Fill the pressure cooker base with water and lemon juice, and then lower the steamer basket into the cooker. Close and lock the lid.
3. The cooking time will depend on the size of the artichokes. A large globe artichoke that almost fills the pressure cooker could take 10 minutes, while medium artichokes only need about 5 minutes.
4. Turn the heat up to high. When the cooker reaches pressure, lower to the minimum heat needed to maintain pressure. Cook 5–10 minutes at high pressure.
5. When time is up, open the pressure cooker by releasing pressure.
6. Lift the artichokes very carefully out of the pressure cooker (they will be so tender, they may fall apart) and serve.

PER SERVING | Calories: 68 | Fat: 0 g | Protein: 4 g | Sodium: 130 mg | Fiber: 7 g | Carbohydrates: 16 g

Steamy Carrot Coins

Carrots can really showcase the vitamin- and flavor-saving capabilities of pressure cookers. Taste the carrots undressed, or try them with any of the sauces or dips in this chapter!

INGREDIENTS | SERVES 6

1 pound thick carrots, peeled and sliced into ¼-inch thick coins
1 cup water

1. Fill the pressure cooker base with water. Place carrot coins in steamer basket and lower the basket into the cooker. Close and lock the lid.
2. Turn the heat up to high. When the cooker reaches pressure, lower to the minimum heat needed to maintain pressure. Cook 3–4 minutes at low pressure (1–2 minutes at high pressure). Open the pressure cooker by releasing pressure.
3. Transfer carrots to serving dish immediately to avoid overcooking.

PER SERVING | Calories: 30 | Fat: 0 g | Protein: 1 g | Sodium: 51 mg | Fiber: 2 g | Carbohydrates: 7 g

Boiled Peanuts

Use "green" raw peanuts, not cooked or dried nuts. The cooking time will depend on how fresh the uncooked peanuts are. Once cooked, store in the refrigerator.

INGREDIENTS | SERVES 8

1 pound raw peanuts
4 cups water
¼ cup salt

Cajun Peanuts

Add a little flavor to plain boiled peanuts by adding Cajun seasoning to the water when boiling. Try a pre-blended seasoning mix or make your own by combining red pepper, black pepper, cayenne pepper, garlic powder, and salt.

1. Rinse the peanuts under cold water and then place in the pressure cooker. Add the water and salt. Close and lock the pressure cooker.
2. Turn the heat up to high. When the cooker reaches pressure, lower to the minimum heat needed to maintain pressure. Cook 20–40 minutes at high pressure.
3. When time is up, open the pressure cooker by releasing pressure. Strain and enjoy!

PER SERVING | Calories: 317 | Fat: 27 g | Protein: 14 g | Sodium: 3550 mg | Fiber: 5 g | Carbohydrates: 9 g

Tomatillo Salsa

Serve with corn tortilla chips or as an accompaniment to any Mexican-themed dish.

INGREDIENTS | SERVES 8

1 pound tomatillos, paper removed

Water, for cooking

2 jalapeños, stemmed, seeded, and chopped

½ onion, chopped

½ cup cold water

½ cup chopped cilantro

2 teaspoons salt

Tomatillo

The tomatillo is the small, yellowish or green fruit of a Mexican ground cherry. Surprisingly, it is not a variety of tomato.

1. Cut the tomatillos in half and place them in the pressure cooker. Add enough water to cover the tomatillos. Close and lock the lid.
2. Turn the heat up to high. When the cooker reaches pressure, lower to the minimum heat needed to maintain pressure. Cook for 2 minutes at high pressure.
3. Open with the natural release method (see Chapter 1).
4. Add the drained, cooked tomatillos, jalapeños, onion, and cold water to a food processor or blender. Blend until well combined. Add the cilantro and salt and pulse until combined. Chill the salsa before serving.

PER SERVING | Calories: 21 | Fat: 0 g | Protein: 1 g | Sodium: 590 mg | Fiber: 1 g | Carbohydrates: 4 g

Steamed Spring Rolls

Serve with your favorite dipping sauce.

INGREDIENTS | SERVES 12

1 cup shredded cabbage

1 cup sliced bamboo shoots

¼ cup chopped cilantro

2 cloves garlic, minced

5 shiitake mushrooms, sliced

2 carrots, grated

1 teaspoon soy sauce

1 teaspoon rice wine vinegar

12 spring roll wrappers

2 cups water

Spring Roll Wrappers

Spring roll wrappers are also known as rice paper. They are made from rice flour and rolled into thin, translucent sheets. Before using, briefly soak the papers in water so they become soft and pliable for rolling up the spring roll filling.

1. Combine the cabbage, bamboo shoots, cilantro, garlic, mushrooms, carrots, soy sauce, and rice wine vinegar in a medium bowl. Stir until just combined.
2. Soak the spring roll wrappers in water and place them on a flat surface.
3. Top each wrapper with an equal amount of the cabbage mixture, making a row down the center. Roll up the wrappers, tuck in the ends, and place side by side in the pressure cooker steamer basket.
4. Add water to the pressure cooker and lower in the steamer basket. Close and lock the lid.
5. Turn the heat up to high. When the cooker reaches pressure, lower to the minimum heat needed to maintain pressure. Cook for 3–4 minutes at high pressure.
6. When time is up, open the pressure cooker by releasing pressure. Remove rolls immediately and place on a serving platter.

PER SERVING | Calories: 14 | Fat: 0 g | Protein: 1 g | Sodium: 40 mg | Fiber: 1 g | Carbohydrates: 3 g

Mini Cabbage Rolls

You can improve the flavor of these cabbage rolls by adding diced roasted red pepper instead of raw red bell pepper.

INGREDIENTS | YIELD: 30 ROLLS

1 medium head Savoy cabbage

3 cups water, divided

1 pound lean ground beef

1 cup long-grain rice

1 red bell pepper, seeded and minced

1 medium onion, peeled and diced

1 cup Vegetable Stock (see recipe in Chapter 4)

1 tablespoon extra-virgin olive oil

2 tablespoons minced, fresh mint

1 teaspoon dried tarragon

1 teaspoon salt

½ teaspoon freshly ground black pepper

2 tablespoons lemon juice

1. Wash the cabbage. Remove the large, outer leaves and set aside. Remove the remaining cabbage leaves and place them in the pressure cooker. Pour in 1 cup water and lock on the lid. Bring to low pressure; maintain the pressure for 1 minute. Quick-release the pressure. Drain the cabbage leaves in a colander and then move them to a cotton towel.

2. In a mixing bowl, add the ground beef, rice, bell pepper, onion, stock, extra-virgin olive oil, mint, tarragon, salt, and pepper. Stir to combine.

3. Place the reserved (uncooked) cabbage leaves on the bottom of the pressure cooker to keep the rolls from getting scorched.

4. Remove the stem running down the center of each steamed cabbage leaf and tear each leaf in half lengthwise. Place 1 tablespoon of the ground beef mixture in the center of each cabbage piece. Loosely fold the sides of the leaf over the filling and then fold the top and bottom of the leaf over the folded sides. As you complete them, place each stuffed cabbage leaf in the pressure cooker.

5. Pour 2 cups water and the lemon juice over the stuffed cabbage rolls. Close and lock the lid.

6. Turn the heat up to high. When the cooker reaches pressure, lower to the minimum heat needed to maintain pressure. Cook 15–20 minutes at high pressure.

7. Open with the natural release method (see Chapter 1).

8. Carefully move the stuffed cabbage rolls to a serving platter by piercing each one with a toothpick.

PER SERVING | Calories: 60 | Fat: 1 g | Protein: 4 g | Sodium: 113 mg | Fiber: 1 g | Carbohydrates: 7 g

CHAPTER 3

Vegetables and Sides

Lemon Zest Asparagus
33

Broccoli and Citrus Salad
33

Garlic Braised Artichokes
34

Golden Beets
35

Braised Beet Greens
36

White Beets and Greens
37

Soy-Glazed Bok Choy
38

Broccoli in Lemon Sauce
39

Spicy Braised Broccoli
39

Spicy Broccoli Rabe
40

Red, White, and Green Brussels
Sprouts Salad
41

Pan-Seared Brussels Sprouts
42

Beer-Braised Savoy Cabbage
43

Red Cabbage and Apples
44

Tie-Dyed Baby Carrots
45

Carrots in Milk
46

Gingered Carrots
46

Southern-Style Collards
47

Corn on the Cob
48

Eggplant Caponata
48

Creamed Corn
49

Milk-Braised Fennel
50

Bavarian Kale
51

Mushy Peas
52

Peperonata (Faux Roasted
Peppers)
53

Potato Stuffed Onions
54

Southern Italian Green Beans
and Tomatoes
55

Green Bean and Pine Nut Salad
56

Boozy Taters
56

Green Bean and Potato Salad
57

Potato and Parsley Salad
58

Curried Yams and Potatoes
59

Herb-Roasted Potatoes
60

Light Scalloped Potatoes
61

Mashed Potatoes
62

Stewed Green Tomatoes
62

Indian-Style Cauliflower and
Potatoes
63

Steamed Pumpkin
64

Spaghetti Squash
64

Swiss Chard and Vegetables in
Parmesan Sauce
65

Spicy and Minty Zucchini
66

Lighter Ratatouille
67

Winter Vegetable Medley
68

Lemon Zest Asparagus

Having lemon zest in the steaming liquid gives this asparagus extra zing. Save the steaming liquid and use it as a base for Lemon Brown and Wild Rice (see Chapter 12).

INGREDIENTS | SERVES 4

1 cup water
Zest of 1 lemon
1 pound asparagus
⅛ teaspoon salt
1 tablespoon olive oil

1. Place water and lemon zest in the pressure cooker and add the steamer basket. Lay asparagus flat in steamer basket. If it does not fit in one layer, make a second layer perpendicular to the first. Sprinkle with salt. Close and lock the lid.
2. Turn the heat up to high. When the cooker reaches pressure, lower the heat to the minimum needed to maintain pressure. Cook for 2–3 minutes at high pressure.
3. Open the pressure cooker by releasing pressure. Transfer immediately to serving dish and dress with olive oil.

PER SERVING | Calories: 52 | Fat: 3 g | Protein: 2 g | Sodium: 75 mg | Fiber: 2 g | Carbohydrates: 4 g

Broccoli and Citrus Salad

Spicy, tangy, and sweet, this salad is the perfect accompaniment to fish and meats. Reserve the steaming liquid in the refrigerator and use it to add flavor to another recipe.

INGREDIENTS | SERVES 6

Zest and juice of 1 orange
1 teaspoon hot pepper flakes
1 tablespoon capers
2 tablespoons extra-virgin olive oil
1 teaspoon salt
¼ teaspoon ground black pepper
1 cup water
2 pounds broccoli florets, trimmed
2 seedless oranges, peeled and thinly sliced

1. Combine zest, juice, pepper flakes, capers, olive oil, salt, and pepper in a small jar. Shake well and set aside.
2. Place water in the cooker and add the steamer basket. Fill the basket with broccoli. Close and lock the lid.
3. Turn the heat up to high. When the cooker reaches pressure, lower to the minimum heat needed to maintain pressure. Cook 4–6 minutes at low pressure (2–3 minutes at high).
4. Open the pressure cooker by releasing pressure. Place broccoli and oranges on a serving platter. Drizzle with the vinaigrette.

PER SERVING | Calories: 112 | Fat: 5 g | Protein: 4 g | Sodium: 486 mg | Fiber: 5 g | Carbohydrates: 15 g

Garlic Braised Artichokes

This is a quick and delicious veggie dish that can also be served on top of rice, pasta, or your favorite grain!

INGREDIENTS | SERVES 4

6 medium artichokes
1 tablespoon olive oil
3 cloves of garlic, smashed
¼ teaspoon salt
¾ cups water

Acidulated Bath

Artichokes oxidize quickly after they've been cut. To prevent this from happening, have a large bowl with the juice of two lemons available and toss the artichoke pieces in as soon as you finish cutting them. Drain before adding to the pressure cooker.

1. Trim the artichokes by cutting off the top third, peeling off the tough exterior leaves, slicing in half, and removing the "choke" using a melon baller. Then cut into wedges.
2. Heat olive oil in an uncovered pressure cooker over medium heat. Add garlic and stir-fry for 30 seconds. Add the artichoke wedges and stir infrequently so that the edges can become golden (about 5 minutes).
3. Sprinkle with salt and add water. Close and lock the lid.
4. Turn the heat up to high. When the cooker reaches pressure, lower the heat to the minimum needed to maintain pressure. Cook for 2–3 minutes at high pressure.
5. When time is up, open the pressure cooker by releasing pressure.
6. Transfer to serving dish immediately to avoid overcooking.

PER SERVING | Calories: 123 | Fat: 4 g | Protein: 6 g | Sodium: 329 mg | Fiber: 10 g | Carbohydrates: 21 g

Golden Beets

You can prepare the unpeeled beets ahead of time.
Cool them, put them in a zip-closure bag, and refrigerate.

INGREDIENTS | SERVES 8

4 large golden or red beets
1 cup water
1 tablespoon olive oil
1 teaspoon salt
½ teaspoon freshly ground black pepper

Beet RX

Beetroot was used in ancient Rome as a treatment for fevers and constipation, among other ailments. Meanwhile, ancient Greeks used the beet leaves to bind wounds.

1. Scrub the beets and trim both ends. Place the beets on the rack in the pressure cooker. Pour in the water. Close and lock the lid.
2. Turn the heat up to high. When the cooker reaches pressure, lower the heat to the minimum needed to maintain pressure. Cook for 15–20 minutes at high pressure.
3. When time is up, open the pressure cooker by releasing pressure.
4. Test beets to see if they are fully cooked. If beets aren't tender, pressure cook for another minute.
5. Remove beets from cooker and let cool. When they are cool enough to handle, use a paring knife to remove the peel. Slice the beets.
6. Season with oil, salt, and pepper.

PER SERVING | Calories: 32 | Fat: 2 g | Protein: 1 g | Sodium: 327 mg | Fiber: 1 g | Carbohydrates: 4 g

Braised Beet Greens

Young, fresh greens will cook more quickly than older, tougher ones.
Adjust the cooking time accordingly.

INGREDIENTS | SERVES 4

1 tablespoon olive oil

1 large shallot or small red onion, peeled and minced

1 pound beet greens

1 teaspoon salt

½ teaspoon freshly ground black pepper

¼ cup chicken broth

1 teaspoon white wine or an infused vinegar (optional)

1. Heat olive oil in an uncovered pressure cooker over medium heat. Add the shallot or onion and sauté for 3 minutes.
2. Add the beet greens. Sprinkle with salt and pepper. Stir the greens to coat them in the oil.
3. Once they're slightly wilted, add the broth, making sure not to exceed the fill line in your pressure cooker. Close and lock the lid.
4. Turn the heat up to high. When the cooker reaches pressure, lower the heat to the minimum needed to maintain pressure. Cook for 1 minute at high pressure.
5. When time is up, open the pressure cooker by releasing pressure.
6. Remove the lid. Simmer and stir for a minute or until the remaining moisture evaporates.
7. Taste for seasoning and add more salt and pepper if needed. Serve warm, with a splash of white wine or an infused vinegar if desired.

PER SERVING | Calories: 92 | Fat: 4 g | Protein: 4 g | Sodium: 703 mg | Fiber: 2 g | Carbohydrates: 12 g

White Beets and Greens

Spring beets are two vegetables in one: the root and the greens!

INGREDIENTS | SERVES 4

3 whole white beets

Water for cooking

1 teaspoon salt

1 tablespoon olive oil

2 cloves garlic, minced

1 lemon wedge, squeezed (about 1 teaspoon lemon juice)

Red Beet Variation

This recipe also works with red beets. Cook them a little longer (20–25 minutes instead of the time listed in the recipe) and be extra careful when peeling. You may want to sauté the greens separately just to keep them green.

1. Cut the greens from the beets and wash well by immersing them in a large bowl of water and swishing them around. Let sit for 30 minutes.
2. When time is up, lift greens out of the water, leaving all of the dirt and sand at the bottom of the bowl. Place greens in a strainer and drain.
3. Put the beet roots in the pressure cooker, fill with just enough water to cover, and add salt. Close and lock the lid.
4. Turn the heat up to high. When the cooker reaches pressure, lower the heat to the minimum needed to maintain pressure. Cook for 5–7 minutes at high pressure.
5. When time is up, open the pressure cooker by releasing pressure.
6. Toss in the beet greens and close the lid. Let them cook in the residual heat and steam of the beets for about 5 minutes.
7. Then, open the cooker again and strain the beets and greens. Peel the beets (tugging on the thin skin with a paper towel) and cut into pieces.
8. Heat the oil in a sauté pan over medium-high heat. When oil is hot, add the beets and sear for about 3 minutes.
9. Add garlic and beet greens to the pan. Stir frequently and cook until the stems are tender.
10. Transfer to serving dish and squirt with lemon.

PER SERVING | Calories: 59 | Fat: 3 g | Protein: 1 g | Sodium: 637 mg | Fiber: 2 g | Carbohydrates: 6 g

Soy-Glazed Bok Choy

Any type of bok choy, such as Chinese cabbage or baby bok choy, works well in this recipe.

INGREDIENTS | SERVES 4

1 pound bok choy
Water for cooking, divided
¼ cup soy sauce
1 teaspoon rice wine vinegar
1 teaspoon peanut oil
1 teaspoon minced ginger
1 teaspoon cornstarch

Vitamin Bomb

Bok choy contains a high concentration of both vitamin A and vitamin C! Each four-ounce serving provides about 3500 IU of vitamin A and 50 mg of vitamin C.

1. Trim the ends off the bok choy and slice in half, lengthwise. Place in the steamer basket.
2. Place ½ cup water in the pressure cooker and add the steamer basket. Close and lock the lid.
3. Turn the heat up to high. When the cooker reaches pressure, lower the heat to the minimum needed to maintain pressure. Cook for 1 minute at high pressure.
4. When time is up, open the pressure cooker by releasing pressure. Remove the steamer basket and drain water from cooker.
5. Add the soy sauce, rice wine vinegar, peanut oil, and ginger to the pressure cooker and bring to medium heat, uncovered.
6. Combine the cornstarch with 2 teaspoons of water in a small bowl, and slowly add to the pressure cooker, stirring constantly.
7. Add the bok choy and stir until it's completely coated.
8. Transfer to serving dish with sauce.

PER SERVING | Calories: 37 | Fat: 1 g | Protein: 3 g | Sodium: 972 mg | Carbohydrates: 4.5 g | Fiber: 1 g

Broccoli in Lemon Sauce

Make this simple dish even healthier by substituting the butter with 1 tablespoon of extra-virgin olive oil.

INGREDIENTS | SERVES 6

4 cups broccoli florets, trimmed
¼ teaspoon salt
1 cup water
2 tablespoons butter, melted
1 tablespoon fresh lemon juice
¼ teaspoon Dijon mustard

1. Put the broccoli, salt, and water in the pressure cooker. Close and lock the lid.
2. Turn the heat up to high. When the cooker reaches pressure, lower to the minimum heat needed to maintain pressure. Cook 4–6 minutes at low pressure (2–3 minutes at high).
3. Open the pressure cooker by releasing pressure. Drain and transfer the broccoli to a serving bowl.
4. Whisk together the butter, lemon juice, and mustard. Pour over the broccoli and toss to mix.

PER SERVING | Calories: 55 g | Fat: 4 g | Protein: 2 g | Sodium: 121 mg | Fiber: 1.5 g | Carbohydrates: 4 g

Spicy Braised Broccoli

This is another quick and multiuse veggie dish that can be served in a variety of different ways. Try it on top of pasta or over a bed of your favorite rice!

INGREDIENTS | SERVES 4

1 tablespoon olive oil
3 cloves garlic, crushed
⅛ teaspoon hot pepper flakes
1 pound broccoli florets, trimmed
¼ teaspoon salt
⅛ teaspoon pepper
¾ cups water

1. Heat olive oil in an uncovered pressure cooker over medium heat. Add garlic and hot pepper and cook for 30 seconds, stirring constantly. Add broccoli and cook about 5 minutes, stirring infrequently so that the edges become golden.
2. Add salt, pepper, and water. Close and lock the lid.
3. Turn the heat up to high. When the cooker reaches pressure, lower the heat to the minimum needed to maintain pressure. Cook for 2–3 minutes at high pressure.
4. Open the pressure cooker by releasing pressure. Transfer to serving dish immediately.

PER SERVING | Calories: 71 | Fat: 4 g | Protein: 3 g | Sodium: 186 mg | Fiber: 3 g | Carbohydrates: 8 g

Spicy Broccoli Rabe

Broccoli rabe, also known as rapini, can be prepared in the same way as regular broccoli.

INGREDIENTS | SERVES 4

1 pound broccoli rabe, trimmed
1 teaspoon salt
1 cup water
1 tablespoon olive oil
2 cloves garlic, sliced
½ teaspoon hot pepper flakes
2 anchovies

Umami Secret

Anchovies add that extra "umph" of flavor known as umami. When you use just a small amount and melt them, as in this recipe, there is no fishy flavor. However, if you prefer, you can leave them out.

1. Put the broccoli rabe, salt, and water in the pressure cooker. Close and lock the lid.
2. Turn the heat up to high. When the cooker reaches pressure, lower the heat to the minimum needed to maintain pressure. Cook for 2 minutes at low pressure or 30 seconds at high pressure.
3. When time is up, open the pressure cooker by releasing pressure.
4. Strain the rabe and rinse out the pressure cooker.
5. Heat olive oil in uncovered pressure cooker over medium heat. Sauté garlic, pepper flakes, and anchovies until the garlic is golden and the anchovies have melted, about 3 minutes.
6. Return the broccoli rabe to the pressure cooker and sauté everything together for about 1 minute.
7. Transfer to serving dish and serve.

PER SERVING | Calories: 92 | Fat: 4 g | Protein: 4 g | Sodium: 713 mg | Carbohydrates: 12 g | Fiber: 2 g

Red, White, and Green Brussels Sprouts Salad

If fresh pomegranate is not available, you can rehydrate dried cranberries by putting them in the steaming liquid under the Brussels sprouts.

INGREDIENTS | SERVES 6

1 pound Brussels sprouts
1 cup water
1 tablespoon olive oil
1 teaspoon salt
¼ teaspoon pepper
½ cup pine nuts, toasted
Seeds of 1 medium pomegranate

Rome Sprouts?

Brussels sprouts are named after the capital of Belgium, though there is little historical evidence that they actually originated there. In fact, varieties that preceded the sprouts we know today were cultivated in ancient Rome!

1. Remove the outer leaves and trim the stems of the Brussels sprouts. Cut larger sprouts in half to get them to a uniform size for even cooking.
2. Put water in the pressure cooker and add the steamer basket. Put the sprouts in the basket. Close and lock the lid.
3. Turn the heat up to high. When the cooker reaches pressure, lower to the minimum heat needed to maintain pressure. Cook 3–4 minutes at high pressure.
4. When time is up, open the pressure cooker by releasing pressure.
5. Quickly transfer the sprouts to a serving dish to avoid overcooking.
6. Toss Brussels sprouts in olive oil, salt, and pepper. Sprinkle with pine nuts and pomegranate seeds.

PER SERVING | Calories: 81 | Fat: 5 g | Protein: 3 g | Sodium: 416 mg | Carbohydrates: 7 g | Fiber: 3 g

Pan-Seared Brussels Sprouts

Pan-searing Brussels sprouts brings out their buttery notes.

INGREDIENTS | SERVES 4

1 pound Brussels sprouts

1 tablespoon olive oil

¾ cup water

½ teaspoon salt

¼ teaspoon pepper

1. Remove the outer leaves and trim the stems of the Brussels sprouts. Cut larger sprouts in half to get them to a uniform size for even cooking.
2. Heat olive oil in an uncovered pressure cooker over medium heat. Sauté sprouts, stirring often, for 5 minutes or until the sides begin to brown. Add the water. Close and lock the lid.
3. Turn the heat up to high. When the cooker reaches pressure, lower the heat to the minimum needed to maintain pressure. Cook for 1 minute at high pressure.
4. When time is up, open the pressure cooker by releasing pressure.
5. Transfer immediately to serving dish to avoid overcooking. Season with salt and pepper.

PER SERVING | Calories: 77 g | Fat: 4 g | Protein: 4 g | Sodium: 324 mg | Carbohydrates: 10 g | Fiber: 4 g

Beer-Braised Savoy Cabbage

You could also braise cabbage in wine, stock, or the reserved steaming liquid from another recipe.

INGREDIENTS | SERVES 6

1 medium Savoy cabbage
1 tablespoon butter
1 medium onion, sliced
¾ cup light beer

Buying Savoy Cabbage

Buy a whole head of cabbage. Pre-sliced or shredded cabbage begins to lose its vitamins almost immediately.

1. Slice the cabbage in half, and then into strips. Wash and dry the cabbage strips.
2. Heat butter in an uncovered pressure cooker over medium heat. Add the onion and cook, stirring occasionally, until softened (about 5 minutes).
3. Add the cabbage and beer. Close and lock the lid.
4. Turn the heat up to high. When the cooker reaches pressure, lower to the minimum heat needed to maintain pressure. Cook 3–5 minutes at high pressure.
5. When time is up, open the pressure cooker by releasing pressure.
6. Transfer to serving platter immediately to avoid overcooking, and serve warm or room temperature.

PER SERVING | Calories: 74 | Fat: 2 g | Protein: 2 g | Sodium: 30 mg | Carbohydrates: 11 g | Fiber: 4 g

Red Cabbage and Apples

Red wine will help preserve the color of the cabbage. Serve with any pork entrée.

INGREDIENTS | SERVES 8

1 (2½-pound) red cabbage
1 tablespoon olive oil
1 medium onion, diced
2 Granny Smith apples, peeled, cored, and sliced
½ cup Merlot
3 tablespoons red wine vinegar
1 teaspoon salt
¼ teaspoon freshly ground black pepper

1. Cut cabbage into quarters. Remove and discard the core. Slice the quarters into thin strips. Put aside.
2. Heat olive oil in an uncovered pressure cooker over medium heat. Sauté the onion until soft (about 5 minutes).
3. Add the apples and stir in the Merlot and red wine vinegar.
4. Gradually add cabbage to the pressure cooker by filling the pressure cooker to the top and loosely covering it with the lid until the cabbage wilts, freeing up more space in the pressure cooker.
5. Stir in enough of the remaining cabbage to bring the pressure cooker to the fill line. Close and lock the lid.
6. Turn the heat up to high. When the cooker reaches pressure, lower the heat to the minimum needed to maintain pressure. Cook for 2–4 minutes at high pressure.
7. When time is up, open the pressure cooker by releasing pressure.
8. Transfer the cabbage to a serving bowl using a slotted spoon. Season with salt and pepper.

PER SERVING | Calories: 88 | Fat: 2 g | Protein: 2 g | Sodium: 321 mg | Fiber: 4 g | Carbohydrates: 15 g

Tie-Dyed Baby Carrots

The name of this recipe comes from the beautiful, mottled color the beets give to the carrots.

INGREDIENTS | SERVES 8

8 small red beets
1 pound peeled baby carrots
¼ cup water
1 tablespoon olive oil
1 teaspoon salt
¼ teaspoon freshly ground black pepper

Beet and Carrot Salad

Toss chilled leftover beets and carrots with honey-mustard salad dressing or your favorite vinaigrette. Stir in some finely diced shallot or red onion and minced fresh parsley, and top with toasted walnuts and feta cheese.

1. Scrub and peel the beets, trim the ends, and then cut into quarters.
2. Add the baby carrots to the pressure cooker and put the beets on top. Pour in the water. Close and lock the lid.
3. Turn the heat up to high. When the cooker reaches pressure, lower the heat to the minimum needed to maintain pressure. Cook for 8 minutes at high pressure.
4. When time is up, open the pressure cooker by releasing pressure.
5. Test the beets and carrots to determine whether or not they're cooked through. If they're not yet tender, return the pan to medium heat. Add more water if necessary, and bring to a simmer. Simmer with pressure cooker loosely covered by the lid until the vegetables are tender.
6. Once they're cooked through, drain off any excess moisture and transfer to a serving bowl. Toss with oil, salt, and pepper.

PER SERVING | Calories: 69 | Fat: 2 g | Protein: 1.5 g | Sodium: 402 mg | Fiber: 4 g | Carbohydrates: 12 g

Carrots in Milk

A side dish that is sure to be appreciated by children of all ages!

INGREDIENTS | SERVES 4

1 pound thick carrots, peeled and cut into 1-inch chunks

¾ cup fat-free milk

¼ cup water

½ teaspoon salt

¼ teaspoon nutmeg

1 tablespoon olive oil

1 tablespoon flour

1. Fill the pressure cooker with carrots, milk, water, salt, nutmeg, and oil. Close and lock the lid.
2. Turn the heat up to high. When the cooker reaches pressure, lower the heat to the minimum needed to maintain pressure. Cook 3–4 minutes at high pressure.
3. Open the pressure cooker by releasing pressure. With a slotted spoon, transfer carrots to serving dish.
4. Place uncovered pressure cooker over medium heat. Add flour to remaining liquid and heat until thickened, stirring constantly. Pour sauce over carrots and serve.

PER SERVING | Calories: 99 | Fat: 4 g | Protein: 3 g | Sodium: 391 mg | Fiber: 3 g | Carbohydrates: 14 g

Gingered Carrots

You can boost the flavor in this dish by adding a dash of cinnamon or allspice after cooking.

INGREDIENTS | SERVES 4

1 pound carrots, peeled and sliced diagonally

2 tablespoons vegetable oil

1 teaspoon minced fresh ginger (or ⅛ teaspoon ground ginger)

1 cup water

½ teaspoon salt

¼ teaspoon black pepper

1. Add the carrots, oil, ginger, and water to the pressure cooker. Stir to mix. Close and lock the lid.
2. Turn the heat up to high. When the cooker reaches pressure, lower the heat to the minimum needed to maintain pressure. Cook for 1 minute at high pressure.
3. Open the pressure cooker by releasing pressure. Strain carrots, season with salt and pepper, and serve.

PER SERVING | Calories: 106 | Fat: 7 g | Protein: 1 g | Sodium: 372 mg | Carbohydrates: 11 g | Fiber: 3 g

Fresh Versus Ground Ginger

Ground ginger is more pungent than fresh so you shouldn't substitute one for the other in all recipes. In this recipe, however, either will work well.

Southern-Style Collards

Collard greens are a Southern staple typically flavored with animal fat, but this tasty vegetarian version is made by adding liquid smoke and soy sauce to the broth.

INGREDIENTS | SERVES 6

1 pound collard greens
1 tablespoon olive oil
½ onion, diced
1 garlic clove, minced
1 chipotle chili pepper
4 cups Vegetable Stock (see recipe in Chapter 4)
1 teaspoon liquid smoke
1 tablespoon soy sauce
1 teaspoon white vinegar
1 teaspoon salt
¼ teaspoon pepper

1. To prepare the greens, cut away the tough stalks and stems and discard any leaves that are bruised or yellow. Wash the collards two or three times thoroughly to remove the grit. Chop into large pieces and set aside.
2. Heat olive oil in an uncovered pressure cooker over medium heat. Add the onion, garlic, and chipotle pepper. Cook until the onions begin to soften (about 5 minutes). Add chopped collards, stock, liquid smoke, soy sauce, and white vinegar. Stir well. Close and lock the lid.
3. Turn the heat up to high. When the cooker reaches pressure, lower the heat to the minimum needed to maintain pressure. Cook for 10–15 minutes at high pressure.
4. Open with the natural release method (see Chapter 1).
5. Remove the chipotle pepper before serving. Season with salt and pepper.

PER SERVING | Calories: 246 | Fat: 5 g | Protein: 10 g | Sodium: 957 mg | Fiber: 22 g | Carbohydrates: 55 g

Corn on the Cob

If you're cutting fat from your diet or watching your calories, you'll love this dish!
Corn served this way tastes delicious without any butter or salt.

INGREDIENTS | SERVES 4

4 ears fresh sweet corn, shucked
¾ cup water
1 lime, quartered
¼ teaspoon freshly ground black pepper

Get the Freshest Corn!

As soon as corn is picked from the farm, the sugars in the kernels begin turning into starch. So get the freshest cobs you can find, and cook them right away!

1. Place the rack in the pressure cooker and put the corn on the rack. Pour in the water. Close and lock the lid.
2. Turn the heat up to high. When the cooker reaches pressure, lower the heat to the minimum needed to maintain pressure. Cook for 3–5 minutes at high pressure.
3. Open the pressure cooker by releasing pressure.
4. Transfer the corn to plates. Squeeze a wedge of lime juice and grind black pepper over each ear of corn.

PER SERVING | Calories: 127 | Fat: 1 g | Protein: 4 g | Sodium: 8 mg | Fiber: 4 g | Carbohydrates: 31 g

Eggplant Caponata

This versatile dish can be served hot, at room temperature, or cold. You can use it as a pasta topping, a side dish, or even a pita filling if you strain all the liquid.

INGREDIENTS | SERVES 8

2 tablespoons extra-virgin olive oil
1 tablespoon white wine vinegar
1 teaspoon ground cinnamon
1 large eggplant, peeled and diced
1 medium onion, peeled and diced
2 cloves garlic, peeled and minced
1 (14½-ounce) can of diced tomatoes
1 stalk celery, diced
½ cup pitted and chopped olives
½ cup golden raisins
2 tablespoons capers
¾ teaspoon salt
½ teaspoon freshly ground black pepper

1. Add all ingredients to the pressure cooker. Stir well to mix. Close and lock the lid
2. Turn the heat up to high. When the cooker reaches pressure, lower the heat to the minimum needed to maintain pressure. Cook for 5–7 minutes at high pressure.
3. Open the pressure cooker by releasing pressure.
4. Remove the lid and stir the contents of the pressure cooker. Taste for seasoning. Add salt and pepper to taste.

PER SERVING | Calories: 100 | Fat: 4 g | Protein: 2 g | Sodium: 511 mg | Fiber: 4 g | Carbohydrates: 15 g

Creamed Corn

Creamed corn is an almost soupy vegetable side dish that is popular in the Midwest and South.

INGREDIENTS | SERVES 6

6 ears sweet corn, shucked
½ cup water
1 tablespoon corn or vegetable oil
2 tablespoons flour
½ cup whole milk or unsweetened soymilk
2 teaspoons salt
1 teaspoon honey

Creamed Corn Variations

Many creamed corn recipes don't call for cream or dairy at all. When scraping kernels from a cob of corn and pressing against the cob, you release starch that makes the corn "creamy."

1. Place the rack in the pressure cooker and place the corn on the rack. Pour in the water. Close and lock the lid.
2. Turn the heat up to high. When the cooker reaches pressure, lower the heat to the minimum needed to maintain pressure. Cook for 3–5 minutes at high pressure.
3. When time is up, open the pressure cooker by releasing pressure.
4. When the corn is cool enough to handle, place each ear of corn over a large mixing bowl and remove the kernels with a knife, using long downward strokes and rotating the cob as you go.
5. Take half of the kernels and pulse in a food processor until just smooth.
6. In a medium saucepan, heat the oil, then stir in the flour, being careful not to brown it. Slowly stir the milk into the roux, and stir until smooth.
7. Add all of the corn to the saucepan and bring to a boil. Reduce heat and simmer for 10 minutes.
8. Stir in salt and honey just before removing from heat. Serve.

PER SERVING | Calories: 167 | Fat: 4 g | Protein: 5 g | Sodium: 800 mg | Carbohydrates: 33 g | Fiber: 3.5 g

Milk-Braised Fennel

An unusual yet delicious accompaniment to meat.

INGREDIENTS | SERVES 4

2 large fennel bulbs
¾ cup fat-free milk
¼ cup water
½ teaspoon salt
¼ teaspoon nutmeg
1 tablespoon olive oil
1 tablespoon flour
1 teaspoon freshly ground black pepper

Just Eat It!

The whole fennel plant is edible. Fennel pollen, seeds, bulbs, and leaves have culinary value—and flavor.

1. Remove the green tips of the fennel and reserve them for garnish. Slice the fennel bulbs into ¼-inch-thick slices.
2. Fill the pressure cooker with fennel, milk, water, salt, nutmeg, and oil. Close and lock the lid.
3. Turn the heat up to high. When the cooker reaches pressure, lower the heat to the minimum needed to maintain pressure. Cook 3–4 minutes at high pressure.
4. When time is up, open the pressure cooker by releasing pressure.
5. With a slotted spoon, carefully remove fennel slices to serving dish. Place uncovered pressure cooker over medium heat.
6. Add flour to the remaining liquid in pressure cooker and heat until thickened, stirring constantly.
7. Pour sauce over cooked fennel and garnish with green fennel tips. Season with pepper before serving.

PER SERVING | Calories: 90 | Fat: 4 g | Protein: 3 g | Sodium: 375 mg | Fiber: 4 g | Carbohydrates: 12 g

Bavarian Kale

Kale is a leafy green vegetable that is both colorful and nutritious. This dish provides all the starch you need from the vegetable portion of your meal.

INGREDIENTS | SERVES 4

2 cups water
½ teaspoon salt
2 bunches kale, washed and drained
2 tablespoons olive or vegetable oil
1 small onion, peeled and diced
1 clove garlic, minced
1½ cups chicken broth
4 medium potatoes, peeled and diced
1 stalk celery, diced
4 teaspoons sour cream

1. Bring water to a boil in the pressure cooker. Stir in the salt.
2. Cut the kale leaves into ½-inch-wide strips. Blanch kale for 1 minute in pressure cooker, drain, and set aside.
3. Heat olive or vegetable oil in the uncovered pressure cooker over medium heat. Add the onion and sauté for 5 minutes.
4. Add the garlic and sauté for 30 seconds. Add the broth, potatoes, celery, and blanched kale. Close and lock the lid.
5. Turn the heat up to high. When the cooker reaches pressure, lower the heat to the minimum needed to maintain pressure. Cook for 6–8 minutes at high pressure.
6. Open with the natural release method (see Chapter 1).
7. Stir, slightly mashing the potatoes into the mixture.
8. Transfer to plates and garnish each serving with a teaspoon of sour cream.

PER SERVING | Calories: 285 | Fat: 9 g | Protein: 7 g | Sodium: 733 mg | Fiber: 6 g | Carbohydrates: 45 g

Mushy Peas

This is a great use for frozen peas, but you can pressure-steam fresh peas as well.

INGREDIENTS | SERVES 6

1 tablespoon olive oil
1 scallion, finely chopped
1 pound frozen peas
1 sprig mint
1 cup water
¾ teaspoon salt
½ teaspoon freshly ground black pepper

Don't Go Dry

As mint dries, it begins to acquire a bitter taste. Use fresh mint if you can find it. If not, substitute with fresh basil or even one lavender flower for the menthol taste that would ordinarily be contributed by fresh mint.

1. Heat olive oil in an uncovered pressure cooker over medium heat. Add the scallion and sauté until softened (approximately 3–5 minutes).
2. Add the peas, mint, and water. Close and lock the lid.
3. Turn the heat up to high. When the cooker reaches pressure, lower to the minimum heat needed to maintain pressure. Then, begin counting 2–3 minutes cooking time at high pressure.
4. When time is up, open the pressure cooker by releasing pressure.
5. Remove mint sprig. Drain about half of cooking liquid, and mash or purée the remainder to desired thickness.
6. Add salt and pepper to taste.

PER SERVING | Calories: 81 | Fat: 2.5 g | Protein: 4 g | Sodium: 400 mg | Fiber: 4 g | Carbohydrates: 11 g

Peperonata (Faux Roasted Peppers)

This Italian pepper recipe is extremely flexible. You can serve this as an appetizer, piled onto crispy crostini, or as a sauce mixed in with freshly cooked pasta.

INGREDIENTS | SERVES 6

1 tablespoon vegetable oil

1 red onion, thinly sliced into strips

2 red bell peppers, seeded and thinly sliced

2 yellow bell peppers, seeded and thinly sliced

1 green bell pepper, seeded and thinly sliced

2 garlic cloves, chopped, divided

3 ripe tomatoes, chopped, or 1 (14½-ounce) can of chopped tomatoes

1 bunch of basil, chopped

2 tablespoons olive oil

½ teaspoon salt

¼ teaspoon pepper

1. Heat vegetable oil in an uncovered pressure cooker over medium heat. Add onion and sauté until soft (about 5 minutes).
2. Add the red, yellow, and green peppers. Let one side of the peppers brown without stirring (about 5 minutes).
3. Add half of the garlic and all of the tomatoes. Mix well. Close and lock the pressure cooker.
4. Turn the heat up to high. When the cooker reaches pressure, lower the heat to the minimum needed to maintain pressure. Cook for 5 minutes at high pressure.
5. When time is up, open the pressure cooker by releasing pressure.
6. Remove the peppers with tongs and put them immediately in a serving bowl. Add the rest of the garlic, basil, olive oil, salt, and pepper to the serving bowl.
7. Mix well and serve.

PER SERVING | Calories: 104 | Fat: 7 g | Protein: 2 g | Sodium: 204 mg | Fiber: 3 g | Carbohydrates: 10 g

Potato Stuffed Onions

Chop the extra onion and freeze it in 1-cup portions to use in other recipes.

INGREDIENTS | SERVES 6

5 medium potatoes, unpeeled

2 cups water, divided

1 egg

¾ cup grated Parmigiano-Reggiano cheese

1 tablespoon thyme

2 teaspoons salt

1 teaspoon white pepper

3 large onions, peeled and halved horizontally

½ cup bread crumbs

Stuff It!

Onions can also be stuffed with ground meat and spices, or even a ricotta-bread crumb mixture!

1. Place potatoes in pressure cooker with 1 cup water. Close and lock the lid.
2. Turn the heat up to high. When the cooker reaches pressure, lower the heat to the minimum needed to maintain pressure. Cook for 10–15 minutes at high pressure.
3. Open with the natural release method (see Chapter 1).
4. Remove potatoes with a slotted spoon and set aside.
5. When cool enough to handle, peel potatoes and mash them with a fork. Spread mashed potatoes on a platter and allow them to cool.
6. Once cool, transfer potatoes to a large mixing bowl and add egg, cheese, thyme, salt, and pepper.
7. Using a melon baller, scoop out all but the outer 2 or 3 layers of the raw onion, making a cup shape.
8. Stuff the onions with the potato mixture and place in steamer basket. Put steamer basket in pressure cooker with remaining cup of water. Close and lock the lid.
9. Turn the heat up to high. When the cooker reaches pressure, lower the heat to the minimum needed to maintain pressure. Cook for 10–15 minutes at high pressure.
10. When time is up, open the pressure cooker by releasing pressure.
11. Carefully transfer the onions to plates and sprinkle with breadcrumbs.

PER SERVING | Calories: 259 | Fat: 6 g | Protein: 9 g | Sodium: 967 mg | Fiber: 6 g | Carbohydrates: 442 g

Southern Italian Green Beans and Tomatoes

To keep your green beans from overcooking, steam them over the tomatoes.
You can use fresh or frozen green beans for this recipe.

INGREDIENTS | SERVES 6

1 tablespoon olive oil

1 clove garlic, crushed

2 cups chopped tomatoes, or 1 (14½-ounce) can of chopped tomatoes

1 pound green beans, trimmed

¼ teaspoon salt

1 sprig basil, chopped

1 tablespoon extra-virgin olive oil

Tomato Magic

In Italy, both meats and vegetables are cooked in tomato sauce, so you can do this recipe with just about any vegetable!

1. Heat olive oil in an uncovered pressure cooker over medium heat. Add garlic and cook until golden (about 30 seconds–1 minute). Add the tomatoes and stir well.
2. Fill steamer basket with green beans and add to pressure cooker. Sprinkle with salt.
3. Turn the heat up to high. When the cooker reaches pressure, lower the heat to the minimum needed to maintain pressure. Cook for 5–7 minutes at low pressure (3 minutes at high pressure).
4. When time is up, open the pressure cooker by releasing pressure.
5. Pull out the steamer basket and mix green beans into tomato sauce.
6. Once mixed, check to see if green beans are tender by gently poking with fork. If the green beans need to cook a little more, simmer them with the sauce on low heat, uncovered.
7. When fork tender, move the mixed contents to a serving bowl. Sprinkle with basil and extra-virgin olive oil. Serve warm or at room temperature.

PER SERVING | Calories: 74 | Fat: 5 g | Protein: 2 g | Sodium: 105 mg | Fiber: 3 g | Carbohydrates: 8 g

Green Bean and Pine Nut Salad

The pressure cooker can bring the bright color back to frozen green beans, and their bright flavors shine in this simple salad.

INGREDIENTS | SERVES 4

1 pound fresh or frozen green beans
1 cup water
¼ cup toasted pine nuts
2 teaspoons white balsamic vinegar
1 tablespoon olive oil

1. Lay green beans in steamer basket. Place water in the pressure cooker and add the steamer basket. Close and lock the lid.
2. Turn the heat up to high. When the cooker reaches pressure, lower the heat to the minimum needed to maintain pressure. Cook for 5–7 minutes at high pressure.
3. Open the pressure cooker by releasing pressure. Transfer to serving dish and dress with pine nuts, vinegar, and olive oil.

PER SERVING | Calories: 154 | Fat: 12 g | Protein: 4 g | Sodium: 17 mg | Fiber: 4.5 g | Carbohydrates: 11 g

Boozy Taters

Here's something a little different to do with your potatoes. They don't have a strong wine flavor, but just a little something "extra."

INGREDIENTS | SERVES 6

1 tablespoon olive oil
5 medium potatoes, peeled and diced
2 teaspoons salt
1 teaspoon black pepper
1 sprig rosemary, chopped
1 cup of Marsala, Vin Santo, or any other sweet dry wine

No Liquor

Don't substitute the wine with liquors like brandy or whisky. They contain a greater amount of alcohol and could ignite when you release pressure!

1. Heat olive oil in an uncovered pressure cooker over medium heat. Add the potatoes, salt, pepper, and rosemary. Add the wine and stir, scraping the bottom of the pan. Close and lock the lid.
2. Turn the heat up to high. When the cooker reaches pressure, lower the heat to the minimum needed to maintain pressure. Cook for 6 minutes at high pressure.
3. Open the pressure cooker by releasing pressure. Serve warm.

PER SERVING | Calories: 177 | Fat: 2.5 g | Protein: 3 g | Sodium: 799 mg | Fiber: 4.5 g | Carbohydrates: 30 g

Green Bean and Potato Salad

Braising potatoes on the bottom of the pressure cooker leaves space at the top for cooking another vegetable. You can replace green beans with baby artichokes, carrots, or zucchini rounds.

INGREDIENTS | SERVES 6

3 pounds red or new potatoes, cut into 1-inch cubes

1 cup water

½ teaspoon salt

1 pound green beans

3 tablespoons white balsamic vinegar

4 tablespoons extra-virgin olive oil

Zest of 1 lemon

1. Add potatoes and water to the pressure cooker and sprinkle with salt. Place the trivet and steamer basket over the potatoes and fill with green beans. Close and lock the lid.
2. Turn the heat up to high. When the cooker reaches pressure, lower the heat to the minimum needed to maintain pressure. Cook for 5 minutes at high pressure.
3. When time is up, open the pressure cooker by releasing pressure.
4. Transfer green beans to a serving bowl. Drain the potatoes and add them to the bowl.
5. In a separate small bowl, whisk vinegar, oil, and lemon zest. Pour over the potatoes and green beans. Toss to coat.
6. Serve warm or chill overnight in the refrigerator.

PER SERVING | Calories: 264 | Fat: 9 g | Protein: 5 g | Sodium: 216 mg | Fiber: 7 g | Carbohydrates: 41 g

Potato and Parsley Salad

Steaming the potatoes that have already been cut helps them to keep their shape. This way, there's no risk of cutting a hot potato and finding out that it's too soft—turning your salad into an unintended purée.

INGREDIENTS | SERVES 6

⅓ cup finely chopped white onion

3 tablespoons white wine vinegar

½ teaspoon black pepper

3 pounds red or new potatoes, cut into 1-inch cubes

1 cup water

1 teaspoon salt

4 tablespoons extra-virgin olive oil

1 bunch parsley, finely chopped

1. Place onion in a small mixing bowl with the vinegar and pepper. Set aside to macerate.
2. Place potatoes in the steamer basket. Place water in the pressure cooker and add the steamer basket. Close and lock the lid.
3. Turn the heat up to high. When the cooker reaches pressure, lower the heat to the minimum needed to maintain pressure. Cook for 10 minutes at high pressure.
4. Open with the natural release method (see Chapter 1).
5. When time is up, transfer potatoes to a large mixing bowl and dress them with the onion, vinegar, and pepper mixture. When they have cooled to room temperature (about 10 minutes) add the salt, olive oil, and parsley.
6. Serve immediately or chill overnight in the refrigerator.

PER SERVING | Calories: 240 | Fat: 9 g | Protein: 4 g | Sodium: 213 mg | Fiber: 6 g | Carbohydrates: 36 g

Curried Yams and Potatoes

Growing your own potatoes is easy, especially if you live in a cooler climate. Purchase seed potatoes from your local gardening store and use organic fertilizers to keep them healthy.

INGREDIENTS | SERVES 8

1 tablespoon butter

1 small onion, peeled and finely diced

2 tablespoons curry paste

3 cloves garlic, peeled and minced

4 large yams, peeled and diced

1 large potato, peeled and diced

¼ cup applesauce

¾ cup water

1 cup frozen extra-fine baby peas, thawed

1 cup plain low-fat yogurt

1 cucumber, peeled and sliced

1. Melt the butter in the pressure cooker over medium-high heat. Add the onion and sauté for 3 minutes.
2. Stir in the curry paste and garlic and sauté for 2 minutes.
3. Stir in the yams and potatoes. Sauté for about 3 minutes or until the pan is sticky and the mixture is about to burn.
4. Stir in the applesauce and water. Close and lock the lid.
5. Turn the heat up to high. When the cooker reaches pressure, lower the heat to the minimum needed to maintain pressure. Cook for 5–7 minutes at high pressure.
6. Open with the natural release method (see Chapter 1).
7. Remove the lid. Stir and slightly mash the potato mixture.
8. Add the peas and stir into the potatoes. Cover and let rest for a few minutes to bring the peas to temperature.
9. Serve with a dollop of plain low-fat yogurt over each serving and garnish with cucumber slices.

PER SERVING | Calories: 152 | Fat: 3 g | Protein: 4 g | Sodium: 56 mg | Fiber: 5 g | Carbohydrates: 28 g

Herb-Roasted Potatoes

These potatoes will brown nicely during the sauté and look like they're from the oven!
Very small or fingerling potatoes can also be used.

INGREDIENTS | SERVES 6

4 tablespoons vegetable oil

2 pounds new potatoes

3 cloves garlic, skin on

1 sprig rosemary, chopped

½ cup Chicken Stock (see recipe in Chapter 4)

1 teaspoon salt

¼ teaspoon pepper

Pressure Pans

Some stovetop pressure cooker manufacturers make a low, wide pressure cooker that is called a "pressure pan" or "pressure braiser." If you have one, it's perfect for this recipe because of the wide area in which to sauté the potatoes!

1. Heat vegetable oil in an uncovered pressure cooker over medium heat. Add as many potatoes as will cover the base of your pressure cooker.
2. Roll the potatoes around and brown the outside on all sides (8–10 minutes). Remove from pressure cooker and repeat with rest of potatoes and the garlic and rosemary.
3. Once all potatoes are cooked and removed from the pressure cooker, pierce each potato in the center with a sharp knife. Return potatoes to the pressure cooker and pour in the stock. Close and lock the lid.
4. Turn the heat up to high. When the cooker reaches pressure, lower the heat to the minimum needed to maintain pressure. Cook for 5 minutes at high pressure.
5. Open with the natural release method (see Chapter 1).
6. Remove the outer skin of the garlic cloves (and serve whole or smash, to taste).
7. Transfer potatoes to serving dish and sprinkle everything with salt and pepper.

PER SERVING | Calories: 194 | Fat: 9 g | Protein: 3 g | Sodium: 431 mg | Fiber: 4 g | Carbohydrates: 25 g

Light Scalloped Potatoes

Using plain yogurt to replace heavy cream and most of the butter makes this a creamy and light dish.

INGREDIENTS | SERVES 6

2 cups plain whole yogurt

5 potatoes, peeled and thinly sliced

1 teaspoon salt

1 teaspoon white pepper

1 teaspoon nutmeg

½ cup grated Parmesan cheese

1 tablespoon butter, cut into small cubes

½ cup bread crumbs

Make and Use a Foil Sling

Getting a heatproof container in the pressure cooker is easy. The hard part is pulling it out when it's hot and slippery! To make things easier, use a foil sling to lower and lift containers from the pressure cooker. Fold an extra-long piece of aluminum foil in half. Place a heatproof dish in the middle of the strip, lift up the sides and use as "handles" to lower into the pressure cooker. Fold the handles down during pressure cooking, and when pressure cooking is finished, unfold the handles and pull your dish out of the pressure cooker.

1. Place the yogurt in a fine mesh strainer over a bowl and let drain in the refrigerator for about 4 hours. Discard liquid and set thickened yogurt aside.
2. In a heatproof baking dish that will fit inside your pressure cooker without touching the sides, layer the potatoes and yogurt, sprinkling each layer of potato with salt, white pepper, and nutmeg. Continue working in layers until the container is full. Top with Parmesan cheese and butter.
3. Place water in the pressure cooker. Add the steamer basket and lower the uncovered baking dish into the pressure cooker. Close and lock the lid.
4. Turn the heat up to high. When the cooker reaches pressure, lower the heat to the minimum needed to maintain pressure. Cook for 15 minutes at high pressure.
5. Open with the natural release method (see Chapter 1).
6. Carefully remove the container from the pressure cooker.
7. Sprinkle with bread crumbs and slide under the broiler. Wait until the top is crisp before serving.

PER SERVING | Calories: 263 | Fat: 8 g | Protein: 10 g | Sodium: 634 mg | Fiber: 5 g | Carbohydrates: 39 g

Mashed Potatoes

A classic dish that can easily be personalized by tossing in a handful of your favorite grated cheese right at the end!

INGREDIENTS | SERVES 6

5 medium potatoes, unpeeled
2 cups water
1 teaspoon coarse or rock salt
½ cup whole milk
1 teaspoon salt
½ teaspoon white pepper

Keep Potato Skins!

According to the Washington State Potato Commission, a 6-ounce potato contains 2 grams of highly digestible protein—almost as much as half a glass of milk—making it a great foundation for a meal.

1. Place the potatoes inside the pressure cooker, add water, and sprinkle with salt. Close and lock the lid.
2. Turn the heat up to high. When the cooker reaches pressure, lower the heat to the minimum needed to maintain pressure. Cook for 10–15 minutes at high pressure.
3. Open with the natural release method (see Chapter 1).
4. Strain out the cooking liquid and mash potatoes with potato masher. Add milk as needed to reach creamy consistency. Season with salt and pepper.
5. Transfer to a serving dish.

PER SERVING | Calories: 135 | Fat: 1 g | Protein: 4 g | Sodium: 807 mg | Fiber: 4 g | Carbohydrates: 29 g

Stewed Green Tomatoes

This dish is great for green tomatoes that have not had time to ripen on the vine.

INGREDIENTS | SERVES 4

1 tablespoon olive oil
2 tablespoons minced onion
4 large green tomatoes, sliced
¾ cup water
½ teaspoon sugar
½ teaspoon salt
¼ teaspoon paprika
½ teaspoon curry powder
½ cup plain bread crumbs
1 tablespoon chopped, fresh parsley

1. In the preheated pressure cooker over medium heat add the oil and onion and sauté for 2 minutes.
2. Add the tomatoes, water, sugar, salt, paprika, and curry powder. Stir to mix. Close and lock the lid.
3. Turn the heat up to high. When the cooker reaches pressure, lower the heat to the minimum needed to maintain pressure. Cook for 8 minutes at high pressure.
4. Open with the natural release method (see Chapter 1).
5. Remove lid from pressure cooker. Return to medium heat and bring to a simmer.
6. Stir in bread crumbs. Simmer and stir until thickened. Transfer to serving dish and top with parsley.

PER SERVING | Calories: 137 | Fat: 7 g | Protein: 3.5 | Sodium: 389 mg | Fiber: 2.5 g | Carbohydrates: 16 g

Indian-Style Cauliflower and Potatoes

Not only is this an easy one-pot-meal that takes just minutes to prepare, the star ingredient, cauliflower, is a great source of vitamin C and manganese—two major antioxidants.

INGREDIENTS | SERVES 4

1 cup water
2 cups peeled and cubed potatoes
2 cups chopped cauliflower
2 tablespoons vegetable oil
1 teaspoon cumin seeds
1 clove garlic, minced
1 teaspoon minced ginger
1 teaspoon turmeric
1 teaspoon garam masala
1 teaspoon salt

1. Add water and potatoes to the pressure cooker. Place the cauliflower in steamer basket and lower into pressure cooker. Close and lock the lid.
2. Turn the heat up to high. When the cooker reaches pressure, lower the heat to the minimum needed to maintain pressure. Cook for 4 minutes at high pressure.
3. When time is up, open the pressure cooker by releasing pressure. Remove and strain potatoes and cauliflower.
4. In the empty, uncovered pressure cooker, heat vegetable oil over medium-high heat. Add cumin seeds, garlic, and ginger, and sauté for 1 minute. Add the turmeric, garam masala, and salt, and sauté for 1 additional minute.
5. Add the cooked potatoes and cauliflower. Simmer over low heat, stirring occasionally, for 5–10 minutes. Serve.

PER SERVING | Calories: 131 | Fat: 7 g | Protein: 2 g | Sodium: 610 | Fiber: 3 g | Carbohydrates: 15 g

Steamed Pumpkin

Make your own pumpkin purée to use in pies or pasta sauce!

INGREDIENTS | SERVES 6

1 medium (4-pound) pumpkin, seeded, cut into large pieces

1 cup water

Save the Seeds!

Rinse the seeds well and spread in an even layer on a cookie sheet to dry. Then toss them with vegetable oil and salt, return them to the cookie sheet, and roast at 300°F for 30 minutes, shaking the pan every 10 minutes.

1. Place pumpkin pieces in the pressure cooker skin-side down. Pour in the water. Close and lock the lid.
2. Turn the heat up to high. When the cooker reaches pressure, lower the heat to the minimum needed to maintain pressure. Cook for 8–10 minutes at high pressure.
3. Open with the natural release method (see Chapter 1).
4. When pumpkin pieces are cool enough to handle, peel off and discard the skin. Mash pumpkin with a fork or purée with an immersion blender.

PER SERVING | Calories: 77 | Fat: 0 g | Protein: 3 g | Sodium: 3 mg | Fiber: 1.5 g | Carbohydrates: 19 g

Spaghetti Squash

Sauté the "spaghetti" in olive oil, garlic, sage, and nutmeg and serve dusted with cheese!

INGREDIENTS | SERVES 6

1 large spaghetti squash, halved or quartered and seeded

1 cup water

1. Place squash halves or quarters in the pressure cooker skin-side down. Pour in the water. Close and lock the lid.
2. Turn the heat up to high. When the cooker reaches pressure, lower the heat to the minimum needed to maintain pressure. Cook for 6–8 minutes at high pressure.
3. Open with the natural release method (see Chapter 1).
4. When squash is cool enough to handle, use a fork to scoop out the "spaghetti" part from the skin.

PER SERVING | Calories: 35 | Fat: 0 g | Protein: 3 g | Sodium: 4 mg | Fiber: 2 g | Carbohydrates: 7.5 g

Swiss Chard and Vegetables in Parmesan Sauce

This rich side dish also goes well with something as simple as leftover roast turkey or chicken.

INGREDIENTS | SERVES 8

½ cup water

1 pound Swiss chard

1 onion, peeled and sliced

3 stalks celery, diced

2 carrots, sliced on the diagonal

1 pound Brussels sprouts

1 medium zucchini

1 cauliflower

4 tablespoons butter

4 cloves garlic, peeled and minced

½ cup grated Parmigiano-Reggiano cheese

⅛ teaspoon crushed and dried red pepper flakes

½ cup whole milk

1. Add the water to the pressure cooker.
2. Wash and drain the chard. Remove and discard the tough stems. Tear the chard into bite-size pieces. Set aside.
3. Layer the onion, celery, carrots, and chard into the pressure cooker.
4. Wash and drain Brussels sprouts. Remove and discard the outer leaves. Cut in half and add on top of the chard.
5. Slice the zucchini and put on top of the Brussels sprouts. Divide the cauliflower into large florets and add on top of the zucchini. Close and lock the lid.
6. Turn the heat up to high. When the cooker reaches pressure, lower the heat to the minimum needed to maintain pressure. Cook for 3 minutes at high pressure.
7. When time is up, open the pressure cooker by releasing pressure.
8. Drain the vegetables and transfer them to a serving bowl.
9. Melt the butter in the empty, uncovered pressure cooker over medium heat. Stir in the garlic and sauté for 30 seconds to 1 minute, being careful not to let the garlic burn. Stir in the cheese and pepper flakes. Slowly whisk in the milk.
10. Continue to cook and stir until the sauce is smooth and bubbling. Pour sauce over the vegetables and toss to coat. Serve.

PER SERVING | Calories: 158 | Fat: 9 g | Protein: 7 g | Sodium: 231 mg | Carbohydrates: 15 g | Fiber: 5 g

Spicy and Minty Zucchini

This easy and quick recipe packs a lot of flavor!

INGREDIENTS | SERVES 4

1 tablespoon olive oil

⅛ teaspoon hot pepper flakes

2 garlic cloves, smashed

1 pound zucchini, sliced into ¼ inch-thick rounds

½ teaspoon salt

½ cup water (if using an electric pressure cooker)

1 bunch fresh mint, chopped

Look Ma, No Water!

Most pressure cookers need at least 1 cup of water to reach pressure, but zucchini is 95 percent water. If 1 cup of water weighs about 8 ounces, then 1 pound of zucchini contains almost 2 cups of cooking liquid—locked in the veggie!

You can actually cook zucchini without water if you like, although this technique works best with stovetop pressure cookers that operate using a spring valve. This doesn't mean that you can't try this technique with your jiggling or puffing pressure cooker, but you may need to add a tablespoon or two of water to ensure they reach pressure. This is NOT recommended for electric pressure cookers—the initial scorch may damage the nonstick liner.

1. Heat olive oil in an uncovered pressure cooker over medium heat. Add pepper flakes, garlic, and half of the zucchini. Brown one side of the zucchini until golden, about 8 minutes. Then add the rest of the zucchini, stir well, and add salt. For electric pressure cookers, add ½ cup of water. Close and lock the lid.
2. Turn the heat up to high. When the cooker reaches pressure, lower the heat to the minimum needed to maintain pressure. Cook for 4–5 minutes at low pressure (1–2 minutes at high pressure).
3. When time is up, open the pressure cooker by releasing pressure.
4. Quickly transfer the zucchini from the cooker to a serving dish to avoid overcooking. Sprinkle with fresh mint leaves and serve hot or at room temperature.

PER SERVING | Calories: 52 | Fat: 4 g | Protein: 1.5 g | Sodium: 305 mg | Fiber: 1 g | Carbohydrates: 4 g

Lighter Ratatouille

The original version of this dish lightly fries each vegetable before combining.
Here, we skip the frying step and steam everything in its own juice.

INGREDIENTS | SERVES 4

2 tablespoons extra-virgin olive oil

½ cup water (if using an electric pressure cooker)

2 (7-inch) zucchini, washed and sliced

1 small or Japanese eggplant, peeled and sliced

1 small onion, peeled and thinly sliced

1 green bell pepper, seeded and diced

8 ounces fresh mushrooms, cleaned and sliced

1 (28-ounce) can diced tomatoes

3 tablespoons tomato paste

3 tablespoons water

2 cloves garlic, peeled and minced

1 teaspoon basil

1 teaspoon oregano

⅛ teaspoon dried red pepper flakes

1 teaspoon salt

½ teaspoon freshly ground black pepper

½ cup grated Parmigiano-Reggiano cheese

1. Coat the bottom and sides of the pressure cooker with oil. If using an electric pressure cooker, add water. Layer the remaining ingredients, except cheese, in the order given. Close and lock the lid.
2. Turn the heat up to high. When the cooker reaches pressure, lower the heat to the minimum needed to maintain pressure. Cook for 6 minutes at high pressure.
3. When time is up, open the pressure cooker by releasing pressure.
4. Remove the lid, stir, and taste for seasoning, adjusting if necessary. Serve topped with the grated cheese.

PER SERVING | Calories: 209 | Fat: 12 g | Protein: 9 g | Sodium: 1060 mg | Fiber: 5 g | Carbohydrates: 20 g

Winter Vegetable Medley

Any earthy herbs, such as rosemary, thyme, or sage, will work well in this delicious recipe.

INGREDIENTS | SERVES 4

2 tablespoons olive oil

1 sprig rosemary

3 carrots, peeled and sliced

1 large sweet potato, diced and peeled

6 red potatoes, quartered

2½ cups peeled and cubed butternut squash

1 cup water

1 teaspoon salt

½ teaspoon black pepper

1. Heat olive oil and rosemary in an uncovered pressure cooker over medium heat. Add all of the carrots, sweet potato, red potato, and butternut squash, stirring until well coated. Cook for 5 minutes.
2. Add water. Close and lock the lid of the pressure cooker.
3. Turn the heat up to high. When the cooker reaches pressure, lower the heat to the minimum needed to maintain pressure. Cook for 6 minutes at high pressure.
4. When time is up, open the pressure cooker by releasing pressure.
5. Drain the water. Season with salt and pepper and remove the rosemary sprig before serving.

PER SERVING | Calories: 378 | Fat: 8 g | Protein: 8 g | Sodium: 670 mg | Carbohydrates: 74 g | Fiber: 11 g

CHAPTER 4

Stocks, Soups, and Chowders

Chicken Stock
70

Fish Stock
71

Beef Stock
72

Vegetable Stock
73

Mushroom Broth
73

Fresh Tomato Soup
74

Lentil Soup
74

White Bean with Garlic and Kale Soup
75

Mushroom-Barley Soup
76

Re-Fashioned Potato Soup
77

Egg Drop Soup
77

Cream of Chestnut Soup
78

Butternut Squash and Ginger Soup
79

French Onion Soup
80

Creamy Lima Bean Soup
81

Corn Chowder
82

Creamy Asparagus Soup
83

Thai Carrot Soup
84

Vietnamese Beef Noodle Soup
85

Cuban Black Bean Soup
86

Greek Meatball Soup
87

Pasta and Chickpea Minestrone
88

New England Clam Chowder
89

Manhattan Clam Chowder
90

Split-Pea Soup
91

Portuguese Kale Soup
91

Cauliflower and Fennel Velouté
92

Chicken Stock

You can use the carcass of a previously roasted chicken for this recipe, too! With this recipe, you'll have concentrated chicken stock that you can use as-is, or add water for a milder flavor.

INGREDIENTS | YIELDS 8 CUPS

1 tablespoon olive oil
2 pounds bone-in chicken pieces
1 bunch fresh parsley
2 carrots, peeled and cut in half
1 yellow onion, quartered
3 celery stalks, cut in half
1 bunch fresh thyme
1 tablespoon sea salt
6 cups water

How Long Will It Take?

A full pressure cooker takes longer time to reach pressure. The pressure cooker cannot begin to build up pressure until all of the contents are brought to a boil and begin to generate pressure.

1. Preheat the pressure cooker on low heat for 2–3 minutes, then add olive oil. When oil begins to simmer, add the chicken pieces. Turn the heat to medium and brown the chicken well, turning frequently (about 7–10 minutes).
2. Add the parsley, carrots, onion, celery, thyme, and salt. Pour in just enough water to cover the vegetables. Close and lock the pressure cooker lid.
3. Turn the heat up to high. When the cooker reaches pressure, lower the heat to the minimum needed to maintain pressure. Cook for 20–25 minutes at high pressure.
4. Open with the natural release method (see Chapter 1).
5. Pour stock through strainer into a large mixing bowl. Let the liquid cool for about an hour before covering with plastic wrap. Refrigerate overnight.
6. The next day, spoon off the fat that has gathered at the top. If it has not solidified (it can depend on how much fat was on the pieces of chicken you used for the stock), you can remove the top layer by dropping a paper towel over the top and removing it as soon as it begins to absorb. You may need to do this several times to fully remove the top layer and clarify the stock.
7. Refrigerate for 3 days or freeze for up to 3 months.

PER CUP | Calories: 30 | Fat: 3 g | Protein: 0 g | Sodium: 952 mg | Fiber: 1 g | Carbohydrates: 3 g

Fish Stock

This stock is perfect to use in place of bottled clam juice as the base for any fish soup or seafood risotto.

INGREDIENTS | SERVES 12

1 pound fish heads, bones, and trimmings

6 black peppercorns

2 stalks celery, cut in two

1 carrot, peeled and cut in quarters

1 small white onion, peeled and quartered

1 bunch fresh parsley

7 cups cold water

1 cup dry (not sweet) white wine

More Seafood Scraps

Great additions to a fish stock include shrimp, crab, and lobster shells.

1. Add all ingredients to the pressure cooker, pouring in enough water to bring the contents to the fill line. Bring to a boil, uncovered, over medium high heat. When a boil is reached, skim and discard any foam from the surface. Close and lock the lid.
2. Turn the heat up to high. When the cooker reaches pressure, lower the heat to the minimum needed to maintain pressure. Cook for 10–12 minutes at high pressure.
3. Open with the natural release method (see Chapter 1).
4. Remove the lid and pour the stock through a fine mesh strainer, using a spatula to push on the remaining solids in the strainer to release their liquid. Discard the solids.
5. Cool and refrigerate for 1 day or freeze for up to 3 months.

PER CUP | Calories: 21 | Fat: 0 g | Protein: 0 g | Sodium: 30 mg | Carbohydrates: 2 g | Fiber: 0 g

Beef Stock

This stock is rather concentrated, so combine one part stock with one part water or to taste. The broth can be kept for one or two days in the refrigerator or frozen for up to three months.

INGREDIENTS | SERVES 12

1 tablespoon vegetable oil

1½ pounds bone-in chuck roast

1 pound cracked or sliced beef bones

1 large onion, quartered

2 large carrots, peeled and cut in two

2 stalks celery, cut in two

4 cups water, or to cover

Disposable Cups to the Rescue!

Do you have leftover, mismatched plastic or paper cups from various picnics, barbeques, and birthday parties? Pour the cooled stock into them, cover with plastic wrap, and freeze. When you need it, simply peel off the cup and toss the "stock-cicle" into the pan!

1. In an uncovered pressure cooker, heat the vegetable oil over high heat. Brown the meat and bones on all sides. Reduce heat to medium and add the onion, carrots, celery, and enough water to cover all ingredients. Close and lock the lid.
2. Turn the heat up to high. When the cooker reaches pressure, lower the heat to the minimum needed to maintain pressure. Cook for 60–90 minutes at high pressure.
3. Open with the natural release method (see Chapter 1).
4. Strain or use a slotted spoon to remove the roast and beef bones. Reserve the roast and the meat removed from the bones for another use. Discard the bones.
5. Cool and refrigerate the broth overnight. The next day, take the stock out of the refrigerator and spoon off the fat that has gathered at the top.
6. Cool and refrigerate for 1 day or freeze for up to 3 months.

PER CUP | Calories: 21 g | Fat: 5 g | Protein: 0 g | Sodium: 46 mg | Carbohydrates: 2 g | Fiber: 1 g

Vegetable Stock

Save scraps of vegetables to make a homemade stock.

INGREDIENTS | YIELDS 4 CUPS

2 large onions, peeled and halved

2 medium carrots, peeled and cut into large pieces

3 stalks celery, cut in half

10 peppercorns

1 bay leaf

4½ cups water

Delicious Scraps

Save carrot tops, onion skins, and herb stems in a plastic freezer zip-top bag. You can use them instead of whole vegetables to make aromatic vegetable stock.

1. Add the onions, carrots, and celery to the pressure cooker. Add the peppercorns, bay leaf, and water to completely cover the vegetables. Close and lock the lid.
2. Turn the heat up to high. When the cooker reaches pressure, lower the heat to the minimum needed to maintain pressure. Cook for 10–15 minutes at high pressure.
3. Open with the natural release method (see Chapter 1).
4. Strain the stock through a fine mesh strainer. Store in the refrigerator for 2–3 days, or freeze for up to 3 months.

PER CUP | Calories: 36 | Fat: 0 g | Protein: 1 g | Sodium: 27 mg | Fiber: 2 g | Carbohydrates: 8 g

Mushroom Broth

Fresh broth can be refrigerated for two or three days or frozen for three months.

INGREDIENTS | YIELDS 8 CUPS

4 carrots, peeled and cut in half

2 large leeks, cleaned and cut into large pieces

2 yellow onions, quartered

1 celery stalk, cut in half

5 whole cloves

2 cups sliced fresh mushrooms (or 3 ounces dried mushrooms)

8 cups water

Mushroom Varieties

You can use button mushrooms for a mellow flavor, or for a more intense flavor, try portobello mushroom cap black gills.

1. Put all ingredients in the pressure cooker. Close and lock the lid.
2. Turn the heat up to high. When the cooker reaches pressure, lower the heat to the minimum needed to maintain pressure. Cook for 10–15 minutes at high pressure.
3. Open with the natural release method (see Chapter 1).
4. Pour through a fine mesh strainer and discard solids. Refrigerate or freeze.

PER CUP | Calories: 46 | Fat: 0 g | Protein: 2 g | Sodium: 42 mg | Carbohydrates: 10 g | Fiber: 2 g

Fresh Tomato Soup

This soup celebrates the simple yet wondrous and summery taste of fresh, vine-ripened tomatoes. You can add sautéed onion or shallots and herbs if you wish.

INGREDIENTS | SERVES 4

8 medium fresh tomatoes, roughly chopped

1 small potato, diced

¼ teaspoon sea salt

¼ teaspoon baking soda

1 cup water

2 cups whole milk

¼ teaspoon freshly ground black pepper

Choosing the Right Tomato

Most types of tomatoes will work in tomato soup, but the key is to find tomatoes that are fresh and ripe. If you have your pick of tomatoes, try a combination of Roma and beefsteak.

1. Add tomatoes and their juice, potato, salt, baking soda, and water to the pressure cooker. Close and lock the lid.
2. Turn the heat up to high. When the cooker reaches pressure, lower the heat to the minimum needed to maintain pressure. Cook for 5–7 minutes at high pressure.
3. Open with the natural release method (see Chapter 1).
4. Stir in milk and simmer until all is well combined (about 2 minutes). Purée with immersion blender to desired consistency, sprinkle with pepper and serve.

PER SERVING | Calories: 148 | Fat: 4 g | Protein: 7 g | Sodium: 295 mg | Carbohydrates: 22 g | Fiber: 4 g

Lentil Soup

Any color lentils—red, yellow, brown, or green—will work in this lentil soup.

INGREDIENTS | SERVES 6

1 tablespoon olive oil

1 yellow onion, sliced

4 garlic cloves, minced

1 carrot, sliced

5 plum tomatoes, chopped

2 teaspoons dried tarragon

1 teaspoon dried thyme

1 teaspoon paprika

6 cups Vegetable Stock (see recipe in this chapter)

2 cups dry lentils, rinsed and drained

1 bay leaf

2 teaspoons salt

½ teaspoon pepper

1. Heat olive oil in an uncovered pressure cooker over medium heat. Add onions and sauté until they begin to turn golden (5–7 minutes). Add the garlic and carrots and sauté for 2–3 minutes. Add remaining ingredients except salt and pepper. Close and lock the lid.
2. Turn the heat up to high. When the cooker reaches pressure, lower the heat to the minimum needed to maintain pressure. Cook for 10–13 minutes at high pressure.
3. Open with the natural release method (see Chapter 1).
4. Remove the bay leaf, season with salt and pepper, and serve.

PER SERVING | Calories: 284 | Fat: 3 g | Protein: 17 g | Sodium: 1352 mg | Fiber: 21 g | Carbohydrates: 47 g

White Bean with Garlic and Kale Soup

This soup is best enjoyed during the winter, when kale is in peak season.

INGREDIENTS | SERVES 8

6 cups water

2 cups dried cannellini beans

2 tablespoons olive oil

½ cup thinly sliced onion

6 garlic cloves, thinly sliced

2 teaspoons dried oregano

1 (6-ounce) can tomato paste

8 cups Vegetable Stock (see recipe in this chapter)

3 cups chopped kale

1 tablespoon salt

1 teaspoon pepper

Queen of Greens

Kale is a nutritional and antioxidant powerhouse. One cup of kale contains 36 calories and 5 grams of fiber. It also contains 180 percent of vitamin A, 200 percent of vitamin C, and 1,020 percent of vitamin K, three powerful antioxidants.

1. Rinse the beans and soak them for 8 hours in enough water to cover them by more than 1 inch. Drain and rinse.
2. Heat olive oil in an uncovered pressure cooker over medium heat. Sauté the onion until soft (about 5 minutes). Add the garlic and sauté for about 1 minute. Add the beans and the rest of the ingredients. Close and lock the lid.
3. Turn the heat up to high. When the cooker reaches pressure, lower the heat to the minimum needed to maintain pressure. Cook for 10–15 minutes at high pressure.
4. Open with the natural release method (see Chapter 1).
5. Taste for seasoning and add more salt and pepper if needed. Serve.

PER SERVING | Calories: 204 | Fat: 1 g | Protein: 12 g | Sodium: 1625 mg | Fiber: 10 g | Carbohydrates: 40 g

Mushroom-Barley Soup

The portobello cap will bring umami, the fifth flavor, to this soup.

INGREDIENTS | SERVES 6

2 tablespoons butter

1 tablespoon olive or vegetable oil

2 stalks celery, diced

1 large carrot, peeled and diced

1 large sweet onion, peeled and sliced

2 cloves garlic, peeled and minced

1 portobello mushroom cap, diced

8 ounces button mushrooms, cleaned and sliced

1 bay leaf

½ cup pearl barley

6 cups water

2 teaspoons salt

½ teaspoon ground black pepper

2 tablespoons vermouth or brandy

Pearl Barley

Pearl barley is the type of barley that has the outer hull and the bran layer removed. It is one of the most commonly used varieties, but not the most nutritious.

1. Heat the butter and oil in an uncovered pressure cooker over medium heat. Add the celery and carrot and sauté for 2 minutes. Add the onion and sauté for 3 minutes, or until the onion is soft and transparent.
2. Stir in the garlic and portobello and button mushrooms. Sauté for 5 minutes, or until the mushrooms begin to release their moisture.
3. Stir in the bay leaf, barley, water, salt, and pepper. Close and lock the lid.
4. Turn the heat up to high. When the cooker reaches pressure, lower the heat to the minimum needed to maintain pressure. Cook for 20–25 minutes at high pressure.
5. Open with the natural release method (see Chapter 1).
6. Remove the lid. Remove and discard the bay leaf and add the vermouth or brandy. Serve.

PER SERVING | Calories: 143 | Fat: 6 g | Protein: 2 g | Sodium: 805 mg | Fiber: 4 g | Carbohydrates: 17 g

Re-Fashioned Potato Soup

This soup is lovely garnished with fresh herbs, or you can add a dollop of sour cream or plain Greek yogurt to each bowl. To turn it into a baked potato soup, top the soup with crumbled bacon and shredded cheese.

INGREDIENTS | SERVES 4

1 tablespoon extra-virgin olive oil

1 onion, diced

1 stalk celery, diced

4 medium potatoes, peeled and diced

6 cups Vegetable Stock (see recipe in this chapter)

2 teaspoons salt

½ teaspoon white pepper

1 cup whole plain yogurt

¼ cup chopped chives or parsley

1. Heat olive oil in an uncovered pressure cooker over medium heat. Sauté the onion and celery (about 5 minutes). Add potatoes and stock. Close and lock the lid.
2. Turn the heat up to high. When the cooker reaches pressure, lower the heat to the minimum needed to maintain pressure. Cook for 5–8 minutes at high pressure.
3. Open with the natural release method (see Chapter 1).
4. Purée with immersion blender, then add salt and white pepper. Stir in the yogurt and ladle into individual bowls. Garnish with chives or parsley.

PER SERVING | Calories: 246 | Fat: 5 g | Protein: 6 g | Sodium: 2053 mg | Fiber: 6 g | Carbohydrates: 44 g

Egg Drop Soup

The eggs for this soup are not cooked under pressure but added at the end, taking advantage of the very hot broth.

INGREDIENTS | SERVES 6

½ teaspoon ginger

1 star anise

2 cloves

3 fennel seeds

⅛ teaspoon cinnamon

2 teaspoons white pepper

8 ounces cherry tomatoes, halved

4 cups water

2 cups Chicken Stock (see recipe in this chapter)

4 eggs, whisked

2 green scallions, chopped

1. Put spices (ginger, star anise, cloves, fennel seeds, cinnamon, and white pepper) in a tea ball or bouquet garni bag. Add the spices, tomatoes, water, and stock to the pressure cooker. Close and lock the lid.
2. Turn the heat up to high. When the cooker reaches pressure, lower the heat to the minimum needed to maintain pressure. Cook for 5–7 minutes at high pressure.
3. Open the pressure cooker by releasing pressure.
4. While stirring clockwise with one hand, slowly pour in the whisked eggs with the other, creating thin strands.
5. Sprinkle with green scallions and serve.

PER SERVING | Calories: 87 | Fat: 4 g | Protein: 7 g | Sodium: 168 mg | Carbohydrates: 5 g | Fiber: 1 g

Cream of Chestnut Soup

This soup is very rich, so make small servings if it's being used as an opener to a meal.
Serve it with a swirl of cream and fresh ground nutmeg.

INGREDIENTS | SERVES 8

½ pound dried chestnuts, or 1 (16-ounce) can or vacuum-packed jar chestnuts

3 tablespoons butter

1 stalk celery, roughly chopped

1 onion, roughly sliced

1 sprig sage

¼ teaspoon white pepper

1 bay leaf

1 medium potato, peeled and roughly chopped

4 cups Chicken Stock (see recipe in this chapter)

2 tablespoons dark rum

¼ teaspoon ground nutmeg

Go Fresh Instead

Fresh chestnuts are only available for a few weeks a year. You can use 1½ pounds of fresh chestnuts instead of the dried or jarred chestnuts. To remove shells from fresh chestnuts, boil them whole in your pressure cooker for 10 minutes and open with the natural release method. Drain the water, strain the chestnuts, and peel immediately.

1. Place dry chestnuts in a large bowl and cover with water. Let them soak in the refrigerator overnight. Drain and rinse. If using canned or jarred chestnuts, drain and rinse.

2. Melt butter in an uncovered pressure cooker over medium heat. Add celery, onion, sage, and pepper and sauté until the onions are soft (about 5 minutes). Add the bay leaf, potato, chestnuts, and stock. Close and lock the lid.

3. Turn the heat up to high. When the cooker reaches pressure, lower the heat to the minimum needed to maintain pressure. Cook for 15–20 minutes at high pressure.

4. Open with the natural release method (see Chapter 1).

5. Remove the bay leaf and add the rum and nutmeg. Purée the contents of the pressure cooker with an immersion blender and serve.

PER SERVING | Calories: 166 | Fat: 6 g | Protein: 4 g | Sodium: 179 mg | Fiber: 3 g | Carbohydrates: 22 g

Butternut Squash and Ginger Soup

This soup showcases the pressure cooker's ability to really magnify the flavor of vegetables.

INGREDIENTS | SERVES 6

1 tablespoon olive oil

1 large onion, roughly chopped

1 sprig sage

1 teaspoon salt

¼ teaspoon white pepper

4 pounds butternut squash, peeled, seeded, and cubed

1 (½-inch) piece of fresh ginger, or 1 teaspoon dry ginger

¼ teaspoon nutmeg

4 cups Vegetable Stock (see recipe in this chapter)

½ cup toasted pumpkin seeds

Squash It!

Use any winter squash or pumpkin to make this soup. If they have a particularly tough skin, simply pressure steam large slices for 5 minutes at high pressure and then pull the skin right off.

1. Heat olive oil in an uncovered pressure cooker over medium heat. Sauté onions with the sage, salt, and pepper. When the onions are soft (approximately 5 minutes), push onions aside and add a handful of squash cubes to cover the bottom of pressure cooker.
2. Let the squash brown for about 10 minutes, stirring infrequently. Add the rest of the squash as well as the ginger, nutmeg, and stock. Close and lock the lid.
3. Turn the heat up to high. When the cooker reaches pressure, lower the heat to the minimum needed to maintain pressure. Cook for 10–15 minutes at high pressure.
4. When time is up, open the pressure cooker by releasing pressure.
5. Remove the piece of ginger (if used) and sage stem. Purée the contents of the pressure cooker with an immersion blender and serve garnished with pumpkin seeds.

PER SERVING | Calories: 237 | Fat: 8 g | Protein: 6 g | Sodium: 773 mg | Fiber: 7 g | Carbohydrates: 40 g

French Onion Soup

You can cut down on the time it takes to make this soup by using a mandoline to thinly slice the onions. The thinner the slices, the faster they will reduce and brown!

INGREDIENTS | SERVES 4

2 tablespoons extra-virgin olive oil

4 white onions, thinly sliced

4 cloves garlic, minced

1 tablespoon dried thyme

1 cup red wine

4 cups Vegetable Stock (see recipe in this chapter)

1 teaspoon salt

¼ teaspoon pepper

4 slices French bread, toasted

4 (1-ounce) slices Swiss cheese

Extra Herbs

To add even more flavor to this rich, brothy soup, use a bouquet garni in place of just one herb. Bouquet garni is a small bundle of parsley, thyme, and bay leaf tied together. Remove the entire bouquet from the soup before serving.

1. Heat olive oil in an uncovered pressure cooker over medium-high heat. Sauté the onions until golden brown (about 8–10 minutes). Add the garlic and sauté for 1 minute. Add the thyme, red wine, and stock. Close and lock the lid.

2. Turn the heat up to high. When the cooker reaches pressure, lower the heat to the minimum needed to maintain pressure. Cook for 5–7 minutes at high pressure.

3. Open with the natural release method (see Chapter 1).

4. Taste for seasoning and add salt and pepper.

5. Preheat the oven to the broiler setting. Lightly toast the slices of French bread.

6. To serve, ladle the soup into a heatproof bowl, place a slice of the toasted French bread on top of the soup, and put a slice of cheese on top of the bread. Place the soup under the broiler until the cheese has melted.

PER SERVING | Calories: 371 | Fat: 15 g | Protein: 12 g | Sodium: 1408 mg | Fiber: 3 g | Carbohydrates: 35 g

Creamy Lima Bean Soup

Use caution when using an immersion blender with hot soups. Immerse the head completely before turning it on and turn it off before pulling the head out to avoid hot splashes.

INGREDIENTS | SERVES 6

2 cups dried lima beans

4 cups water

1 tablespoon olive oil

1 small onion, diced

1 clove garlic, minced

4½ cups Vegetable Stock (see recipe in this chapter)

1 teaspoon salt

¼ teaspoon pepper

2 tablespoons chopped chives

1. Rinse the lima beans and soak for 8 hours in 4 cups water. Drain and rinse.
2. Heat olive oil in an uncovered pressure cooker over medium-high heat. Sauté the onion until golden brown (about 8–10 minutes). Add the garlic and cook for 1 minute more.
3. Add the stock and lima beans. Close and lock the lid.
4. Turn the heat up to high. When the cooker reaches pressure, lower the heat to the minimum needed to maintain pressure. Cook for 6–8 minutes at high pressure.
5. Open with the natural release method (see Chapter 1).
6. Purée the soup using an immersion blender.
7. Season with salt and pepper, then garnish with chives before serving.

PER SERVING | Calories: 232 | Fat: 3 g | Protein: 12 g | Sodium: 679 mg | Fiber: 11 g | Carbohydrates: 40 g

Corn Chowder

For an extra kick, add a fresh hot chili pepper to this soup, sliced in half.

INGREDIENTS | SERVES 6

4 large leeks

1 tablespoon olive oil

4 cups Vegetable Stock (see recipe in this chapter)

2 cups water

6 medium potatoes, diced

1 bay leaf

1 teaspoon salt

¼ teaspoon black pepper

1½ cups fresh or frozen corn

½ teaspoon dried thyme

½ teaspoon honey

1 cup whole plain yogurt

What Is Chowder?

Chowder originally indicated a thick soup made with chunks of seafood, but the meaning has been expanded to include other main ingredients, such as corn.

1. Cut off the root end of the leeks and discard any bruised outer leaves. Slice the leeks.
2. Heat olive oil in an uncovered pressure cooker over medium heat. Add the leeks and cook until soft (about 3 minutes). Stir in the stock, water, and potatoes. Add the bay leaf, salt, and pepper. Close and lock the lid.
3. Turn the heat up to high. When the cooker reaches pressure, lower the heat to the minimum needed to maintain pressure. Cook for 4–6 minutes at high pressure.
4. When time is up, open the pressure cooker by releasing pressure.
5. Remove and discard the bay leaf. Stir in the corn, thyme, honey, and yogurt. Simmer for about 1 minute and serve.

PER SERVING | Calories: 245 | Fat: 4 g | Protein: 6 g | Sodium: 795 mg | Fiber: 6 g | Carbohydrates: 48 g

Creamy Asparagus Soup

To bulk up the protein of this soup, add 1 cup cooked navy beans before blending.

INGREDIENTS | SERVES 6

2 pounds asparagus

1 tablespoon olive oil

1 large onion, diced

1½ teaspoons salt

1 teaspoon thyme

5 cups Vegetable Stock (see recipe in this chapter)

¼ cup whole milk

1 teaspoon lemon juice

Peak Season

Asparagus is in peak season during the spring, and during this time there are plenty of the flavorful stalks for sale at grocery stores or farmers' markets. Use asparagus in a soup, grilled or baked, or even battered and fried.

1. Trim the hard ends off the asparagus and cut it into 1-inch pieces.
2. Heat olive oil in an uncovered pressure cooker over medium heat. Sauté the onion until golden brown (5–7 minutes). Add the asparagus, salt, and thyme and sauté for about 5 minutes. Add the stock, then close and lock the lid.
3. Turn the heat up to high. When the cooker reaches pressure, lower the heat to the minimum needed to maintain pressure. Cook for 3–5 minutes at high pressure.
4. Open with the natural release method (see Chapter 1).
5. Add the milk and lemon juice to the soup. Purée using an immersion blender and serve.

PER SERVING | Calories: 76 | Fat: 3 g | Protein: 4 g | Sodium: 1056 mg | Fiber: 4 g | Carbohydrates: 11 g

Thai Carrot Soup

Carrots are loaded with vitamin A and help maintain good vision. Coconut milk is very rich, so serve this soup in small portions or make it a meal.

INGREDIENTS | SERVES 8

1 tablespoon olive oil

1 onion, diced

2 cloves garlic, minced

3 teaspoons curry powder

1 bay leaf

1 pound carrots, peeled and roughly chopped

4 cups Vegetable Stock (see recipe in this chapter)

1 cup unsweetened coconut milk

1 teaspoon salt

½ teaspoon pepper

¼ cup thinly sliced basil

Chiffonade

Chiffonade is a technique for cutting herbs and greens. To chiffonade basil, stack the cleaned and dried leaves, roll the leaves loosely, and slice from end to end. You'll be left with thin ribbons of basil.

1. Heat olive oil in an uncovered pressure cooker over medium heat. Sauté the onion until soft (about 5 minutes). Add the garlic and curry powder and sauté for an additional 30 seconds. Then, add the rest of the ingredients except for the basil. Close and lock the lid.
2. Turn the heat up to high. When the cooker reaches pressure, lower the heat to the minimum needed to maintain pressure. Cook for 5–7 minutes at high pressure.
3. Open with the natural release method (see Chapter 1).
4. Remove the bay leaf. Purée using an immersion blender. Add salt and pepper, garnish individual bowls with basil, and serve.

PER SERVING | Calories: 109 | Fat: 8 g | Protein: 1 g | Sodium: 613 mg | Carbohydrates: 9 g | Fiber: 2 g

Vietnamese Beef Noodle Soup

This is a simplified, Americanized version of pho, substituting brown sugar for the yellow rock sugar found in Asian markets.

INGREDIENTS | SERVES 10

1 (3-pound) chuck roast, trimmed of fat and cut into bite-size pieces

3 medium yellow onions (2 quartered and 1 thinly sliced)

4 (1-inch) pieces of ginger

5 star anise

6 whole cloves

1 (3-inch) cinnamon stick

¼ teaspoon salt

2 cups beef broth

Water for cooking

2 pounds small dried banh pho noodles

4 tablespoons fish sauce

1 tablespoon brown sugar

4 scallions, green part only, cut into thin rings

⅓ cup chopped fresh cilantro

½ teaspoon freshly ground black pepper

Optional Garnishes for Pho

If desired, have these additional garnishes available at the table: sprigs of spearmint (*hung lui*), sprigs of Asian/Thai basil (*hung que*), thorny cilantro leaves (*ngo gai*), bean sprouts, blanched and thinly sliced hot chilies (such as Thai bird or dragon), or lime wedges.

1. Add beef, quartered onions, ginger, star anise, cloves, cinnamon stick, salt, broth, and enough water to cover by about 1 inch to the pressure cooker. Close and lock the lid.
2. Turn the heat up to high. When the cooker reaches pressure, lower the heat to the minimum needed to maintain pressure. Cook for 25–30 minutes at high pressure.
3. Open with the natural release method (see Chapter 1).
4. About 30 minutes before serving, soak the sliced onion in cold water. In a separate bowl, cover the banh pho noodles with hot water and allow to soak for 15–20 minutes, or until softened and opaque white. Drain and set aside.
5. Remove the meat from the broth with a slotted spoon and shred the meat. Strain the broth, discarding solids. Return strained broth to the pressure cooker along with the shredded meat. Bring the meat and broth to a boil over medium-high heat. Stir in fish sauce and brown sugar.
6. Add as many noodles to a strainer as you can submerge in the boiling broth without causing the pressure cooker to boil over. Cook noodles for 15–20 seconds, then pull strainer from the broth.
7. Pour noodles into individual serving bowls and ladle broth and beef over the noodles. Garnish with onion slices, scallions, cilantro, and black pepper.

PER SERVING | Calories: 570 | Fat: 13 g | Protein: 42 g | Sodium: 309 mg | Fiber: 3 g | Carbohydrates: 68 g

Cuban Black Bean Soup

As with almost any bean dish, you can add diced celery and carrot slices to this soup when you add the onion. In fact, adding some along with another cup of chicken broth will increase the servings.

INGREDIENTS | SERVES 8

2 strips of bacon, chopped

1 green bell pepper, seeded and diced

1 large yellow onion, peeled and diced

4 ounces smoked sausage, diced

3 cloves garlic, peeled and minced

3 teaspoons paprika

½ teaspoon ground cumin

½ teaspoon chili powder

¼ teaspoon coriander

1 bay leaf

6 cups chicken broth

1 smoked turkey wing

1 pound dried black beans, soaked overnight, rinsed, and drained

⅛ teaspoon cayenne pepper or dried red pepper flakes

1 tablespoon red wine vinegar

1 teaspoon salt

¼ teaspoon black pepper

1. Add bacon to the pressure cooker and fry over medium-high heat until the bacon begins to render its fat (about 5–7 minutes). Reduce the heat to medium and add the green pepper. Sauté for 3 minutes.
2. Stir in the onion and sausage and sauté for 3 minutes or until the onion is tender. Add the garlic, paprika, cumin, chili powder, coriander, bay leaf, broth, turkey wing, and beans. Close and lock the lid.
3. Turn the heat up to high. When the cooker reaches pressure, lower the heat to the minimum needed to maintain pressure. Cook for 5–7 minutes at high pressure.
4. Open with the natural release method (see Chapter 1).
5. Remove the turkey wing and take the meat off of the bones. Return meat to the pot. Remove and discard the bay leaf.
6. Use a potato masher or immersion blender to partially purée the soup.
7. Return uncovered pan to medium heat and bring to a simmer. Stir in the cayenne pepper or dried red pepper flakes and vinegar. Simmer for 5 minutes.
8. Add salt and pepper and serve.

PER SERVING | Calories: 418 | Fat: 14 g | Protein: 26 g | Sodium: 1309 mg | Fiber: 10 g | Carbohydrates: 47 g

Greek Meatball Soup

This recipe is adapted from a Greek soup (youvarlakia avgolemono). The traditional version doesn't have the vegetables added to the broth, but those vegetables make this soup a one-pot meal.

INGREDIENTS | SERVES 6

1 pound lean ground beef

¼ pound ground pork

1 small onion, peeled and minced

1 clove garlic, peeled and minced

6 tablespoons uncooked converted long-grain white rice

1 tablespoon dried parsley

2 teaspoons dried dill or mint

1 teaspoon dried oregano

1 teaspoon salt

¼ teaspoon black pepper

3 large eggs, divided

6 cups chicken broth

1 medium onion, peeled and chopped

1 cup baby carrots, each sliced into thirds

1 stalk celery, finely chopped

⅓ cup fresh lemon juice

1. In a large bowl, mix the ground beef, ground pork, minced onion, garlic, rice, parsley, dill or mint, oregano, salt, pepper, and 1 egg. Shape into small meatballs and set aside.
2. Add 2 cups of broth to the pressure cooker. Add the meatballs, chopped onion, carrots, and celery, and then pour in the remaining broth to cover. Close and lock the lid.
3. Turn the heat up to high. When the cooker reaches pressure, lower the heat to the minimum needed to maintain pressure. Cook for 5–7 minutes at high pressure.
4. Open with the natural release method (see Chapter 1).
5. Use a slotted spoon to move the meatballs to a soup tureen. Cover and keep warm. Return the pressure cooker to medium heat and bring to a simmer.
6. In a small bowl, beat the two remaining eggs. Gradually whisk in the lemon juice.
7. Ladle in about a cup of the hot broth in a slow, steady stream, beating continuously until all of the hot liquid has been incorporated into the egg mixture. Stir this mixture into the pressure cooker. Stir and simmer for 5 minutes or until mixture is thickened.
8. Pour over the meatballs and serve.

PER SERVING | Calories: 356 | Fat: 14 g | Protein: 28 | Sodium: 1588 mg | Fiber: 1 g | Carbohydrates: 27 g

Pasta and Chickpea Minestrone

This minestrone is delicious topped with a dusting of Pecorino Romano cheese. Keep in mind that once the chickpeas, also known as garbanzo beans, are soaked and ready to go, they only need about 15 minutes under pressure and 10 more minutes of rest to be fully cooked.

INGREDIENTS | SERVES 6

1 cup dried chickpeas

7 cups water, divided

1 tablespoon olive oil

1 onion, chopped

1 carrot, chopped

1 celery stalk, chopped

1 sprig rosemary

1 sprig sage

1 bay leaf

1 garlic clove, pressed

2 tablespoons tomato purée, or one teaspoon of tomato concentrate

1 cup ditalini (or other small pasta shape)

2 teaspoons salt

1 teaspoon pepper

Less Gassy Chicks!

Changing the chickpeas' soaking water often can remove some of the indigestible sugars that could translate into gas after being consumed. Strain and rinse the beans and soaking container every six hours or so (two or three times during the soak).

1. Soak chickpeas in 4 cups water for at least 24 hours. Drain and set aside.

2. Heat olive oil in an uncovered pressure cooker over medium heat. Sauté the onion, carrot, and celery until softened, about 5 minutes. Add rosemary, sage, bay leaf, and garlic and stir for about 1 minute.

3. Add the chickpeas, 3 cups water, and tomato purée. Close and lock the lid.

4. Turn the heat up to high. When the cooker reaches pressure, lower the heat to the minimum needed to maintain pressure. Cook for 13–18 minutes at high pressure.

5. Open with the natural release method (see Chapter 1).

6. Bring the contents of the pressure cooker to a boil, uncovered, and add pasta. Cook until pasta is tender, about 8–10 minutes.

7. Season with salt and pepper before serving.

PER SERVING | Calories: 149 | Fat: 3 g | Protein: 5 g | Sodium: 945 mg | Fiber: 3 g | Carbohydrates: 26 g

New England Clam Chowder

The clams and their liquid will be salty, so wait until the chowder is cooked to add salt.
Serve with oyster crackers or sourdough crostini.

INGREDIENTS | SERVES 4

2 (6½-ounce) cans chopped clams
2 slices bacon
1 stalk celery, finely diced
2 large shallots, peeled and minced
1 pound red potatoes, peeled and diced
2½ cups unsalted chicken broth
1 tablespoon fresh chopped thyme
1 cup frozen corn, thawed
2 cups whole milk
1 tablespoon flour

1. Drain the clams, reserving the liquid. Set the clams and liquid aside.
2. In an uncovered pressure cooker, fry bacon over medium-high heat until crispy. Drain bacon on paper towels and crumble. Return bacon to pressure cooker.
3. Add celery and sauté for 3 minutes. Add shallots and sauté for 3 minutes. Stir in the potatoes and stir-fry to coat the potatoes in the fat. Stir in clam liquid, broth, and thyme. Close and lock the lid.
4. Turn the heat up to high. When the cooker reaches pressure, lower the heat to the minimum needed to maintain pressure. Cook for 5–7 minutes at high pressure.
5. Open with the natural release method (see Chapter 1).
6. Stir in the corn, milk, flour, and clams. Bring to a simmer for 5 minutes, and then serve.

PER SERVING | Calories: 448 | Fat: 14 g | Protein: 35 g | Sodium: 919 mg | Fiber: 3 g | Carbohydrates: 46 g

Manhattan Clam Chowder

You should wait until the chowder is cooked to add any salt to this recipe as well. Serve with oyster crackers, dinner rolls, or toasted garlic bread.

INGREDIENTS | SERVES 6

2 (6½-ounce) cans minced clams
2 slices bacon
2 stalks celery, finely diced
2 large carrots, peeled and finely diced
1 large sweet onion, peeled and diced
1 pound red potatoes, peeled and diced
1 (28-ounce) can diced tomatoes
1 teaspoon dried parsley
¼ teaspoon dried thyme
⅛ teaspoon dried oregano
½ teaspoon freshly ground black pepper

1. Drain the clams, reserving the liquid. Set the clams and liquid aside.
2. In an uncovered pressure cooker, fry bacon over medium-high heat until crispy. Drain bacon on paper towels and crumble. Return to pressure cooker.
3. Add celery and carrots and sauté for 3 minutes. Add onion and sauté for 3 minutes. Stir in the potatoes and stir-fry to coat the potatoes in the fat. Stir in clam liquid, tomatoes, parsley, thyme, and oregano. Close and lock the lid.
4. Turn the heat up to high. When the cooker reaches pressure, lower the heat to the minimum needed to maintain pressure. Cook for 5–7 minutes at high pressure.
5. Open with the natural release method (see Chapter 1).
6. Stir in the reserved clams and pepper. Bring to a simmer and then serve.

PER SERVING | Calories: 173 | Fat: 4 g | Protein: 11 g | Sodium: 314 | Fiber: 4 g | Carbohydrates: 23 g

Split-Pea Soup

This is a comforting, creamy, and nutritious soup! There is no need to add vegetable stock since you are making it on the fly, but for a more intense flavor, replace water with stock.

INGREDIENTS | SERVES 4

1 tablespoon olive oil
1 onion, finely chopped
1 stalk celery, finely chopped
1 carrot, finely chopped
⅛ teaspoon cumin
1½ cups split peas, rinsed
4 cups water

1. Heat olive oil in an uncovered pressure cooker over medium heat. Add onion, celery, carrot, and cumin. Sauté until the onions are soft (about 5 minutes). Add the split peas and water. Close and lock the lid.
2. Turn the heat up to high. When the cooker reaches pressure, lower the heat to the minimum needed to maintain pressure. Cook for 8–10 minutes at high pressure.
3. Open with the natural release method (see Chapter 1).
4. Serve as-is or use an immersion blender to make the soup smoother and creamier.

PER SERVING | Calories: 94 | Fat: 4 g | Protein: 3 g | Sodium: 31 mg | Carbohydrates: 12 g | Fiber: 4 g

Peas and Ham

When you sauté the vegetables in this recipe, you can add about 4 ounces of bacon, cooked ham, or smoky pancetta cut into cubes to turn this soup into a classic!

Portuguese Kale Soup

Collard greens can be substituted for the kale, but be sure to increase the cooking time slightly by 3–4 minutes at high pressure.

INGREDIENTS | SERVES 6

1 tablespoon olive oil
1 large yellow onion, peeled and thinly sliced
4 ounces linguiça or kielbasa, sliced
4 large potatoes, peeled and diced
4 cups chicken broth
1½ cups dried cannellini beans, soaked overnight
1 pound kale, sliced into thin strips
1 teaspoon salt
¼ teaspoon pepper

1. Heat olive oil in an uncovered pressure cooker over medium heat. Sauté onion and linguiça until the onions are soft (about 5 minutes). Add potatoes, broth, and beans. Place kale on top without stirring further. Close and lock the lid.
2. Turn the heat up to high. When the cooker reaches pressure, lower the heat to the minimum needed to maintain pressure. Cook for 6–8 minutes at high pressure.
3. Open with the natural release method (see Chapter 1).
4. Season with salt and pepper, stir to combine, and serve.

PER SERVING | Calories: 482 | Fat: 7 g | Protein: 23 g | Sodium: 1157 mg | Carbohydrates: 84 g | Fiber: 16 g

Cauliflower and Fennel Velouté

This is a delicious blend of flavors that does not weigh you down.
Try it with grated gorgonzola cheese and a fennel leaf garnish.

INGREDIENTS | SERVES 6

1 tablespoon olive oil

1 medium onion, chopped

½ fennel bulb (about the same quantity chopped as the onion)

1½ teaspoons salt

1 teaspoon white pepper

1 large head of cauliflower, cut into florets

1 bay leaf

5 cups Vegetable Stock (see recipe in this chapter)

2 tablespoons butter

¼ cup flour

1. Heat olive oil in an uncovered pressure cooker over medium heat. Add the onion, fennel, salt, and pepper, and sauté until the onion and fennel are softened, about 5 minutes. Add the cauliflower, bay leaf, and stock. Scrape the brown bits off the bottom of the pan and incorporate into the liquid. Close and lock the lid.
2. Turn the heat up to high. When the cooker reaches pressure, lower the heat to the minimum needed to maintain pressure. Cook for 5–7 minutes at high pressure.
3. Open the pressure cooker by releasing pressure.
4. Remove the bay leaf and add the butter and flour. Simmer for 3–5 minutes.
5. Before serving, use an immersion blender to purée the contents of the cooker.

PER SERVING | Calories: 121 | Fat: 7 g | Protein: 3 g | Sodium: 1088 mg | Carbohydrates: 15 g | Fiber: 3 g

CHAPTER 5

Legumes

Adzuki Beans
94

Black Beans
94

Black-Eyed Peas
95

Chickpeas
95

Lima Beans
96

Lentils
96

Pinto Beans
97

Split Peas
97

Soybeans
98

White Beans
98

Chipotle-Cilantro Black Beans
99

Lentil and Black Bean Chili
99

Italian Lentils in Tomato Sauce
100

Yellow Lentil and Spinach Curry
101

Red Lentil Curry
101

Not Refried Beans
102

Three Bean Salad
103

Cannellini and Mint Bean Salad
104

Black Bean Salad
104

Chana Masala
105

Red Bean Chili
105

Chickpea Caprese Salad
106

Wild Rice and Black Soybeans
106

White Beans and Brown Rice
107

Spicy Black Beans and Rice
108

Southern Black-Eyed Peas
109

Five Pepper Chili
110

Veggie Chili
111

Chickpea, Cannellini, and
Barley Stew
112

Succotash
112

Adzuki Beans

Adzuki beans are also known as red soybeans.

INGREDIENTS | SERVES 4

2 cups adzuki beans, soaked
8 cups water
2 tablespoons vegetable oil

Using Dried Beans (Nonsoaked)

You can skip the soaking step and make this recipe using dried beans. Cover the beans with water and pressure cook for 15–20 minutes at high pressure. Open with the natural release method, then strain and rinse before serving.

1. Put all of the ingredients in the pressure cooker. Close and lock the lid.
2. Turn the heat up to high. When the cooker reaches pressure, lower the heat to the minimum needed to maintain pressure. Cook for 6–9 minutes at high pressure.
3. Open with the natural release method (see Chapter 1).
4. Strain and serve.

PER SERVING | Calories: 167 | Fat: 7 g | Protein: 7 g | Sodium: 4 mg | Fiber: 7 g | Carbohydrates: 19 g

Black Beans

Compared to other legumes, black beans take a very short time to cook. When they are soaked, they cook faster than lentils!

INGREDIENTS | SERVES 4

2 cups black beans, soaked
8 cups water
2 tablespoons vegetable oil

Using Dried Beans (Nonsoaked)

You can skip the soaking step. Cover dried beans with water and cook for 20–25 minutes at high pressure. Open with the natural release method, then strain and rinse before serving.

1. Put all of the ingredients in the pressure cooker. Close and lock the lid. Turn the heat up to high. When the cooker reaches pressure, lower the heat to the minimum needed to maintain pressure. Cook for 5–6 minutes at high pressure.
2. Open with the natural release method (see Chapter 1).
3. Strain and serve.

PER SERVING | Calories: 165 | Fat: 7.5 g | Protein: 6 g | Sodium: 9 mg | Fiber: 7 g | Carbohydrates: 18 g

Black-Eyed Peas

Black-eyed peas do not need to be soaked. However, if you need them to cook more quickly, you can soak them for about 4 hours and their cooking time will halved (3 minutes on high pressure).

INGREDIENTS | SERVES 4

2 cups black-eyed peas, dried
8 cups water
2 tablespoons vegetable oil

1. Put all of the ingredients in the pressure cooker. Close and lock the lid. Turn the heat up to high. When the cooker reaches pressure, lower the heat to the minimum needed to maintain pressure. Cook for 6–7 minutes at high pressure.
2. Open with the natural release method (see Chapter 1).
3. Strain and serve.

PER SERVING | Calories: 340 | Fat: 8 g | Protein: 19 g | Sodium: 7 mg | Fiber: 9 g | Carbohydrates: 50 g

Chickpeas

Did you know that you can also find black chickpeas? They are actually just dark brown, and take the same amount of time to cook as regular chickpeas!

INGREDIENTS | SERVES 4

2 cups chickpeas, soaked
8 cups water
2 tablespoons vegetable oil

Using Dried Chickpeas (Nonsoaked)

You can skip the soaking step. Cover chickpeas with water and cook for 30–40 minutes at high pressure. Open with the natural release method, then strain and rinse before serving.

1. Put all of the ingredients in the pressure cooker. Close and lock the lid. Turn the heat up to high. When the cooker reaches pressure, lower the heat to the minimum needed to maintain pressure. Cook for 13–15 minutes at high pressure.
2. Open with the natural release method (see Chapter 1).
3. Strain and serve.

PER SERVING | Calories: 194 | Fat: 9 g | Protein: 7 g | Sodium: 5 mg | Fiber: 6 g | Carbohydrates: 22 g

Lima Beans

It doesn't matter what size lima beans you use! It takes the same amount of time to cook baby and large limas.

INGREDIENTS | SERVES 4

2 cups lima beans, soaked
8 cups water
2 tablespoons vegetable oil

Using Dried Beans (Nonsoaked)

You can skip the soaking step. Cover the beans with water and cook for 12–15 minutes at high pressure. Open with the natural release method, then strain and rinse before serving.

1. Put all of the ingredients in the pressure cooker. Close and lock the lid. Turn the heat up to high. When the cooker reaches pressure, lower the heat to the minimum needed to maintain pressure. Cook for 5–7 minutes at high pressure.
2. Open with the natural release method (see Chapter 1).
3. Strain and serve.

PER SERVING | Calories: 361 | Fat: 7 g | Protein: 19 g | Sodium: 16 mg | Fiber: 16 g | Carbohydrates: 56 g

Lentils

Lentils do not need to be soaked. However, you can soak them for about 4 hours and their cooking time will be almost halved (5–6 minutes).

INGREDIENTS | SERVES 4

2 cups lentils, dry
6 cups water
2 tablespoons vegetable oil

Other Lentils

This recipe refers to the most common type of brown lentil. Red, yellow, or split lentils only need 4–6 minutes at high pressure. Green, mini, French, and beluga lentils need 8–10 minutes at high pressure.

1. Put all of the ingredients in the pressure cooker. Close and lock the lid. Turn the heat up to high. When the cooker reaches pressure, lower the heat to the minimum needed to maintain pressure. Cook for 10–12 minutes at high pressure.
2. Open with the natural release method (see Chapter 1).
3. Strain and serve.

PER SERVING | Calories: 399 | Fat: 8 g | Protein: 24 g | Sodium: 6 mg | Fiber: 29 g | Carbohydrates: 57 g

Pinto Beans

Pinto beans can be substituted with borlotti and cranberry beans.

INGREDIENTS | SERVES 4

2 cups pinto beans, soaked

8 cups water

2 tablespoons vegetable oil

Using Dried Pinto Beans (Nonsoaked)

You can skip the soaking step. Cover dried beans with water and cook for 22–24 minutes at high pressure. Open with the natural release method, then strain and rinse before serving.

1. Put all of the ingredients in the pressure cooker. Close and lock the lid. Turn the heat up to high. When the cooker reaches pressure, lower the heat to the minimum needed to maintain pressure. Cook for 4–6 minutes at high pressure.
2. Open with the natural release method (see Chapter 1).
3. Strain and serve.

PER SERVING | Calories: 163 | Fat: 8 g | Protein: 6 g | Sodium: 5 mg | Fiber: 5 g | Carbohydrates: 18 g

Split Peas

Split peas do not need to be soaked before cooking.

INGREDIENTS | SERVES 4

2 cups dried split peas

8 cups water

2 tablespoons vegetable oil

Release Pressure Naturally

Legumes foam when cooked under pressure. If pressure is released by the valve, foam could squirt out and some of the legumes could obstruct the valve. Always release pressure naturally when pressure cooking legumes.

1. Put all of the ingredients in the pressure cooker. Close and lock the lid. Turn the heat up to high. When the cooker reaches pressure, lower the heat to the minimum needed to maintain pressure. Cook for 4–6 minutes at high pressure.
2. Open with the natural release method (see Chapter 1).
3. Strain and serve.

PER SERVING | Calories: 396 | Fat: 8 g | Protein: 24 g | Sodium: 14 mg | Fiber: 25 g | Carbohydrates: 59 g

Soybeans

The same cooking time applies to black, yellow, or beige soy beans.
Red soybeans (adzuki beans) need 6–9 minutes at high pressure.

INGREDIENTS | SERVES 4

2 cups soybeans, soaked

8 cups water

2 tablespoons vegetable oil

Using Dried Soybeans (Nonsoaked)

You can skip the soaking step. Cover dried soybeans with water and pressure cook for 35–40 minutes at high pressure. Open with the natural release method, then strain and rinse before serving.

1. Put all of the ingredients in the pressure cooker. Close and lock the lid. Turn the heat up to high. When the cooker reaches pressure, lower the heat to the minimum needed to maintain pressure. Cook for 20–22 minutes at high pressure.
2. Open with the natural release method (see Chapter 1).
3. Strain and serve.

PER SERVING | Calories: 475 | Fat: 25 g | Protein: 33 g | Sodium: 2 mg | Fiber: 8 g | Carbohydrates: 28 g

White Beans

White beans include navy, cannellini, and haricot.

INGREDIENTS | SERVES 4

2 cups white beans, soaked

8 cups water

2 tablespoons vegetable oil

Using Dried White Beans (Nonsoaked)

You can skip the soaking step. Cover dried beans with water and pressure cook for 18–20 minutes at high pressure. Open with the natural release method, then strain and rinse before serving.

1. Put all of the ingredients in the pressure cooker. Close and lock the lid. Turn the heat up to high. When the cooker reaches pressure, lower the heat to the minimum needed to maintain pressure. Cook for 6–8 minutes at high pressure.
2. Open with the natural release method (see Chapter 1).
3. Strain and serve.

PER SERVING | Calories: 361 | Fat: 7 g | Protein: 19 g | Sodium: 16 mg | Fiber: 17 g | Carbohydrates: 56 g

Chipotle-Cilantro Black Beans

The chipotle powder gives a rich, smoky flavor to this dish. You can substitute chopped dried chipotle pepper for the powder, or if you prefer, dice a small pepper instead for a crisp, fresh flavor.

INGREDIENTS | SERVES 6

1 tablespoon vegetable oil
1 onion, chopped
1 teaspoon chipotle powder
¼ teaspoon cumin
1 bunch cilantro (or parsley), leaves and stems separated and chopped
2 cups dried black beans, soaked
2 cups water
1 teaspoon salt

1. Heat oil in an uncovered pressure cooker over medium heat. Add onion, chipotle powder, cumin, and cilantro stems. Sauté until onions are soft (about 5 minutes). Add beans and water. Close and lock the lid.
2. Turn the heat up to high. When the cooker reaches pressure, lower the heat to the minimum needed to maintain pressure. Cook for 5–6 minutes at high pressure.
3. Open with the natural release method (see Chapter 1).
4. Stir in the salt and cilantro leaves before serving.

PER SERVING | Calories: 249 | Fat: 3 g | Protein: 14 g | Sodium: 403 mg | Fiber: 10 g | Carbohydrates: 42 g

Lentil and Black Bean Chili

Serve with a dollop of sour cream or Greek yogurt.

INGREDIENTS | SERVES 4

1 tablespoon vegetable oil
1 red onion, diced
1 green bell pepper, chopped
1 yellow bell pepper, chopped
2 cloves garlic, smashed
½ teaspoon cumin
½ teaspoon hot pepper flakes
1 teaspoon oregano
1 cup dried lentils
1 cup black beans, soaked
2½ cups water
1 cup fresh or frozen corn
Zest and juice of 1 lime

1. Add all of the ingredients, except for the corn and lime, to the pressure cooker. Close and lock the lid.
2. Turn the heat up to high. When the cooker reaches pressure, lower the heat to the minimum needed to maintain pressure. Cook for 8–10 minutes at high pressure.
3. Open with the natural release method (see Chapter 1).
4. Add the corn, stir well, then close the pressure cooker. Let sit (without turning it on again) to allow the residual heat of the pressure cooker to warm the corn for 5 minutes.
5. Stir in the lime juice and zest just before serving.

PER SERVING | Calories: 320 | Fat: 5 g | Protein: 18 g | Sodium: 202 mg | Fiber: 20 g | Carbohydrates: 54 g

Italian Lentils in Tomato Sauce

This recipe can be served as a side dish, as a sauce for pasta, or over rice.

INGREDIENTS | SERVES 6

1 tablespoon olive oil

1 stalk celery, chopped

1 medium green pepper, chopped

1 medium onion, chopped

1 cup dried lentils

1 (14½-ounce) can chopped tomatoes

2 cups water

1 tablespoon extra-virgin olive oil

1 teaspoon salt

¼ teaspoon pepper

New Year Tradition

On New Year's Eve in Italy, this dish is served with a stuffed pork-foot sausage, *cotechino*. Since lentils look like little coins, tradition dictates that the more lentils you eat, the more you will prosper in the next year. This is enough to get even the most finicky eater to consume large portions!

1. Heat olive oil in an uncovered pressure cooker over medium heat. Add celery, pepper, and onion. Sauté until onion has softened (about 5 minutes). Then add the lentils, tomatoes, and water and stir well. Close and lock the lid.
2. Turn the heat up to high. When the cooker reaches pressure, lower the heat to the minimum needed to maintain pressure. Cook for 10–12 minutes at high pressure.
3. Open with the natural release method (see Chapter 1).
4. Finish with a swirl of extra-virgin olive oil and add salt and pepper to taste before serving.

PER SERVING | Calories: 177 | Fat: 5 g | Protein: 9 g | Sodium: 407 mg | Fiber: 11 g | Carbohydrates: 24 g

Yellow Lentil and Spinach Curry

This color combination is particularly attractive, but you can make this curry with any lentils of your choice. Adjust the cooking time accordingly.

INGREDIENTS | SERVES 4

1 tablespoon olive oil
1 onion, diced
¼ teaspoon red pepper flakes
¼ teaspoon coriander
¼ teaspoon turmeric
⅛ teaspoon cumin
1 cup dried yellow lentils
1 cup chopped tomatoes
½ cup water
2 cups chopped fresh baby spinach

1. Heat olive oil in an uncovered pressure cooker over medium heat. Add onion, pepper flakes, coriander, turmeric, and cumin. Sauté until onion has softened (about 5 minutes), then add lentils, tomatoes, and water. Stir well. Close and lock the lid.
2. Turn the heat up to high. When the cooker reaches pressure, lower the heat to the minimum needed to maintain pressure. Cook for 10–12 minutes at high pressure.
3. Open with the natural release method (see Chapter 1).
4. Mix in the baby spinach and serve.

PER SERVING | Calories: 223 | Fat: 4 g | Protein: 13 g | Sodium: 19 mg | Fiber: 16 g | Carbohydrates: 33 g

Red Lentil Curry

The tomatoes make this a particularly delicious dish. Serve with a dollop of sour cream or Greek yogurt.

INGREDIENTS | SERVES 6

2 tablespoons vegetable oil
1 cup diced onion
1 teaspoon minced garlic
1 teaspoon peeled and minced ginger
3 tablespoons curry powder
1 teaspoon turmeric
1 teaspoon cumin
½ teaspoon cayenne pepper
2 cups dried red lentils
1 (14½-ounce) can of chopped tomatoes
1½ cups water
1 teaspoon salt
½ teaspoon of pepper

1. Heat oil in an uncovered pressure cooker over medium heat. Add onion, garlic, ginger, curry powder, turmeric, cumin, and cayenne pepper. Sauté until onion has softened (about 5 minutes). Add the lentils, tomatoes, and water and stir well. Close and lock the lid.
2. Turn the heat up to high. When the cooker reaches pressure, lower the heat to the minimum needed to maintain pressure. Cook for 10–12 minutes at high pressure.
3. Open with the natural release method (see Chapter 1).
4. Add salt and pepper before serving.

PER SERVING | Calories: 303 | Fat: 6 g | Protein: 18 g | Sodium: 499 mg | Fiber: 22 g | Carbohydrates: 46 g

Not Refried Beans

*Traditionally, the beans are cooked first and then transferred to a hot pan—
hence the "fry" in the refried beans. Instead, we fry the aromatics and cook them
with the beans for a healthier and more flavorful "refried" bean.*

INGREDIENTS | SERVES 6

1 bunch parsley, washed

1 tablespoon vegetable oil

1 onion, chopped

2 cloves garlic, smashed

¼ teaspoon chipotle powder

½ teaspoon cumin

2 cups pinto or borlotti beans, soaked

2 cups water

1 teaspoon salt

1. Separate the parsley leaves from the stems. Chop the stems and set aside, then chop the leaves and set aside.

2. Heat oil in an uncovered pressure cooker over medium heat. Add onion, garlic, chipotle powder, cumin, and parsley stems. Sauté until the onions are soft (about 5 minutes). Add the beans and water. Close and lock the lid.

3. Turn the heat up to high. When the cooker reaches pressure, lower the heat to the minimum needed to maintain pressure. Cook for 6–8 minutes at high pressure.

4. Open with the natural release method (see Chapter 1).

5. Add salt and use a potato masher to mash about half of the beans. Stir in salt and sprinkle with parsley leaves before serving.

PER SERVING | Calories: 112 | Fat: 3 g | Protein: 5 g | Sodium: 653 mg | Fiber: 5 g | Carbohydrates: 16 g

Three Bean Salad

Cook the three beans at once, instead of each one individually.

INGREDIENTS | SERVES 8

1½ cups frozen green beans

½ red onion, chopped finely

5 tablespoons apple cider vinegar

1 tablespoon white sugar

4 cups water

1 cup chickpeas, soaked and rinsed

1 bay leaf

1 clove of garlic, lightly crushed

1 cup borlotti, cranberry, or pinto beans, soaked and rinsed

2 celery stalks, chopped finely

1 bunch parsley, finely chopped

4 tablespoons olive oil

2 teaspoons salt

1 teaspoon pepper

1. Wrap frozen green beans tightly in heavy duty aluminum foil and set aside.
2. In a small bowl, mix together onion, vinegar, and sugar. Set aside.
3. Pour water into the pressure cooker and add chickpeas, bay leaf, and garlic. Next, add the steamer basket with the borlotti beans. Finally, add the tin foil packet of green beans. Close and lock the pressure cooker.
4. Turn the heat up to high. When the cooker reaches pressure, lower the heat to the minimum needed to maintain pressure. Cook for 13–15 minutes at high pressure.
5. Open with the natural release method (see Chapter 1).
6. Remove and open the tinfoil packet of green beans. Pour the beans from the steamer basket and the chickpeas from bottom of the pressure cooker into a strainer and rinse under cold water to stop them from cooking. Slice the green beans into pieces and mix in with the other beans.
7. In a serving bowl, combine all the beans, onion mixture, celery, parsley, olive oil, salt, and pepper and mix well.
8. Serve immediately or refrigerate several hours or overnight.

PER SERVING | Calories: 149 | Fat: 8 g | Protein: 5 g | Sodium: 708 mg | Fiber: 5 g | Carbohydrates: 16 g

Cannellini and Mint Bean Salad

This refreshing salad can be served as a side dish or on top of your favorite rice or pasta.

INGREDIENTS | SERVES 6

2 cups cannellini beans, soaked
4 cups water
1 tablespoon vegetable oil
1 clove garlic, smashed
1 bay leaf
3 teaspoons olive oil
1 teaspoon white wine vinegar
1 teaspoon salt
¼ teaspoon white pepper
1 sprig fresh mint, chopped

1. Add beans, water, oil, garlic, and bay leaf to the pressure cooker. Close and lock the lid.
2. Turn the heat up to high. When the cooker reaches pressure, lower the heat to the minimum needed to maintain pressure. Cook for 6–8 minutes at high pressure.
3. Open with the natural release method (see Chapter 1).
4. Strain the beans and discard the bay leaf. Dress with olive oil, vinegar, salt, and pepper. Sprinkle with mint before serving.

PER SERVING | Calories: 249 | Fat: 5 g | Protein: 13 g | Sodium: 409 mg | Fiber: 12 g | Carbohydrates: 39 g

Black Bean Salad

This is another healthy salad that can be served as either a side dish or on top of your favorite rice or pasta.

INGREDIENTS | SERVES 6

2 cups black beans, soaked
4 cups water
1 tablespoon vegetable oil
1 clove garlic, smashed
1 bay leaf
2 medium tomatoes, chopped
1 cup fresh or frozen corn kernels
½ red onion, finely chopped
3 teaspoons olive oil
1 teaspoon lemon juice
1 teaspoon salt
¼ teaspoon white pepper
1 sprig fresh oregano

1. Add beans, water, oil, garlic, and bay leaf to the pressure cooker. Close and lock the lid.
2. Turn the heat up to high. When the cooker reaches pressure, lower the heat to the minimum needed to maintain pressure. Cook for 6–8 minutes at high pressure.
3. Open with the natural release method (see Chapter 1).
4. Strain the beans and discard the bay leaf. Let cool. Mix in tomatoes, corn, onion, olive oil, lemon juice, salt, and pepper. Sprinkle with fresh oregano leaves before serving.

PER SERVING | Calories: 150 | Fat: 5 g | Protein: 6 g | Sodium: 654 mg | Fiber: 6 g | Carbohydrates: 21 g

Chana Masala

*You can make this recipe totally vegan by substituting the butter with
1 tablespoon of vegan margarine such as Earth Balance.*

INGREDIENTS | SERVES 6

1 tablespoon vegetable oil

1 tablespoon butter or vegan margarine

1 onion, diced

1 garlic clove, minced

1 teaspoon grated ginger

1 teaspoon ground cumin

¼ teaspoon ground cayenne pepper

¼ teaspoon ground turmeric

1 teaspoon paprika

1 teaspoon garam masala

2 cups chickpeas, soaked

3 cups water

2 medium tomatoes, diced and drained

1. Heat oil and butter in an uncovered pressure cooker over medium heat. Add onion, garlic, and spices. Sauté until onion has softened (about 5 minutes). Add chickpeas and water. Close and lock the lid.
2. Turn the heat up to high. When the cooker reaches pressure, lower the heat to the minimum needed to maintain pressure. Cook for 13–15 minutes at high pressure.
3. Open with the natural release method (see Chapter 1).
4. Mix in the tomatoes and let them warm in the uncovered pressure cooker for 5 minutes before serving.

PER SERVING | Calories: 147 | Fat: 6 g | Protein: 6 g |
Sodium: 15 mg | Fiber: 5 g | Carbohydrates: 20 g

Red Bean Chili

Perfect when served over a fluffy bed of white rice.

INGREDIENTS | SERVES 4

1 tablespoon olive oil

1 onion, diced

2 cloves garlic, minced

1 tablespoon hot pepper flakes

½ teaspoon chipotle powder

½ teaspoon cumin

1 tablespoon paprika

2 cups kidney beans, soaked

3 cups Vegetable Stock (see recipe in Chapter 4)

2 cups diced fresh tomatoes

2 teaspoons salt

1. In preheated pressure cooker, add all of the ingredients except for the tomatoes and salt. Close and lock the lid.
2. Turn the heat up to high. When the cooker reaches pressure, lower the heat to the minimum needed to maintain pressure. Cook for 8–10 minutes at high pressure.
3. Open with the natural release method (see Chapter 1).
4. Mix in the chopped tomatoes and salt. Simmer, uncovered, for 5 minutes to further reduce the liquid before serving.

PER SERVING | Calories: 186 | Fat: 4 g | Protein: 8 g |
Sodium: 1932 mg | Fiber: 9 g | Carbohydrates: 31 g

Chickpea Caprese Salad

The fresh basil plays double duty in this recipe. The stems flavor the beans during cooking, and the leaves give this dish a classic Caprese feel.

INGREDIENTS | SERVES 6

1 bunch basil

2 cups chickpeas, soaked

4 cups water

1 tablespoon vegetable oil

1 clove garlic, smashed

3 medium tomatoes, diced

4 ounces fresh mozzarella cheese, diced

3 teaspoons olive oil

1 teaspoon salt

1 teaspoon white pepper

1. Separate the basil leaves from the stems. Chop the leaves and put aside.
2. Add chickpeas, water, oil, garlic, and basil stems to the pressure cooker. Close and lock the lid.
3. Turn the heat up to high. When the cooker reaches pressure, lower the heat to the minimum needed to maintain pressure. Cook for 13–15 minutes at high pressure.
4. Open with the natural release method (see Chapter 1).
5. Strain the chickpeas and discard the basil stems. Rinse chickpeas under water and let cool. In a serving bowl, mix chickpeas, tomatoes, mozzarella, basil leaves, olive oil, salt, and pepper. Serve immediately or refrigerate.

PER SERVING | Calories: 207 | Fat: 10 g | Protein: 11 g | Sodium: 523 mg | Fiber: 6 g | Carbohydrates: 19 g

Wild Rice and Black Soybeans

This combination is easy to make because both wild rice and soybeans need the same pressure cooking time.

INGREDIENTS | SERVES 4

3 cloves garlic, smashed

4 cups vegetable broth

1 cup black soybeans, soaked

1 cup wild rice

1 teaspoon salt

¼ teaspoon pepper

1. Place all ingredients in the pressure cooker. Close and lock the lid. Turn the heat up to high. When the cooker reaches pressure, lower the heat to the minimum needed to maintain pressure. Cook for 22–25 minutes at high pressure.
2. Open with the natural release method (see Chapter 1).
3. Stir well and serve.

PER SERVING | Calories: 394 | Fat: 10 g | Protein: 20 g | Sodium: 1924 mg | Fiber: 6 g | Carbohydrates: 54 g

White Beans and Brown Rice

Naturally nutty brown rice is a perfect pairing with the licorice-flavored anise and the bright lemon zest.

INGREDIENTS | SERVES 6

1 tablespoon vegetable oil
1 small onion, chopped
½ teaspoon anise
Zest and juice of 1 lemon
2 cups brown rice
4 cups water, divided
1 cup cannellini beans, soaked
2 teaspoons salt
1 teaspoon white pepper
1 bunch mint leaves, torn

Anise

Since it is sweet and very aromatic, anise is a spice usually used in desserts. Even though it is part of the parsley family, it is under-utilized in savory dishes.

1. Heat oil in an uncovered pressure cooker over medium heat. Add onion and sauté until soft (about 5 minutes). Add anise, lemon zest, and rice. Sauté for about 3 minutes and then add 3 cups water. Close and lock the lid.
2. Turn the heat up to high. When the cooker reaches pressure, lower the heat to the minimum needed to maintain pressure. Cook for 15–20 minutes at high pressure.
3. When time is up, open the pressure cooker by releasing pressure.
4. Add the beans and 1 cup water, then mix well. Close and lock the lid.
5. Turn the heat up to high. When the cooker reaches pressure, lower to the heat to the minimum needed to maintain pressure. Cook for 6–9 minutes at high pressure.
6. Open with the natural release method (see Chapter 1).
7. Add lemon juice, salt, pepper, and mint before serving.

PER SERVING | Calories: 396 | Fat: 6 g | Protein: 14 g | Sodium: 1039 mg | Fiber: 15 g | Carbohydrates: 75 g

Spicy Black Beans and Rice

The water used to cook the beans is discarded to keep the rice from turning an unappetizing black!

INGREDIENTS | SERVES 4

1 cup dried black beans, soaked

4 cups water

2 tablespoons vegetable oil, divided

1 medium onion, diced

1 stalk celery, finely diced

1 carrot, peeled and grated

1 medium green bell pepper, diced

2 cloves garlic, minced

2 teaspoons paprika

½ teaspoon cumin

¼ teaspoon chili powder

1 cup medium- or long-grain white rice

2 cups Vegetable Stock (see recipe in Chapter 4)

Everything's Better with Bacon

Make this dish meatier by adding 2 chopped bacon strips during the sauté (omit the oil as the fat from the bacon will be enough to keep the rice and beans from foaming).

1. Place black beans, water, and 1 tablespoon oil in the pressure cooker. Close and lock the lid.
2. Turn the heat up to high. When the cooker reaches pressure, lower the heat to the minimum needed to maintain pressure. Cook for 5–6 minutes at high pressure.
3. Open with the natural release method (see Chapter 1).
4. Strain and rinse the beans and set aside. Rinse the pressure cooker well.
5. Heat remaining tablespoon oil in the uncovered pressure cooker over medium heat. Add onion, celery, carrot, and bell pepper and sauté for 5 minutes.
6. Add garlic, paprika, cumin, and chili powder. Sauté for 5 more minutes and add the rice, stock, and black beans. Close and lock the lid.
7. Turn the heat up to high. When the cooker reaches pressure, lower the heat to the minimum needed to maintain pressure. Cook for 3–4 minutes at high pressure.
8. Open with the natural release method again.
9. Mix well and serve.

PER SERVING | Calories: 439 | Fat: 8 g | Protein: 15 g | Sodium: 310 mg | Fiber: 10 g | Carbohydrates: 77 g

Southern Black-Eyed Peas

Make a meatless version by substituting the bacon with a teaspoon of smoky paprika.

INGREDIENTS | SERVES 8

½ pound thick-cut bacon, diced

1 stalk celery, finely diced

1 pound bag baby carrots

1 large onion, peeled and diced

3 cups black-eyed peas, soaked

1 cup long-grain white rice, rinsed

4 cups chicken broth

1 teaspoon salt

¼ teaspoon pepper

Happy New Year!

In the South, black-eyed peas are a tradition on New Year's Day. The tradition is to eat modestly on the first day of the year to symbolize prosperity every day thereafter. If you are not a fan of black-eyed peas, substitute lentils—that's what Italians eat on New Year's Eve to ensure a prosperous new year.

1. Heat an uncovered pressure cooker over medium heat and add bacon. Fry the bacon until the fat begins to render. Pour out all of the fat, except for about a tablespoon. Add celery, carrots, and onions and sauté until the onions are soft (about 5 minutes). Add the black-eyed peas, rice, and chicken broth. Close and lock the lid.
2. Turn the heat up to high. When the cooker reaches pressure, lower the heat to the minimum needed to maintain pressure. Cook for 5–7 minutes at high pressure.
3. Open with the natural release method (see Chapter 1).
4. Season with salt and pepper and serve.

PER SERVING | Calories: 507 | Fat: 16 g | Protein: 23 g | Sodium: 1105 mg | Fiber: 9 g | Carbohydrates: 70 g

Five Pepper Chili

*This chili is very spicy! Adjust the peppers accordingly if you would like
a milder version or if you are sharing this with children.*

INGREDIENTS | SERVES 8

1 tablespoon vegetable oil

1 onion, diced

1 jalapeño, seeded and minced

1 habanero pepper, seeded and minced

1 bell pepper, diced

1 poblano pepper, seeded and diced

2 cloves garlic, minced

2 (14½-ounce) cans crushed tomatoes

2 cups diced fresh tomatoes

2 tablespoons chili powder

1 tablespoon cumin

2 teaspoons cayenne pepper

⅛ cup Worcestershire sauce

4 cups cooked Pinto Beans (see recipe in this chapter)

2 teaspoons salt

1 teaspoon pepper

1. Heat vegetable oil in an uncovered pressure cooker over medium heat. Sauté the onion until it has caramelized (about 10–15 minutes). Add the jalapeño, habanero, bell, and poblano peppers and sauté for 1 minute more.
2. Add the garlic, crushed tomatoes, fresh tomatoes, chili powder, cumin, cayenne pepper, Worcestershire sauce, beans, salt, and pepper. Close and lock the lid.
3. Turn the heat up to high. When the cooker reaches pressure, lower the heat to the minimum needed to maintain pressure. Cook for 10–12 minutes at high pressure.
4. Open with the natural release method (see Chapter 1).
5. Stir well and serve.

PER SERVING | Calories: 163 | Fat: 3 g | Protein: 8 g | Sodium: 1011 mg | Fiber: 8 g | Carbohydrates: 27 g

Veggie Chili

This is a flavorful medley of vegetables and beans. It's delicious as a chili or, with just a little more vegetable broth, a soup.

INGREDIENTS | SERVES 8

1 tablespoon olive oil

1 onion, diced

3 cloves garlic, pressed

1½ cups cooked Pinto Beans (see recipe in this chapter)

1½ cups cooked kidney beans

1½ cups cooked White Beans (see recipe in this chapter)

1 large green bell pepper, seeded and diced

2 medium zucchini, diced

1½ cups corn

1 (28-ounce) can diced tomatoes

2 cups vegetable broth

2 tablespoons chili powder

1 teaspoon cumin

1 teaspoon dried oregano

¼ teaspoon freshly ground black pepper

⅛ teaspoon cayenne pepper

2 teaspoons salt

1 cup Monterey jack cheese, grated

1. Heat olive oil in an uncovered pressure cooker over medium heat. Add onion and sauté until it begins to soften (about 5 minutes). Stir in the garlic, beans, bell pepper, zucchini, corn, tomatoes, broth, chili powder, cumin, oregano, black pepper, cayenne pepper, and salt. Close and lock the lid.
2. Turn the heat up to high. When the cooker reaches pressure, lower the heat to the minimum needed to maintain pressure. Cook for 5–7 minutes at high pressure.
3. Open with the natural release method (see Chapter 1).
4. Ladle into individual bowls and serve with a dusting of cheese.

PER SERVING | Calories: 270 | Fat: 8 g | Protein: 14 g | Sodium: 979 mg | Fiber: 10 g | Carbohydrates: 39 g

Chickpea, Cannellini, and Barley Stew

This dish has a very light and delicate flavor. If you find the taste too simple, fry some sage leaves in a little garlic and butter for extra flavor and garnish.

INGREDIENTS | SERVES 6

1 whole clove

3 coriander seeds

1 heaping cup dried chickpeas, soaked

1 heaping cup dried cannellini (or navy) beans

½ cup pearl barley

1 clove garlic

2 tablespoons vegetable oil

1 teaspoon white pepper

4 cups water

1 teaspoon salt

¼ cup grated Pecorino Romano cheese

1 tablespoon extra-virgin olive oil

1. Put the clove and coriander seeds in a tea ball or bouquet garni bag and place in pressure cooker. Add chickpeas, beans, barley, garlic, vegetable oil, white pepper, and water to the pressure cooker. Close and lock the lid.
2. Turn the heat up to high. When the cooker reaches pressure, lower the heat to the minimum needed to maintain pressure. Cook for 15 minutes at high pressure.
3. Open with the natural release method (see Chapter 1).
4. Season with salt to taste and top each serving with cheese and a swirl of olive oil.

PER SERVING | Calories: 218 | Fat: 9 g | Protein: 7 g | Sodium: 548 mg | Fiber: 7 g | Carbohydrates: 27 g

Succotash

Succotash can be made with a variety of beans, but the staple ingredients are lima beans and corn.

INGREDIENTS | SERVES 4

1 tablespoon olive oil

1 bell pepper, chopped

1 cup fresh lima beans

1 cup whole kernel corn

1 cup chopped tomatoes

1 cup water

1 teaspoon salt

1. Heat olive oil in an uncovered pressure cooker over medium heat. Add pepper and sauté for 3 minutes. Add lima beans, corn, tomatoes, water, and salt. Close and lock the lid.
2. Turn the heat up to high. When the cooker reaches pressure, lower the heat to the minimum needed to maintain pressure. Cook for 8–10 minutes at high pressure.
3. Open with the natural release method (see Chapter 1).
4. Serve with a slotted spoon to strain any excess liquid.

PER SERVING | Calories: 227 | Fat: 4 g | Protein: 11 g | Sodium: 734 mg | Fiber: 10 g | Carbohydrates: 39 g

Origin of Succotash

The word succotash derives from the Native American word *msickquatash*, which, according to *www.epicurious.com*, means "boiled whole kernels of corn."

CHAPTER 6

Chicken and Turkey

Chicken with Mushrooms in
White Wine
114

Chicken Masala
115

Italian Herb and Lemon Chicken
116

Spicy Ginger Chicken
117

Citrus Spice Chicken
118

Chicken Paprika
119

Whole Beer-Can-Chicken
120

Curry Yogurt Chicken
121

Satay-Flavored Chicken
121

Turkey Thighs in Fig Sauce
122

Turkey in Tarragon Sauce
123

Turkey Breast in Yogurt Sauce
124

Turkey Breast with Mushrooms
125

Cranberry and Walnut Braised
Turkey Wings
126

Turkey Cacciatore
127

Petit Turkey Meatloaf
128

Chicken with Mushrooms in White Wine

For a more intense flavor, substitute the white wine for a very strong and aged red—
you only need half a cup, so use whatever you're serving with dinner.

INGREDIENTS | SERVES 6

1 tablespoon olive oil

1 clove garlic, peeled and crushed

3 pounds bone-in chicken pieces

1 teaspoon cracked black pepper

½ cup dry white wine

1 (15-ounce) can diced tomatoes

4 ounces mushrooms, sliced

2 teaspoons salt

Chicken Bordeaux

Often called Chicken Bordeaux, this simple and delicious chicken dish is perfect with egg noodles or cooked rice. Opt for whole-grain rice for extra fiber and nutrients.

1. Heat olive oil in an uncovered pressure cooker over medium heat. Sauté the garlic until golden (about 1 minute).
2. Rub chicken with pepper. Arrange the chicken pieces skin-side down in the pressure cooker and brown well (approximately 5 minutes). You may need to work in batches.
3. Remove chicken from pan and deglaze the bottom with wine until the liquid is almost completely evaporated (about 3 minutes). Arrange all pieces skin-side up in the pressure cooker, then add tomatoes, mushrooms, and salt. Close and lock the lid.
4. Turn the heat up to high. When the cooker reaches pressure, lower the heat to the minimum needed to maintain pressure. Cook for 8–10 minutes at high pressure.
5. When time is up, open the pressure cooker by releasing pressure.
6. Transfer chicken to a serving platter and keep warm.
7. In the uncovered pressure cooker, reduce the sauce until thickened. Pour over chicken and serve.

PER SERVING | Calories: 320 | Fat: 9 g | Protein: 49 g | Sodium: 964 | Fiber: 1 g | Carbohydrates: 4 g

Chicken Masala

With your pressure cooker, now you can make this delicious Indian dish at home in no time!

INGREDIENTS | SERVES 4

1 tablespoon vegetable oil
1 onion, peeled and diced
1 stalk celery, finely diced
1 large carrot, peeled and grated
1½ tablespoons garam masala
1 clove garlic, peeled and minced
½ cup chicken broth
3 tomatoes, chopped
1 cup coconut milk
1 pound boneless, skinless chicken breasts, diced
⅓ cup flour
1 cup frozen peas
1 teaspoon salt
¼ teaspoon pepper

Garam Masala

Garam masala, meaning "hot mixture," is a blend of ground spices commonly used in Indian and South Asian cuisines. It is easy to find in the spice section of most supermarkets.

1. Heat olive oil in an uncovered pressure cooker over medium heat. Add onion and sauté until transparent (about 3 minutes). Add the celery, carrot, garam masala, and garlic and sauté for 1 more minute. Pour in the chicken broth, tomatoes, coconut milk, and chicken. Close and lock the lid.
2. Turn the heat up to high. When the cooker reaches pressure, lower the heat to the minimum needed to maintain pressure. Cook for 4–5 minutes at high pressure.
3. When time is up, open the pressure cooker by releasing pressure.
4. Stir in the flour and peas and simmer uncovered for 5 minutes until thickened. Season with salt and pepper before serving.

PER SERVING | Calories: 395 | Fat: 20 g | Protein: 30 g | Sodium: 914 mg | Fiber: 5 g | Carbohydrates: 26g

Italian Herb and Lemon Chicken

Black olives are almost never pressure cooked. They have a very strong and decisive flavor that would overwhelm all other flavors if they were added to the pressure cooker.

INGREDIENTS | SERVES 6

4 lemons, divided

2 garlic cloves, chopped

3 sprigs of fresh rosemary, divided

2 sprigs of fresh sage

½ bunch of parsley

5 tablespoons extra-virgin olive oil, divided

1 teaspoon salt

½ teaspoon pepper

1 chicken, cut into parts, or 1 package of bone-in chicken pieces, skin removed

½ cup of dry white wine

4 ounces pitted black salt-cured olives (Taggiesche, French, or Kalamata)

1. Juice 3 lemons and pour the juice in a small bowl. Chop together the garlic, 2 rosemary sprigs, sage, and parsley and add to the lemon juice, along with 4 tablespoons olive oil, salt, and pepper. Mix well and set aside.
2. Place the chicken in a deep dish and cover well with the marinade. Cover with plastic wrap and marinate in the refrigerator for 2–4 hours.
3. Remove chicken from dish, reserving marinade. Heat 1 tablespoon olive oil in an uncovered pressure cooker over medium heat. Brown the chicken pieces on all sides for about 5 minutes. Remove chicken from pan and deglaze pan with the white wine. Cook until liquid is almost completely evaporated (about 3 minutes).
4. Return chicken pieces to pressure cooker. Place dark-meat pieces (wings, legs, and thighs) on the bottom of the pan, topped with the breasts (breasts should not touch the bottom of the pressure cooker.) Pour in the reserved marinade. Close and lock the lid.
5. Turn the heat up to high. When the cooker reaches pressure, lower the heat to the minimum needed to maintain pressure. Cook for 8–10 minutes at high pressure.
6. Open the pressure cooker by releasing pressure.
7. Move the chicken pieces out of the cooker and place on a serving platter. Cover with foil and keep warm.
8. Reduce the liquid in the uncovered cooker, over medium-high heat, to ¼ of its amount, or until it becomes thick and syrupy.
9. Pour reduced pan juices over chicken. Slice the remaining lemon and chop 1 sprig of rosemary. Serve chicken garnished with lemon slices, rosemary, and olives.

PER SERVING | Calories: 336 | Fat: 19 g | Protein: 25 g | Sodium: 662 mg | Fiber: 7 g | Carbohydrates: 14 g

Spicy Ginger Chicken

A very simple way to prepare chicken with a kick!

INGREDIENTS | SERVES 6

1 tablespoon vegetable oil

1 teaspoon fresh grated ginger

3 cloves garlic, minced

½ teaspoon crushed red pepper flakes

1 teaspoon white pepper

3 pounds skinless, bone-in chicken pieces

1 tablespoon soy sauce

1 tablespoon honey

¾ cup water

1. Heat oil in an uncovered pressure cooker over medium heat. Sauté the ginger, garlic, crushed pepper, and white pepper for about 2 minutes. Add the chicken pieces and drizzle with soy sauce and honey. Add the water. Close and lock the lid.
2. Turn the heat up to high. When the cooker reaches pressure, lower the heat to the minimum needed to maintain pressure. Cook for 8–10 minutes at high pressure.
3. When time is up, open the pressure cooker by releasing pressure.
4. Remove the chicken pieces to a serving platter and cover loosely with foil. Reduce the liquid in the uncovered cooker over medium-high heat to ¼ of its amount, or until it becomes thick and syrupy.
5. Pour reduced pan juices over chicken and serve.

PER SERVING | Calories: 303 | Fat: 9 g | Protein: 48 g | Sodium: 323 mg | Fiber: 0 g | Carbohydrates: 4 g

Citrus Spice Chicken

Hints of spice round out the overall flavors of this dish, which are enhanced by the natural citric acid in the juices.

INGREDIENTS | SERVES 6

2 tablespoons vegetable oil

3 pounds boneless, skinless chicken thighs

1 teaspoon paprika

½ teaspoon sea salt

⅛ teaspoon cinnamon

⅛ teaspoon ginger

⅛ teaspoon ground cloves

½ cup white raisins

½ cup slivered almonds

¾ cup orange juice

¼ cup lemon juice

½ cup apple juice

1 pound baby carrots

1 tablespoon cornstarch

¼ cup cold water

Love Orange?

Enjoy this same recipe but with a focus on orange. Instead of using the combination of orange, lemon, and apple juices, use 1½ cups of orange juice for a dish that is equally flavorful and easy. Top with freshly chopped mint leaves for a refreshing finish.

1. Heat olive oil in an uncovered pressure cooker over medium heat. Fry chicken thighs for 2 minutes on each side. Add the paprika, salt, cinnamon, ginger, cloves, raisins, almonds, orange juice, lemon juice, apple juice, and carrots. Close and lock the lid.
2. Turn the heat up to high. When the cooker reaches pressure, lower the heat to the minimum needed to maintain pressure. Cook for 8–10 minutes at high pressure.
3. When time is up, open the pressure cooker by releasing pressure.
4. Remove the chicken from pressure cooker and transfer to a serving platter. Keep warm.
5. In a separate bowl, combine cornstarch with the water and whisk into the remaining liquid in the pressure cooker. Stir and boil over high heat for 3 minutes or until the sauce is thickened.
6. Pour sauce over chicken and serve.

PER SERVING | Calories: 448 | Fat: 17 g | Protein: 46 g | Sodium: 452 mg | Fiber: 4 g | Carbohydrates: 25 g

Chicken Paprika

Paprika is a spice that is made by grinding varieties of dried peppers. Paprika can be spicy, sweet, mild, or even smoked.

INGREDIENTS | SERVES 4

1 tablespoon vegetable oil

1 onion, peeled and sliced into strips

1 green bell pepper, sliced into strips

4 bone-in chicken breast halves

5 cloves garlic, smashed

¼ cup tomato purée

2 tablespoons Hungarian paprika

¾ cup Chicken Stock (see recipe in Chapter 4)

¾ cup plain whole-milk yogurt

2 teaspoons sea salt

1 teaspoon pepper

Spice It Up or Cool It Down

If you like your meals spicy, add cayenne pepper to this dish. If you don't like spice, sour cream, yogurt, or any milk product is a great way to cool down spicy flavor. Also, if you accidentally consume something super spicy, don't drink water. Reach for the milk instead!

1. Heat oil in an uncovered pressure cooker over medium heat. Add onion and pepper and sauté for about 3 minutes. Add the chicken skin-side down and brown for about 5 minutes. Turn chicken and add garlic, tomato purée, paprika, and stock. Close and lock the lid.
2. Turn the heat up to high. When the cooker reaches pressure, lower the heat to the minimum needed to maintain pressure. Cook for 7–9 minutes at high pressure.
3. When time is up, open the pressure cooker by releasing pressure.
4. Transfer the chicken to a serving platter and keep warm.
5. Stir in the yogurt and simmer in the uncovered cooker for 5 minutes or until the sauce has thickened. Stir in salt and pepper.
6. Pour sauce over chicken and serve.

PER SERVING | Calories: 248 | Fat: 9 g | Protein: 29 | Sodium: 1467 mg | Fiber: 3 g | Carbohydrates: 12 g

Whole Beer-Can-Chicken

Be sure to measure the height of your pressure cooker before buying a chicken. You don't want it to be too tall to fit! If the can doesn't fit in the chicken, use a trivet (pointing up into the cavity) as a stand.

INGREDIENTS | SERVES 6

2 tablespoons chopped rosemary (reserve a teaspoon for garnish)

2 tablespoons chopped sage

2 tablespoons chopped thyme

2 tablespoons olive oil

Juice and zest of 1 lemon

1 teaspoon salt

½ teaspoon black pepper

3½ pounds chicken

1 can beer (your choice)

2 bay leaves, divided

Lying or Sitting

Sitting a chicken in the pressure cooker, as opposed to laying it down as you would in the oven, keeps all of the dark meat in contact with the base of the pressure cooker (where there is the most heat) and the breast meat up high, where it is cooked more delicately by the super-heated steam.

1. In a bowl, prepare the seasoning by mixing the rosemary, sage, thyme, olive oil, lemon juice, salt, and pepper.
2. Rinse chicken inside and out and pat dry. Tuck the tips of the wings behind the neck opening of the chicken and brush on the seasoning.
3. In a separate pan (or your pressure cooker if it is large enough) brown the seasoned chicken well on all sides (about 10 minutes).
4. Pour ⅓ of the beer out of the can and place half the lemon zest and one bay leaf into the can. Place the can in the middle of the pressure cooker. Lower the chicken over the can of beer so that the can is inside the cavity. Pour any of the remaining seasoning and liquid from the sauté pan over the chicken.
5. Add the remaining lemon zest and bay leaf. Close and lock the lid.
6. Turn the heat up to high. When the cooker reaches pressure, lower the heat to the minimum needed to maintain pressure. Cook for 20–25 minutes at high pressure.
7. Open with the natural release method (see Chapter 1).
8. Carefully remove the chicken and the beer can from the pressure cooker. Place the chicken on the serving platter to rest tented with aluminum foil, pour in the remaining beer from the can and discard. Simmer the contents of the uncovered cooker for about 5 minutes or until reduced by half.
9. Strain the pan sauce and pour over the chicken. Sprinkle with fresh rosemary before serving.

PER SERVING | Calories: 429 | Fat: 14 g | Protein: 64 g | Sodium: 626 mg | Fiber: 1 g | Carbohydrates: 4 g

Curry Yogurt Chicken

Serve this East Indian–style dish with basmati rice, couscous, or lentils.

INGREDIENTS | SERVES 6

1 cup water

½ cup plain low-fat yogurt

1 tablespoon lemon juice

2 cloves garlic, peeled and minced

2 teaspoons grated fresh ginger, or ½ teaspoon ground ginger

1 teaspoon turmeric

¼ teaspoon sea salt

1 teaspoon paprika

1 teaspoon curry powder

¼ teaspoon freshly ground black pepper

6 boneless, skinless chicken breasts

2 teaspoons cornstarch

2 teaspoons cold water

1. Mix water, yogurt, lemon juice, garlic, ginger, turmeric, salt, paprika, curry powder, and pepper in a bowl. Add the chicken and marinate in refrigerator for 1 hour.
2. Turn the heat up to high. When the cooker reaches pressure, lower the heat to the minimum needed to maintain pressure add the chicken mixture to the cooker. Cook for 4–5 minutes at high pressure.
3. When time is up, open the pressure cooker by releasing pressure.
4. Transfer the chicken to a serving platter and keep warm.
5. Mix the cornstarch with the cold water. Stir into the cooker and boil for 3 minutes or until mixture thickens.
6. Pour sauce over the chicken. Serve immediately.

PER SERVING | Calories: 291 | Fat: 7 g | Protein: 51 g | Sodium: 382 mg | Fiber: 0 g | Carbohydrates: 3 g

Satay-Flavored Chicken

Inspired by the delicious Thai appetizer, Chicken Satay with Peanut Sauce, this main dish can be quickly pressure cooked and served on top of a pillow of jasmine rice.

INGREDIENTS | SERVES 4

½ cup coconut milk

1 tablespoon fish sauce

2 teaspoons red curry paste

½ teaspoon ground turmeric

½ teaspoon white pepper

½ teaspoon powdered ginger

1 pound boneless chicken tenders (or breasts sliced into strips)

3 cups cooked Jasmine Rice (see Chapter 12)

½ cup ground peanuts

1. Put all of the ingredients, except rice and peanuts, in the pressure cooker. Stir to mix. Close and lock the lid.
2. Turn the heat up to high. When the cooker reaches pressure, lower the heat to the minimum needed to maintain pressure. Cook for 4–5 minutes at high pressure.
3. When time is up, open the pressure cooker by releasing pressure.
4. Simmer uncovered until the sauce is thickened. Pour sauce over cooked jasmine rice and sprinkle with ground peanuts.

PER SERVING | Calories: 350 | Fat: 24 g | Protein: 29 g | Sodium: 97 mg | Fiber: 2 g | Carbohydrates: 5 g

Turkey Thighs in Fig Sauce

Both balsamic vinegar and figs are tart, so this sauce tastes great with both pork and chicken.

INGREDIENTS | SERVES 4

1 tablespoon olive oil

4 bone-in turkey thighs, skin removed (about 3 pounds)

1 large onion, cut into thin strips

2 large carrots, peeled and sliced diagonally

1 stalk celery, finely diced

½ cup balsamic vinegar

1 cup chicken, turkey, or veal stock

Zest and juice of 1 lemon

2 teaspoons salt

1 teaspoon black pepper

12 dried figs, cut in half

1 tablespoon flour

1 sprig fresh rosemary, chopped

Fresh Fig Variation

You can use fresh figs instead of dried, but they will cook much more quickly. Slice them in half and add to the turkey thighs for the last 5 minutes of cooking time. Do not stir them in; sprinkle them on top of the contents in the pressure cooker. They will steam delicately and release their juice.

1. Heat olive oil in an uncovered pressure cooker over medium heat. Brown the turkey thighs on all sides, working in batches if they are particularly large. Add the onion, carrots, and celery and sauté until the onions begin to soften (about 5 minutes).

2. Deglaze the pan with vinegar, and then add stock, lemon juice, and zest. Return thighs to the cooker. If they do not all fit in the base, stand them with the bone pointing up to ensure even braising. Sprinkle with salt and pepper and add the figs. Close and lock the lid.

3. Turn the heat up to high. When the cooker reaches pressure, lower the heat to the minimum needed to maintain pressure. Cook for 25–30 minutes at high pressure.

4. Open with the natural release method (see Chapter 1).

5. Transfer the thighs, carrots, and figs to a serving platter. Tent loosely with aluminum foil and keep warm.

6. Complete the sauce in the cooker by stirring in flour and boiling over high heat until thickened and reduced. Pour sauce over turkey thighs, carrots, and figs and serve with a sprinkle of fresh rosemary.

PER SERVING | Calories: 431 | Fat: 8 g | Protein: 53 g | Sodium: 1621 | Fiber: 4 g | Carbohydrates: 33 g

Turkey in Tarragon Sauce

Serve this delicious turkey with mashed potatoes and steamed asparagus.

INGREDIENTS | SERVES 4

2 slices bacon, cut in half
1 pound skinless, boneless turkey breast
1 onion, peeled and diced
2 cloves garlic, peeled and minced
½ cup dry white wine
2 tablespoons minced fresh tarragon
1 cup heavy cream
1 teaspoon salt
½ teaspoon white pepper

Fresh Tarragon

Tarragon is a leafy herb that has a licorice flavor. Because of its strong flavor, it pairs nicely with other strong-flavored ingredients such as heavy cream. Other great herbs to use in this recipe are Italian flat-leaf parsley or dill.

1. Cook the bacon in an uncovered pressure cooker over medium heat until crisp. Drain the cooked bacon on paper towels and set aside.
2. Cut the turkey into bite-size pieces and add to the pressure cooker along with the onion. Sauté for 5 minutes or until the turkey is lightly browned and the onion is transparent. Add garlic and deglaze the pan with the wine. Close and lock the lid.
3. Turn the heat up to high. When the cooker reaches pressure, lower the heat to the minimum needed to maintain pressure. Cook for 7–9 minutes at high pressure.
4. When time is up, open the pressure cooker by releasing pressure.
5. Using a slotted spoon, transfer the cooked turkey to a serving dish and keep warm. Stir the fresh tarragon into the cooker and bring to a simmer. Stir in the cream until incorporated. Add salt and pepper.
6. Pour the sauce over the cooked turkey. Crumble the bacon over the top of the dish and serve.

PER SERVING | Calories: 421 | Fat: 28 g | Protein: 30 g | Sodium: 764 mg | Fiber: 0 g | Carbohydrates: 6 g

Turkey Breast in Yogurt Sauce

Serve over cooked rice or couscous with a cucumber-yogurt salad. To make the salad, combine plain yogurt, garlic, mint, salt, ginger, and lemon juice. Mix with thinly sliced cucumbers.

INGREDIENTS | SERVES 4

1 cup plain low-fat yogurt

1 teaspoon ground turmeric

1 teaspoon ground cumin

1 teaspoon yellow mustard seeds

¼ teaspoon salt

½ teaspoon freshly ground black pepper

1 pound boneless turkey breast, cut into bite-size pieces

1 tablespoon butter

1 (1 pound bag) frozen baby peas and pearl onions

1. In a large bowl, mix together the yogurt, turmeric, cumin, mustard seeds, salt, and pepper. Stir turkey into the yogurt mixture. Cover and marinate in the refrigerator for 4 hours.
2. Heat butter in an uncovered pressure cooker over medium heat. Add turkey and yogurt mixture. Close and lock the lid.
3. Turn the heat up to high. When the cooker reaches pressure, lower the heat to the minimum needed to maintain pressure. Cook for 7–9 minutes at high pressure.
4. When time is up, open the pressure cooker by releasing pressure.
5. Stir the peas and pearl onions into the cooker and simmer until the vegetables are cooked and the sauce has thickened. Serve.

PER SERVING | Calories: 239 | Fat: 6 g | Protein: 33 g | Sodium: 234 mg | Fiber: 3 g | Carbohydrates: 12 g

Turkey Breast with Mushrooms

The cooking liquid thickens at the end of pressure cooking to form a delicious mushroom gravy topping.

INGREDIENTS | SERVES 6

1 tablespoon vegetable oil

3 tablespoons butter, divided

1 large onion, peeled and diced

1 pound button mushrooms, sliced

4 cloves garlic, smashed

2 pounds boneless turkey breast, sliced

1¾ cups chicken or turkey stock

½ cup sweet Madeira or Port wine

1 bay leaf

¼ cup all-purpose flour

1 teaspoon salt

½ teaspoon black pepper

Super Turkey?

Yes! Turkey is an excellent source of lean protein. One serving of turkey provides more than 50 percent of your body's daily protein requirement—with half the fat of beef and 30 percent fewer calories, too!

1. Heat oil and 1 tablespoon butter in an uncovered pressure cooker over medium heat. Add the onion and sauté for 3 minutes, or until transparent. Add the mushrooms and sauté for 3 minutes (stirring infrequently), then add garlic.
2. Push the sautéed vegetables to the sides of the pan and add the turkey breast. Cook the turkey for 3 minutes or until it browns on one side. Turn turkey and add the stock, wine, and bay leaf. Close and lock the lid.
3. Turn the heat up to high. When the cooker reaches pressure, lower the heat to the minimum needed to maintain pressure. Cook for 5–7 minutes at high pressure.
4. Open with the natural release method (see Chapter 1).
5. Transfer the turkey to a serving platter and tent with foil.
6. Discard the bay leaf. Over medium heat, add flour and remaining butter to the liquid in the pressure cooker. Whisk constantly and simmer uncovered until thickened (about 5 minutes).
7. Season with salt and pepper. Serve turkey breast covered with mushroom gravy.

PER SERVING | Calories: 329 | Fat: 10 g | Protein: 39 g | Sodium: 775 mg | Fiber: 1 g | Carbohydrates: 13 g

Cranberry and Walnut Braised Turkey Wings

This dish is a perfect solution for a small Thanksgiving feast or a hearty winter meal.

INGREDIENTS | SERVES 6

2 tablespoons butter

1 tablespoon vegetable oil

4 turkey wings (about 3 pounds)

1 teaspoon salt

½ teaspoon pepper

1 onion, roughly sliced

1 cup dry cranberries (soaked in boiling water for 5 minutes)

1 cup shelled walnuts

1 bunch fresh thyme, tied with twine

1 cup freshly squeezed orange juice, or prepared juice without sugar

Fresh and Canned Cranberries

Substitute the dried cranberries in this recipe with 1½ cups fresh cranberries or 1 cup canned cranberries, drained and rinsed.

1. Heat butter and oil in an uncovered pressure cooker over medium heat. Sprinkle salt and pepper over turkey wings, and brown wings on both sides, making sure that the skin side is nicely colored.
2. Remove the wings from the pressure cooker and add the onion. Return wings to the pan, skin side up, along with cranberries, walnuts, and thyme. Pour the orange juice over the turkey. Close and lock the lid.
3. Turn the heat up to high. When the cooker reaches pressure, lower the heat to the minimum needed to maintain pressure. Cook for 12–15 minutes at high pressure.
4. Open with the natural release method (see Chapter 1).
5. Remove and discard the thyme bundle and carefully move the turkey wings to a serving dish. Tent with foil.
6. Reduce the contents of the liquid in the uncovered pressure cooker to about half. Pour the liquid, walnuts, onions, and cranberries over the wings and serve.

PER SERVING | Calories: 501 | Fat: 23 g | Protein: 55 g | Sodium: 535 mg | Fiber: 8 g | Carbohydrates: 20 g

Turkey Cacciatore

This dish is sort of like a stew and would be perfect on a pillow of warm polenta.

INGREDIENTS | SERVES 8

1 tablespoon butter

1 tablespoon olive oil

1 (12-pound) turkey cut into 8 pieces (wings, legs, thighs, and breast)

1 cup red wine

1 onion, roughly diced

1 carrot, roughly diced

1 celery stalk, roughly diced

1 clove garlic, smashed

1 (28-ounce) can of whole tomatoes

2 teaspoons salt

1 teaspoon black pepper

2 sprigs of rosemary, divided

1 sprig of sage

1 cup of black salt-cured olives (Taggiesche, French, or Kalamata)

The Hunter's Meat

In Italian, cacciatore means "hunter." This simple preparation is reserved for "caught" meat. For example, in Italy, chickens and lambs have been domesticated for millennia and would not be something that might be "hunted," or served "alla cacciatora!"

1. Heat butter and olive oil in an uncovered pressure cooker over medium heat. Brown the turkey pieces on all sides for about 5 minutes, remove, and set aside. Deglaze the pan with wine and reduce until it is almost all evaporated (about 3 minutes).
2. Add the onion, carrot, celery, and garlic. Top with turkey pieces. Pour the tomatoes over the turkey and sprinkle with salt and pepper. Add 1 rosemary sprig and sage. Close and lock the lid.
3. Turn the heat up to high. When the cooker reaches pressure, lower the heat to the minimum needed to maintain pressure. Cook for 25–30 minutes at high pressure.
4. Open with the natural release method (see Chapter 1).
5. Pour black olives into cooker and stir to warm through. Transfer turkey and sauce to a serving platter and garnish with a sprig of rosemary.

PER SERVING | Calories: 636 | Fat: 14 g | Protein: 102 g | Sodium: 1163 | Fiber: 8 g | Carbohydrates: 17 g

Petit Turkey Meatloaf

The flavor of this meatloaf can be changed up, depending on what you have on hand. Try freshly chopped Italian flat-leaf parsley, snipped chives, Worcestershire sauce, and a little lemon zest.

INGREDIENTS | SERVES 4

1 pound lean ground turkey
1 onion, peeled and diced
1 stalk celery, minced
1 carrot, peeled and grated
½ cup butter cracker crumbs
½ cup grated Pecorino Romano cheese
1 clove garlic, peeled and minced
1 teaspoon fresh chopped basil
1 teaspoon mustard
1 teaspoon sea salt
¼ teaspoon pepper
1 large egg
3 tablespoons ketchup
1 cup water

1. Add all ingredients to a large bowl and mix well. Divide the mixture between 2 mini loaf pans. Pack the mixture down into the pans.
2. Place water in the pressure cooker and add the steamer basket. Lower the little pans onto the basket. Close and lock the lid.
3. Turn the heat up to high. When the cooker reaches pressure, lower the heat to the minimum needed to maintain pressure. Cook for 15–20 minutes at high pressure.
4. Open with the natural release method (see Chapter 1).
5. Use oven mitts or tongs to lift the pans out of the pressure cooker. Serve directly from the pans or transfer to a serving platter.

PER SERVING | Calories: 318 | Fat: 17 g | Protein: 26 g | Sodium: 1031 mg | Fiber: 1 g | Carbohydrates: 13 g

Individual Loaves

Making individual loaves is a great idea no matter how many people you're cooking for. Serve ½–1 loaf per person, then freeze the remaining individual loaves for a quick meal anytime.

CHAPTER 7

Beef and Veal

South African Ground
Beef Casserole
130

Italian Boiled Beef Roast
131

Sloppy Joes
132

Beef and Guinness Stew
133

Beef Biryani
134

Pot Roast
135

Citrus Corned Beef
and Cabbage
136

Ropa Vieja
137

Texas Firehouse Chili
137

Cincinnati Chili
138

Mushroom-Stuffed Veal Roll
139

Beef Rogan Josh
140

Italian Summer Veal Roast
141

Pam's Osso Buco
142

South African Ground Beef Casserole

Serve with yellow rice, a fluffy white rice spiced with turmeric, sugar, cinnamon, and raisins, fresh slices of tropical fruits like mango or papaya, or a chutney.

INGREDIENTS | SERVES 8

1 cup 1% milk

2 slices stale white bread, torn in small pieces

2 tablespoons peanut oil

2 onions, chopped

1 tablespoon curry powder

¾ teaspoon turmeric

1 teaspoon salt

¼ teaspoon pepper

2 pounds ground beef

2 tablespoons raw sugar

Zest and juice of 1 lemon

¼ cup sliced almonds, toasted

½ cup raisins, soaked and drained

1 tablespoon butter

1 cup water

5 eggs

4 bay leaves

Babotie

This dish is called Babotie in South Africa, and it's practically the national dish. It's a surprisingly elegant casserole that traditionally takes 1–1½ hours to bake in the oven. You can have this dish ready in 30 minutes, including the broiled finish!

1. In a bowl, pour milk over bread and set aside.
2. In a large sauté pan over medium heat, heat the oil. Add onions and sauté until soft (about 5 minutes). Add the curry powder, turmeric, salt, and pepper. Add ground beef and cook, stirring to crumble, until beef is browned and all of the liquid has evaporated (about 5–7 minutes). Turn off the heat and mix in the sugar.
3. Squeeze the bread and add it to the pan (keep the milk to use later for the topping). Add the lemon juice and zest, almonds, and raisins. Mix well.
4. Butter a 7½-inch wide (or smaller) heatproof baking dish. Pour mixture into buttered baking dish and flatten slightly.
5. Prepare the pressure cooker by inserting the trivet, or steamer basket, and add water. Make a sling by folding a long piece of foil into three and lower the uncovered dish into the pressure cooker. Close and lock the lid.
6. Turn the heat up to high. When the cooker reaches pressure, lower the heat to the minimum needed to maintain pressure. Cook for 15–20 minutes at high pressure.
7. Open the pressure cooker by releasing pressure. Mix the eggs into the milk to make a custard mixture.
8. Carefully remove the baking dish from the pressure cooker and pour the custard mixture over the meat. Add the bay leaves and cover with foil. Lower dish into the pressure cooker again. Close and lock the lid.
9. Turn the heat up to high. When the cooker reaches pressure, lower the heat to the minimum needed to maintain pressure. Cook for 3–5 minutes at high pressure.
10. Open the cooker by releasing pressure. Serve as is or brown the custard under a broiler for about 5 minutes.

PER SERVING | Calories: 353 | Fat: 19 g | Protein: 26 g | Sodium: 436 mg | Fiber: 2 g | Carbohydrates: 20 g

Italian Boiled Beef Roast

Even the toughest cut of beef can be softened by simply being boiled—tough ligaments and nerves are reduced to gelatin. Serve with a fresh and tangy Italian Salsa Verde (see sidebar).

INGREDIENTS | SERVES 6

1 medium onion, halved (ends removed, skin still on)

8 whole cloves

6 cups water

1 large carrot, peeled and halved

1 celery stalk, halved

1 small tomato, chopped

1 bay leaf

1 sprig sage

1 sprig rosemary

2 sprigs thyme

3 tablespoons salt

1 tablespoon black peppercorns

3 pounds beef round roast

Italian Salsa Verde

Pour ½ cup white wine vinegar over ½ cup unseasoned bread crumbs and set aside. Purée the following in a food processor until smooth: 2 anchovies (optional), 1 teaspoon capers, 2 peeled garlic cloves, 2 bunches parsley (about 4½ ounces), and ¼ cup olive oil. Add the soaked bread crumbs and purée for about 30 seconds to combine. Continue adding more olive oil and pulsing until a sauce consistency is reached. Season with salt and pepper.

1. Cut onion in half and remove ends, but leave skin on. Pierce each half with 4 cloves. Place onion halves in pressure cooker.
2. Add water, carrot, celery, tomato, bay leaf, sage, rosemary, thyme, salt, and peppercorns. In the uncovered pressure cooker, bring the contents to a boil over high heat, then carefully add the meat. If the water does not cover the beef, add more until it does. Bring the contents to a boil. Close and lock the lid.
3. Turn the heat up to high. When the cooker reaches pressure, lower the heat to the minimum needed to maintain pressure. Cook for 50–60 minutes at high pressure.
4. Open with the natural release method (see Chapter 1).
5. Remove beef to a serving platter and tent loosely with foil.
6. Reduce the broth in the uncovered pressure cooker over high heat for about 5 minutes. Strain the broth and remove visible fat.
7. Thinly slice the meat and pour broth over the slices before serving.

PER SERVING | Calories: 533 | Fat: 22 g | Protein: 52 g | Sodium: 3701 mg | Fiber: 23 g | Carbohydrates: 38 g

Sloppy Joes

Serve on hamburger buns with potato chips and coleslaw. Depending on the size of the buns (and individual appetites), this recipe can be stretched to 8 servings.

INGREDIENTS | SERVES 6

1 tablespoon peanut oil
1 large onion, peeled and diced
2 cloves garlic, peeled and minced
1½ pounds lean ground beef
½ cup Beef Stock (see recipe in Chapter 4)
¼ cup tomato paste
1 teaspoon sugar
1 teaspoon salt
½ teaspoon pepper
⅛ teaspoon red pepper flakes
1 teaspoon mustard powder
1 tablespoon Worcestershire sauce
⅛ teaspoon ground cinnamon
⅛ teaspoon ground cloves
6 hamburger rolls

Sloppy Who?

The Original Sloppy Joe Sandwich was invented by a cook aptly named Joe. He worked in a café in Sioux City, Iowa, and served up his sandwich as a variation of the "loose meat" sandwich (which does not contain tomatoes).

1. Heat oil in an uncovered pressure cooker over medium heat. Sauté the onion until soft (about 5 minutes). Add garlic and sauté for another minute. Add all other ingredients, except hamburger rolls, to the pressure cooker and mix well. Close and lock the lid.
2. Turn the heat up to high. When the cooker reaches pressure, lower the heat to the minimum needed to maintain pressure. Cook for 5–7 minutes at high pressure.
3. When time is up, open the pressure cooker by releasing pressure.
4. Stir and simmer, uncovered, over medium heat, breaking apart the cooked meat and thickening the sauce until it's the desired consistency. Spoon mixture onto hamburger rolls to serve.

PER SERVING | Calories: 320 | Fat: 9.6 g | Protein: 27 g | Sodium: 738 mg | Fiber: 2.8 g | Carbohydrates: 29 g

Beef and Guinness Stew

This stew is filled with vegetables and is very flavorful. The small amounts of sugar and cocoa eliminate the bitterness occasionally found in similar stews.

INGREDIENTS | SERVES 8

2 teaspoons canola oil

1 large onion, diced

2 parsnips, diced

2 carrots, diced

2 stalks celery, diced

3 cloves garlic, minced

2 russet potatoes, peeled and diced

2 tablespoons minced fresh rosemary

2 pounds lean top round roast, cut into 1-inch cubes

1 tablespoon honey

1 teaspoon salt

½ teaspoon pepper

1 teaspoon unsweetened cocoa powder

1½ cups Guinness extra stout beer

1 cup frozen peas

1. Heat canola oil in an uncovered pressure cooker over medium heat. Sauté the onion, parsnips, carrots, celery, garlic, potatoes, rosemary, and beef until the ingredients begin to soften and brown, about 5–7 minutes. Drain excess fat. Add honey, salt, pepper, and cocoa powder. Pour in the beer. Close and lock the lid.
2. Turn the heat up to high. When the cooker reaches pressure, lower the heat to the minimum needed to maintain pressure. Cook for 13–15 minutes at high pressure.
3. When time is up, open the pressure cooker by releasing pressure.
4. Add the peas and simmer uncovered for 5 minutes before serving.

PER SERVING | Calories: 302 | Fat: 6 g | Protein: 29 g | Sodium: 393 mg | Fiber: 4.5 g | Carbohydrates: 26 g

Lean Cuts of Beef

Leaner cuts like top round are excellent choices for pressure cooking because they are tenderized in no time. Look for cuts that have minimal marbling and trim off any excess fat before cooking. Searing and sautéing are good ways to cook off some external fat before adding the meat to the cooker. Drain any excess fat before pressure cooking.

Beef Biryani

Biryani is a one-dish meal that is well spiced but not spicy. Traditionally it is made using large amounts of ghee, a type of clarified butter, but pressure cooking it brings out the flavor without adding unnecessary fat.

INGREDIENTS | SERVES 6

1 tablespoon ghee

1 onion, sliced

1 pound top round, cut into strips

1 tablespoon minced fresh ginger

2 cloves garlic, minced

½ teaspoon ground cloves

½ teaspoon ground cardamom

½ teaspoon ground coriander

½ teaspoon freshly ground black pepper

½ teaspoon cinnamon

½ teaspoon cumin

1 teaspoon salt

1 cup whole-milk plain yogurt

1 (28-ounce) can of whole stewed tomatoes

2 cups cooked basmati rice

1. Heat ghee in an uncovered pressure cooker over medium heat. Add onion and sauté until softened (about 5 minutes). Add the rest of the ingredients, except for the rice, to the pressure cooker.
2. Turn the heat up to high. When the cooker reaches pressure, lower the heat to the minimum needed to maintain pressure. Cook for 13–15 minutes at high pressure.
3. When time is up, open the pressure cooker by releasing pressure.
4. Simmer uncovered until most of the liquid has evaporated (about 10 minutes).
5. Serve over cooked basmati rice.

PER SERVING | Calories: 249 | Fat: 7 g | Protein: 21 g | Sodium: 646 mg | Fiber: 2 g | Carbohydrates: 24 g

Make Your Own Ghee

In a heavy-bottomed pan, on low heat, melt an unsalted stick of butter. Simmer until white foam appears, then turn off the heat. Spoon off the foam and discard. Pour through a fine sieve or cheesecloth into jar and refrigerate. The resulting liquid should be clear and golden, like vegetable oil, that solidifies when placed in the refrigerator.

Pot Roast

Turn this into two meals for four people by making roast beef sandwiches the next day. The meat will be tender and moist if you refrigerate the leftovers in the pan juices.

INGREDIENTS | SERVES 8

1 (3-pound) boneless chuck roast
1 pound bag of baby carrots
2 stalks celery, diced
1 green bell pepper, seeded and diced
2 large yellow onions, peeled and sliced
¼ teaspoon onion powder
¼ teaspoon celery seeds
⅛ teaspoon paprika
2 tablespoons sea salt
1 teaspoon white pepper
2 cups Beef Stock (see recipe in Chapter 4)
2 tablespoons tomato paste
2 cloves garlic, peeled and minced
1 tablespoon Worcestershire sauce
1 tablespoon steak sauce

1. Cut the roast into serving-size chunks (remember that it will shrink a bit during cooking), and place all of the ingredients in the pressure cooker. Close and lock the lid.
2. Turn the heat up to high. When the cooker reaches pressure, lower the heat to the minimum needed to maintain pressure. Cook for 18–20 minutes at high pressure.
3. Open with the natural release method (see Chapter 1).
4. Serve with drizzle of cooking liquid.

PER SERVING | Calories: 472 | Fat: 31 g | Protein: 34 g | Sodium: 1920 mg | Fiber: 3 g | Carbohydrates: 11 g

Citrus Corned Beef and Cabbage

Add 6 peeled and diced potatoes to make this a one-pot meal. Potatoes should be added when you open the pressure cooker to add the cabbage.

INGREDIENTS | SERVES 8

1 tablespoon vegetable oil

2 medium onions, peeled and sliced

1 (3-pound) corned beef brisket

1 cup apple juice

¼ cup brown sugar, packed

2 teaspoons finely grated orange zest

2 teaspoons Dijon mustard

6 whole cloves

6 cabbage wedges

Can't Fit the Leafy Greens?

If a large amount of leafy greens threatens to rise over your pressure cooker's maximum fill line or obstruct the pressure valve, simply push them down and cook them with a smaller metal lid from another pan on top, or use a small, heatproof plate. This will weigh down the greens and keep them out of the safety mechanism.

1. Pour the oil in the pressure cooker, and spread evenly inside using a paper towel. Arrange the onion slices across the bottom of the pan. Trim and discard excess fat from the brisket and place it on top of the onions. In a bowl, combine the apple juice, brown sugar, zest, mustard, and cloves and stir to mix. Pour over the brisket. Close and lock the lid.

2. Turn the heat up to high. When the cooker reaches pressure, lower the heat to the minimum needed to maintain pressure. Cook for 30 minutes at high pressure.

3. When time is up, open the pressure cooker by releasing pressure.

4. Place the cabbage on top of the brisket. Close and lock the lid.

5. Turn the heat up to high. When the cooker reaches pressure, lower the heat to the minimum needed to maintain pressure. Cook for 5 minutes at high pressure.

6. When time is up, open the pressure cooker by releasing pressure.

7. Transfer the cabbage and meat to a serving platter, spooning some of the pan juices over the meat. Tent with aluminum foil and let rest for 15 minutes. Carve the brisket by slicing it against the grain. Remove and discard the cloves and fat from the remaining pan sauce. Pour into gravy boat to pass at the table.

PER SERVING | Calories: 543 | Fat: 27 g | Protein: 48 g | Sodium: 1635 mg | Fiber: 6 g | Carbohydrates: 26 g

Ropa Vieja

Serve this Cuban shredded beef with yellow rice and spicy black beans.

INGREDIENTS | SERVES 8

2 pounds top round roast

1 cubanelle pepper, diced

1 large onion, diced

2 carrots, diced

1 (28-ounce) can crushed tomatoes

2 cloves garlic

1 tablespoon oregano

2 teaspoons cumin

½ cup green pimento-stuffed olives

1. Place all ingredients, except for olives, in the pressure cooker. Close and lock the lid.
2. Turn the heat up to high. When the cooker reaches pressure, lower the heat to the minimum needed to maintain pressure. Cook for 60 minutes at high pressure.
3. Open with the natural release method (see Chapter 1).
4. Shred the meat with two forks. Add the olives and mash with a potato masher until well mixed. Serve.

PER SERVING | Calories: 196 | Fat: 5.7 g | Protein: 27 g | Sodium: 295 mg | Fiber: 2.2 g | Carbohydrates: 8.6 g

More Uses for Shredded Beef

Use this delicious shredded beef as filling for tacos, burritos, enchiladas, and quesadillas.

Texas Firehouse Chili

This no-bean chili is similar to dishes entered into firehouse chili cook-offs all over Texas.

INGREDIENTS | SERVES 4

1 pound cubed lean beef

2 tablespoons onion powder

1 tablespoon garlic powder

2 tablespoons Mexican-style chili powder

1 tablespoon paprika

1 teaspoon oregano

½ teaspoon freshly ground black pepper

1 teaspoon white pepper

½ teaspoon cayenne pepper

1 teaspoon chipotle pepper

8 ounces chopped tomatoes

1. Put all ingredients in the pressure cooker. Close and lock the lid.
2. Turn the heat up to high. When the cooker reaches pressure, lower the heat to the minimum needed to maintain pressure. Cook for 15–20 minutes at high pressure.
3. Open with the natural release method (see Chapter 1).
4. Simmer, uncovered, over medium heat, for about 5 minutes to reduce the liquids and thicken. Serve.

PER SERVING | Calories: 210 | Fat: 8 g | Protein: 25 g | Sodium: 67 mg | Fiber: 2.4 g | Carbohydrates: 8 g

Cincinnati Chili

*Cincinnati chili is typically eaten over spaghetti or on hot dogs,
but it is also delicious in a nontraditional bread bowl.*

INGREDIENTS | SERVES 6

1 tablespoon vegetable oil

1 pound lean ground beef

2 onions, finely chopped

1 (14½-ounce) can tomato sauce

2 tablespoons vinegar

2 teaspoons Worcestershire sauce

4 cloves garlic, minced

½ (1-ounce) square unsweetened chocolate

¼ cup chili powder

1½ teaspoons salt

1 teaspoon ground cumin

1 teaspoon ground cinnamon

½ teaspoon ground cayenne pepper

5 whole cloves

5 whole allspice berries

1 bay leaf

1. Put all ingredients in the pressure cooker. Close and lock the lid.
2. Turn the heat up to high. When the cooker reaches pressure, lower the heat to the minimum needed to maintain pressure. Cook for 15–20 minutes at high pressure.
3. Open with the natural release method (see Chapter 1).
4. Simmer, uncovered, over medium heat, for about 5 minutes to reduce the liquids and thicken. Serve.

PER SERVING | Calories: 201 | Fat: 8 g | Protein: 18 g | Sodium: 1054 mg | Fiber: 3.7 g | Carbohydrates: 11 g

Chili Five Ways

Cincinnati Chili can be served up to five ways: "Two-way" means chili and spaghetti; "three-way" means chili, spaghetti, and cheese; "four-way" means chili, spaghetti, cheese, and onions or beans; and "five-way" means all of the above!

Mushroom-Stuffed Veal Roll

You can just as easily substitute a butterflied pork roast for the veal. Serve with a salad, baked potatoes, steamed vegetables, and dinner rolls.

INGREDIENTS | SERVES 8

½ tablespoon unsalted butter

2 tablespoons olive oil, divided

8 ounces fresh button mushrooms, cleaned and sliced

4 ounces fresh shiitake mushrooms, cleaned and sliced

2 large shallots, peeled and minced

2 cloves garlic, peeled and minced, divided

3 tablespoons all-purpose flour

1½ teaspoons salt, divided

½ teaspoon freshly ground black pepper

4 ounces prosciutto, thinly sliced

1 (3½-pound) boneless veal shoulder roast, butterflied

1 large carrot, peeled and grated

1 stalk celery, finely diced

1 small onion, peeled and diced

1 cup dry white wine

1 cup veal or chicken broth

1. Heat butter and 1 tablespoon olive oil in an uncovered pressure cooker over medium heat. Sauté mushrooms for 3 minutes. Stir in the shallots, 1 clove garlic, and 1 teaspoon salt. Sauté for another 10 minutes.
2. Add flour, ½ teaspoon salt, and pepper to a bowl. Stir to mix and set aside.
3. Arrange the prosciutto over the cut side of the roast, overlapping the edges by several inches. Spread all but ¼ cup of the mushroom mixture over the prosciutto up to where it overlaps the edges of the roast. Fold the edges over the mushroom mixture and roll the prosciutto-mushroom layers to the center of the roast. Pull the edges of the roast over the prosciutto-mushroom roll and secure at 1-inch intervals with butcher's twine.
4. Heat the remaining oil in the cooker over medium-high heat. Brown the roast for 5 minutes on each side.
5. Remove roast from the cooker and add the carrot, celery, onion, and remaining clove of garlic to the pressure cooker and sauté for 5 minutes. Deglaze the cooker with the wine and broth, and add the roast on top of the sautéed vegetables. Close and lock the lid.
6. Turn the heat up to high. When the cooker reaches pressure, lower the heat to the minimum needed to maintain pressure. Cook for 25–30 minutes at high pressure.
7. Open with the natural release method (see Chapter 1).
8. Transfer to a serving platter and tent loosely with foil. Let rest for at least 10 minutes before slicing.
9. Use an immersion blender to purée the pan juices and vegetables in the pressure cooker.
10. Slice the roast into ½-inch slices and serve with the sauce on the side.

PER SERVING | Calories: 385 | Fat: 16 g | Protein: 43 g | Sodium: 944 mg | Fiber: 1.2 g | Carbohydrates: 8.5 g

Beef Rogan Josh

Traditionally made with lamb, this lean beef version is lower in fat but still full of flavor. Serve it over rice.

INGREDIENTS | SERVES 6

1 tablespoon ghee (or vegetable oil)
1 onion, diced
1 pound cubed bottom round
3 cloves garlic, minced
2 teaspoons minced fresh ginger
2 tablespoons cumin
2 tablespoons coriander
1 tablespoon turmeric
2 teaspoons cardamom
2 teaspoons freshly ground black pepper
1 teaspoon chili powder
1 (28-ounce) can crushed tomatoes
1 cup whole-milk plain yogurt

1. Heat ghee or oil in an uncovered pressure cooker over medium heat. Sauté onion until softened (about 5 minutes). Add the rest of the ingredients except for the yogurt to the pressure cooker.
2. Turn the heat up to high. When the cooker reaches pressure, lower the heat to the minimum needed to maintain pressure. Cook for 13–15 minutes at high pressure.
3. Open the pressure cooker by releasing pressure. Stir in the yogurt and simmer uncovered until thickened (about 10 minutes).

PER SERVING | Calories: 213 | Fat: 10 g | Protein: 19 g | Sodium: 256 mg | Fiber: 3.3 g | Carbohydrates: 13 g

Italian Summer Veal Roast

Vitello Tonnato is a popular veal roast in Italy, especially enjoyed during hot summer days. The tuna sauce is surprisingly not fishy-tasting.

INGREDIENTS | SERVES 8

3 anchovies

1 (6-ounce) can Italian tuna in olive oil

1 cup good-quality mayonnaise

1 tablespoon olive oil

1 (2-pound) veal roast, or 2 small ones

1 onion, roughly sliced

1 carrot, roughly sliced

1 celery stalk, roughly sliced

2 cloves garlic, peeled

1 cup white wine

1 cup water

4 whole cloves

5 bay leaves

1 sprig rosemary

2 teaspoons salt

½ teaspoon white pepper

2 tablespoons capers, rinsed and drained, for garnish

1. In a blender, purée anchovies, tuna, and mayonnaise until smooth. Refrigerate sauce.
2. Heat olive oil in an uncovered pressure cooker over medium heat. Brown roast on all sides. Add all of the other ingredients, except for the capers. Close and lock the lid.
3. Turn the heat up to high. When the cooker reaches pressure, lower the heat to the minimum needed to maintain pressure. Cook for 20–30 minutes (depending on the thickness of the meat) at high pressure.
4. When time is up, open the pressure cooker by releasing pressure.
5. Remove the roast and place it on a serving platter. Tent with foil and let cool. Strain and reserve the cooking liquid. When the roast is relatively cool, wrap the dish well with plastic wrap and refrigerate 3–4 hours.
6. To serve, slice the roast thinly. Remove tuna sauce from refrigerator and thin with reserved cooking liquid, if necessary. Cover veal slices with tuna sauce and sprinkle with capers.

PER SERVING | Calories: 415 | Fat: 28 g | Protein: 29 g | Sodium: 1035 mg | Fiber: 0.6 g | Carbohydrates: 4.2 g

Pam's Osso Buco

Pam combines spices with tomatoes and gremolata in this recipe. Traditionally, this dish is served with risotto or polenta, but Americans often prefer eating this dish paired with a baked potato, steamed vegetables, and/or tossed salad.

INGREDIENTS | SERVES 8

1 cup all-purpose flour

1 teaspoon salt

½ teaspoon freshly ground black pepper

8 veal shanks, cross-cut ½-inch thick

3 tablespoons extra-virgin olive oil

3 tablespoons unsalted butter

1 celery stalk, diced

2 carrots, diced

1 medium onion, peeled and diced

1 cup Beef Stock (see recipe in Chapter 4)

1 head garlic, cut horizontally through the middle

1 (28-ounce) can diced tomatoes

¼ teaspoon cinnamon

⅛ teaspoon allspice

2 bay leaves

¼ cup dry white wine

Osso Buco Originals . . .

There are several regional variations of Osso Buco: alla Milanese, which is braised in white wine and topped with freshly chopped parsley, garlic, and lemon zest gremolata; alla Romana, in which the veal is cooked with peas; and alla Fiorentina, which includes tomatoes and is similar to this recipe, but is *not* topped with gremolata.

1. Place flour, salt, and pepper in a large plastic bag. Add the veal shanks to the bag and shake to coat them.
2. Heat olive oil and butter in an uncovered pressure cooker over medium heat. Remove 4 veal shanks from the plastic bag, shake off any excess flour (too much could prevent the cooker from reaching pressure). Brown them on each side for about 5 minutes or until golden. Move the browned meat to a platter. Repeat with the remaining 4 veal shanks and remove when done.
3. Add the celery, carrots, and onion and sauté until the vegetables start to get some color and develop an intense aroma (about 8 minutes). Deglaze the cooker with the stock, and scrape the bottom of the pan well to incorporate the delicious browned bits into the sauce.
4. Return the veal shanks to the pan. Add the garlic, tomatoes, cinnamon, allspice, bay leaves, and wine. Close and lock the lid.
5. Turn the heat up to high. When the cooker reaches pressure, lower the heat to the minimum needed to maintain pressure. Cook for 18–20 minutes at high pressure.
6. When time is up, open the pressure cooker by releasing pressure.
7. Simmer uncovered for about 5 minutes or until the liquid is reduced. Carefully move the tender meat to each plate and cover with a generous spoonful of tomato sauce.

PER SERVING | Calories: 302 | Fat: 12 g | Protein: 26 g | Sodium: 605 mg | Fiber: 2.2 g | Carbohydrates: 19 g

CHAPTER 8

Pork, Lamb, and Game

Pork Sausage with Bell Peppers
and Onions
144

Balsamic and Fig Pork Chops
145

Beer BBQ Pork Sliders
with Apple
146

Barbecue Pork Ribs
147

Milk-Braised Pork Loin
148

Pork Roast with Apples
149

Pork with Black Beans
150

Carnitas in Lettuce Cups
151

Maple-Glazed Ham with Raisins
152

Sesame Pork with Pineapple
153

Mediterranean Braised
Lamb Shanks
154

Moroccan Lamb Tagine
155

Braised Quail
156

Rabbit Cacciatore
157

Pork Sausage with Bell Peppers and Onions

Use a combination of spicy Italian sausage, bratwurst, or mild sausage links, if desired.

INGREDIENTS | SERVES 6

½ tablespoon vegetable oil

6 pork sausages

1 large green bell pepper, seeded and sliced

1 large red bell pepper, seeded and sliced

1 large yellow bell pepper, seeded and sliced

1 large onion, sliced

2 cloves garlic, minced

⅓ cup Chicken Stock (see recipe in Chapter 4)

Pork Sausage Hoagies

Serve this recipe on hoagies or hot dog buns for a delicious pork sausage sandwich. Perfect for leftovers, if there are any!

1. Poke each sausage several times with a fork.
2. Heat oil in an uncovered pressure cooker over medium heat. Add 3 sausages to the pressure cooker and brown for about 5 minutes. Move to a plate and brown the remaining sausages. Discard all but one tablespoon of rendered fat in the pressure cooker.
3. Add the peppers and onions and sauté for about 3 minutes or until they begin to soften. Add garlic and return the sausages to the pressure cooker, pushing them down into the peppers and onions. Pour in the stock. Close and lock the lid.
4. Turn the heat up to high. When the cooker reaches pressure, lower the heat to the minimum needed to maintain pressure. Cook for 5–8 minutes at high pressure.
5. When time is up, open the pressure cooker by releasing pressure.
6. Serve with a slotted spoon.

PER SERVING | Calories: 227 | Fat: 13 g | Protein: 12 g | Sodium: 891 mg | Fiber: 2 g | Carbohydrates: 14 g

Balsamic and Fig Pork Chops

Add two chopped apples and handful of toasted walnuts when serving for a fresh and crunchy finish.

INGREDIENTS | SERVES 4

4 (1-inch thick) bone-in pork loin chops
½ teaspoon salt
¼ teaspoon pepper
1 tablespoon butter
1 teaspoon olive oil
2 medium onions, peeled and sliced
4 cloves garlic, peeled and minced
1 teaspoon fresh thyme
3 tablespoons balsamic vinegar
2 tablespoons dry white wine
½ cup chicken broth
1½ cups dried figs

More Fruit Variations

Other delicious fruits for this recipe are dried apricots, dried cherries, dried cranberries, and even dried plums.

1. Sprinkle chops with salt and pepper. Heat butter and oil in an uncovered pressure cooker over medium heat. Brown two pork chops at a time for 3 minutes on each side. Move chops to a plate and keep warm.
2. Sauté the onions and garlic with thyme until soft (about 5 minutes). Add balsamic vinegar, wine, and broth. Stir to deglaze the pan. Return the pork chops to the pressure cooker and top with figs. Close and lock the lid.
3. Turn the heat up to high. When the cooker reaches pressure, lower the heat to the minimum needed to maintain pressure. Cook for 8–10 minutes at high pressure.
4. When time is up, open the pressure cooker by releasing pressure.
5. Serve immediately.

PER SERVING | Calories: 447 | Fat: 11 g | Protein: 39 g | Sodium: 536 mg | Fiber: 6.5 g | Carbohydrates: 45 g

Beer BBQ Pork Sliders with Apple

Beer and apples provide a tangy sweetness to these already delicious sandwiches.
Serve with a salad or coleslaw.

INGREDIENTS | SERVES 6

1½ pounds pork western ribs

½ cup beer (your choice)

1 apple, peeled, cored, and roughly sliced

1 onion, peeled and diced

1 teaspoon raw sugar

1 teaspoon salt

½ teaspoon black pepper

12 whole wheat slider buns, or 6 whole wheat hamburger buns

Sliders

Pork and beef sliders are delicious as an appetizer or an entrée. Make in advance and reheat for parties or dinner.

1. Place ribs in the pressure cooker. Pour in beer and add the apple, onion, sugar, salt, and pepper. Close and lock the lid.
2. Turn the heat up to high. When the cooker reaches pressure, lower the heat to the minimum needed to maintain pressure. Cook for 15–20 minutes at high pressure.
3. Open with the natural release method (see Chapter 1).
4. Move the meat and bones to a cutting board using a slotted spoon. Remove and discard any fat still on the meat. Use two forks to shred the meat.
5. Skim and discard any fat from the top of the pan juices. Blend the contents of the pressure cooker using an immersion blender. Stir the shredded pork back into the cooker and simmer, uncovered, on medium heat for 5 minutes.
6. Spoon the meat onto hamburger buns and serve.

PER SERVING | Calories: 340 | Fat: 9. 6 g | Protein: 29 g | Sodium: 737 mg | Fiber: 1.7 g | Carbohydrates: 31 g

Barbecue Pork Ribs

By the time the pressure finishes, the meat on these ribs will be falling off the bone. Use this as a standalone dish or for pork sandwiches.

INGREDIENTS | SERVES 4

1 cup barbecue sauce
½ cup apple jelly
1 (3-inch) cinnamon stick
6 whole cloves
1 large onion, peeled and diced
1 cup water
3 pounds pork western ribs

1. Add the barbecue sauce, jelly, cinnamon stick, cloves, onion, and water to the pressure cooker. Stir to mix. Add the ribs, ladling some of the sauce over them. Close and lock the lid.
2. Turn the heat up to high. When the cooker reaches pressure, lower the heat to the minimum needed to maintain pressure. Cook for 10–15 minutes at high pressure.
3. Open with the natural release method (see Chapter 1).
4. Move the meat and bones to a serving platter and cover with foil to keep warm. Skim any fat from the sauce in the cooker. Remove and discard the cinnamon stick and cloves.
5. Return the pressure cooker to medium-high heat and simmer uncovered for 15 minutes or until the sauce is reduced to desired thickness. Either remove the meat from the bones and stir back into the sauce or pour the sauce into a gravy boat and pass at the table.

PER SERVING | Calories: 594 | Fat: 19 g | Protein: 70 g | Sodium: 928 mg | Fiber: 1 g | Carbohydrates: 29 g

Milk-Braised Pork Loin

This recipe is adapted from Marcella Hazan's "Pork Loin Braised in Milk" roast from The Classic Italian Cookbook. *Hazan's pork loin simmers for 1½ hours! Yours will be ready in just 30 minutes.*

INGREDIENTS | SERVES 6

1 tablespoon butter

2 tablespoons olive oil

2 pounds pork loin in one piece, with some fat on it, securely tied

2 teaspoons salt

1 teaspoon white pepper

1 bay leaf

2½ cups whole milk

Curdled Milk?

When the roast is finished cooking, there will be what looks like chunks of curdled milk. It's not. It's coagulated milk, and they are little bundles of concentrated flavor. If they are not aesthetically pleasing, simply disintegrate them into the rest of the cooking liquid by using an immersion blender.

1. Heat butter and olive oil in an uncovered pressure cooker over medium heat. When the butter is melted, add the pork loin, fat-side facing down. Brown thoroughly on all sides, and finish on the side where you began, about 10 minutes.
2. Add the salt, pepper, and bay leaf. Pour in the milk. If the roast is not covered to the halfway mark, add more milk. Close and lock the lid.
3. Turn the heat up to high. When the cooker reaches pressure, lower the heat to the minimum needed to maintain pressure. Cook for 25–30 minutes at high pressure.
4. Open with the natural release method (see Chapter 1).
5. Move the roast to a serving dish tented with tinfoil to rest.
6. Discard the bay leaf and reduce the cooking liquid in the uncovered pressure cooker over medium heat for about 5 minutes.
7. Slice the roast and arrange on platter. Pour the warm sauce over the slices and serve.

PER SERVING | Calories: 309 | Fat: 14 g | Protein: 36 g | Sodium: 903 mg | Fiber: 0 g | Carbohydrates: 5 g

Pork Roast with Apples

This is a classic American combination of flavors—sweet and salty. You make the applesauce together with the roast to infuse the apples directly into the meat and to flavor the applesauce with the pork.

INGREDIENTS | SERVES 6

2 pounds pork loin in one piece, with some fat on it, securely tied

2 tablespoons olive oil, divided

2 teaspoons salt

1 teaspoon white pepper

1 onion, peeled and roughly sliced

2 Granny Smith apples (or other green, tart apple), peeled, cored, and sliced

½ cup white wine

½ cup water

Apple Slicer

Use an apple slicer for this recipe. It will slice and core the apples at the same time, making this recipe even faster!

1. Rub the roast with 1 tablespoon of oil, salt, and pepper. Heat the remaining tablespoon of olive oil in an uncovered pressure cooker over medium heat. Place the roast in the pan, fat-side facing down. Brown well on all sides, and finish on the side where you began. Add the onions, apples, wine, and water. Close and lock the lid.
2. Turn the heat up to high and when the cooker reaches pressure, lower to the heat to the minimum needed to maintain pressure. Cook for 25–30 minutes at high pressure.
3. Open with the natural release method (see Chapter 1).
4. Move the roast to a serving dish tented with tinfoil to rest.
5. Using an immersion blender, blend the cooking liquid into an applesauce.
6. Slice the roast and serve with applesauce.

PER SERVING | Calories: 253 | Fat: 7.4 g | Protein: 33 g | Sodium: 861 mg | Fiber: 1.2 g | Carbohydrates: 7.5 g

Pork with Black Beans

*Spice up your lunch or dinner with this easy dish. Serve with corn tortillas
or over rice with guacamole and sour cream.*

INGREDIENTS | SERVES 4

1 tablespoon chili powder

⅛ teaspoon cumin powder

1 teaspoon salt

½ teaspoon black pepper

⅛ teaspoon cayenne pepper

1 pound pork loin, cut into 1-inch cubes

1 tablespoon butter

1 yellow onion, peeled and chopped

2 cloves garlic, minced

1 jalapeño pepper, seeded and minced

½ red bell pepper, diced

2 cups dry black beans, soaked for at least 4 hours (or overnight) and rinsed

2 cups chicken broth

Tex-Mex

Tex-Mex indicates a combination of flavors commonly used in traditional Mexican or Spanish cooking infused with Southwestern American cooking traditions. Make your dish more or less spicy by adding or using less cayenne pepper, jalapeño, and either mild, medium, or hot taco sauce.

1. In pressure cooker, combine chili powder, cumin, salt, pepper, and cayenne pepper and mix well. Add pork and toss to coat. Add butter and heat over medium heat, browning pork for about 4 minutes.
2. Add remaining ingredients to cooker. Stir to combine. Close and lock the lid.
3. Turn the heat up to high. When the cooker reaches pressure, lower the heat to the minimum needed to maintain pressure. Cook for 15–20 minutes at high pressure.
4. Open with the natural release method (see Chapter 1).
5. Serve with warm corn or flour tortillas (use whole wheat tortillas for extra fiber), or over rice.

PER SERVING | Calories: 344 | Fat: 9.5 g | Protein: 34 g | Sodium: 1449 mg | Fiber: 7 g | Carbohydrates: 28 g

Carnitas in Lettuce Cups

The addition of bitter chocolate adds a deep flavor to the pork. You can add carnitas to tacos, burritos, tamales, empanadas, or use it for a pulled pork sandwich.

INGREDIENTS | SERVES 8

1 tablespoon unsweetened cocoa powder

1 tablespoon salt

1 teaspoon red pepper flakes

2 teaspoons oregano

1 teaspoon white pepper

1 teaspoon garlic powder

1 teaspoon cumin

⅛ teaspoon coriander

⅛ teaspoon cayenne pepper

1 large onion, finely chopped

4 pounds pork roast, leg or shoulder

3 tablespoons vegetable oil, divided

Water for cooking

1 head butter lettuce, washed and dried

2 carrots, grated

2 limes, cut into wedges

1. The day before, make the rub spice mix. Combine cocoa powder, salt, red pepper flakes, oregano, white pepper, garlic powder, cumin, coriander, cayenne pepper, and onion. Cut the roast into pieces and rub with the spice mixture. Wrap the meat in butcher's paper or foil and refrigerate overnight.
2. Heat 2 tablespoons oil in an uncovered pressure cooker over medium heat. Brown the roast on all sides. Add enough water to almost cover the meat (2–3 cups). Close and lock the lid.
3. Turn the heat up to high. When the cooker reaches pressure, lower the heat to the minimum needed to maintain pressure. Cook for 45–60 minutes at high pressure.
4. Open with the natural release method (see Chapter 1).
5. Remove the pork from the cooker and place on a platter. Using two forks, shred the meat into strips. Set aside.
6. Reduce the cooking liquid in the cooker by half. Cool the liquid and remove the layer of fat that rises to the top.
7. In a large, wide sauté pan, heat 1 tablespoon oil and fry the shredded pork until it becomes lightly brown, (5 minutes). Pour the cooking liquid over the pulled pork and heat through.
8. To make lettuce wraps, carefully remove the outer leaves of the lettuce and arrange on a platter with carrots. Fill with pork and finish with a squirt of fresh lime before serving.

PER SERVING | Calories: 353 | Fat: 13 g | Protein: 51 g | Sodium: 1009 mg | Fiber: 1.5 g | Carbohydrates: 5 g

Maple-Glazed Ham with Raisins

Why buy expensive honey-baked ham when you can make your own in minutes? Make this for dinner, Sunday brunch, or just to have around for delicious ham sandwiches.

INGREDIENTS | SERVES 6

1 (2-pound) ready-to-eat ham

1 large onion, peeled and sliced

⅛ teaspoon ground cloves

¼ teaspoon ground ginger

½ teaspoon ground cinnamon

1 cup water

2 tablespoons raw sugar

½ cup raisins

1 small pineapple, peeled, cored, and chopped; or 1 (14-ounce) can pineapple chunks, drained

½ cup apple butter

¼ cup maple syrup

1 tablespoon balsamic vinegar

1. Add the ham and onion to the pressure cooker. In a separate bowl, stir together the cloves, ginger, cinnamon, water, sugar, and raisins. Pour over the ham. Close and lock the lid.

2. Turn the heat up to high. When the cooker reaches pressure, lower the heat to the minimum needed to maintain pressure. Cook for 15–18 minutes at high pressure.

3. Open with the natural release method (see Chapter 1).

4. Move the ham to a serving platter and keep warm with a foil tent while you finish the sauce.

5. Skim and remove any fat from the pan juices in the pressure cooker. Put the cooker over medium heat and simmer to reduce the pan juices to about 1 cup. Stir in the pineapple chunks, apple butter, maple syrup, and vinegar.

6. Taste for seasoning and adjust if necessary, adding additional maple syrup if you want a sweeter sauce or more vinegar if you need to cut the sweetness.

7. Spoon over individual servings or pour over all ham slices.

PER SERVING | Calories: 372 | Fat: 11 g | Protein: 33 g | Sodium: 1973 mg | Fiber: 1.8 g

Sesame Pork with Pineapple

This dish is similar to the classic Chinese restaurant favorite, sweet and sour pork.
Serve it with Chinese noodles or steamed white rice.

INGREDIENTS | SERVES 6

1 (14-ounce) can pineapple chunks

2 pounds pork shoulder

1 tablespoon all-purpose flour

2 tablespoons sesame oil

1 tablespoon raw sugar

⅛ teaspoon mustard powder

½ teaspoon ground ginger

2 tablespoons apple cider vinegar

1 tablespoon soy sauce

4 medium carrots, peeled and sliced

1 large red bell pepper, seeded and diced into 1-inch pieces

½ pound fresh sugar snap peas

1½ cups fresh broccoli florets, cut into bite-size pieces

2 cloves garlic, peeled and thinly sliced

1 large onion, peeled and sliced

2 tablespoons cornstarch

2 tablespoons cold water

¼ cup bean sprouts

1 tablespoon sesame seeds

Switch Vegetables

This vegetable combination keeps with the Asian sweet and sour pork style; however, feel free to use your favorite vegetables instead!

1. Drain pineapple, reserving juice. Set both aside.
2. Cut the pork into bite-size pieces. Add to a zip-closure bag along with the flour. Seal bag and shake to coat the pork in the flour. Remove pork from bag with tongs and shake off excess flour (too much flour in the cooker could prevent it from reaching pressure).
3. Heat oil in an uncovered pressure cooker over medium heat. Sauté the pork for 3 minutes or until it begins to brown.
4. Deglaze the pan with the pineapple juice. Stir and scrape up any bits stuck to the bottom of the pan. Add the sugar, mustard powder, ginger, vinegar, soy sauce, carrots, red pepper, peas, broccoli, garlic, and onion. Close and lock the lid.
5. Turn the heat up to high. When the cooker reaches pressure, lower the heat to the minimum needed to maintain pressure. Cook for 18–20 minutes at high pressure.
6. Open the pressure cooker by releasing pressure.
7. Using a slotted spoon, move pork and vegetables to a serving bowl and keep warm using foil tent.
8. To make the glaze, mix together the cornstarch and water in a small bowl. Stir in a couple of tablespoons of the pan juices.
9. Put the uncovered pressure cooker over medium heat. Bring pan juices to a boil and whisk in the cornstarch mixture.
10. Reduce the heat to maintain a simmer for 3 minutes or until the mixture is thickened. Stir in the bean sprouts and reserved pineapple chunks. Pour over the cooked pork and vegetables in the serving bowl. Stir to combine.
11. Sprinkle with sesame seeds and serve.

PER SERVING | Calories: 397 | Fat: 16 g | Protein: 33 g | Sodium: 305 mg | Fiber: 4.8 g | Carbohydrates: 29 g

Mediterranean Braised Lamb Shanks

Serve over creamy polenta.

INGREDIENTS | SERVES 4

2 tablespoons flour

1 teaspoon salt

½ teaspoon ground black pepper

4 large lamb shanks, trimmed (3 pounds)

1 tablespoon olive oil

1 red onion, peeled and chopped

1 carrot, peeled and chopped

2 stalks celery, chopped

½ cup red wine

2 garlic cloves, thinly sliced

2 red bell peppers, seeded and cut into thick 1-inch strips

3 medium zucchini, thickly sliced into 1-inch rounds

1 eggplant, cut into 1-inch dice

5 fresh Roma tomatoes, halved; or 1 (28-ounce) can whole stewed tomatoes

1 tablespoon tomato paste

½ cup Vegetable Stock (see recipe in Chapter 4)

1 bunch fresh basil, torn

1. Put the flour, salt, black pepper, and lamb in a large plastic bag and shake to coat. Heat olive oil in an uncovered pressure cooker over medium heat. Brown the shanks on all sides and set aside. Add the onion, carrots, and celery and sauté until softened (about 5 minutes).
2. Deglaze the pressure cooker with the wine and let the liquid almost completely evaporate. Return the shanks to the cooker, along with the rest of the ingredients except for the basil. Close and lock the lid.
3. Turn the heat up to high. When the cooker reaches pressure, lower the heat to the minimum needed to maintain pressure. Cook for 40–45 minutes at high pressure.
4. When time is up, open the pressure cooker by releasing pressure.
5. Move the shanks and vegetables to a serving platter using a slotted spoon. Cover with foil and keep warm. Skim any fat from the cooker.
6. Return the pressure cooker to medium-high heat and simmer sauce uncovered for 10–15 minutes or until the sauce is reduced to desired thickness.
7. Pour over shanks and serve.

PER SERVING | Calories: 591 | Fat: 15 g | Protein: 76 g | Sodium: 1007 mg | Fiber: 10 g | Carbohydrates: 29 g

Moroccan Lamb Tagine

For a traditional Moroccan flavor, you can serve this dish with a cardamom-infused basmati rice. Just make your rice in the usual way and throw in a few crushed cardamom pods.

INGREDIENTS | SERVES 6

1 teaspoon cinnamon powder

1 teaspoon ginger powder

1 teaspoon turmeric powder

1 teaspoon cumin powder

2 cloves garlic, crushed

1 (3-pound) lamb shoulder, cut into 1-inch pieces

10 ounces dried plums

3 tablespoons olive oil, divided

2 onions, roughly sliced

1 cup Vegetable Stock (see recipe in Chapter 4)

1 bay leaf

1 (3-inch) cinnamon stick

3 tablespoons honey

1 teaspoon salt

1 teaspoon pepper

½ cup sliced almonds, toasted

1 tablespoon sesame seeds

Meat Switcheroo

You can make this same dish with chicken or beef by adjusting the cooking times accordingly, but it should not be made with pork. The majority of Moroccans are Muslim and adhere to a halal diet, which forbids consuming pork.

1. Mix the cinnamon powder, ginger, turmeric, cumin, and garlic with 2 tablespoons of olive oil to make a paste. Cover the lamb with this paste and set aside.
2. Place the dried plums in a bowl and cover with boiling water. Set aside.
3. Heat 1 tablespoon olive oil in an uncovered pressure cooker over medium heat. Add onions and cook until softened (about 5 minutes). Remove onions and set aside.
4. Add the meat and brown on all sides (about 10 minutes). Deglaze the pressure cooker with the stock, scraping the bottom well and incorporating any brown bits into the rest of the sauce. Return onions to the pan and add the bay leaf and cinnamon stick. Close and lock the lid.
5. Turn the heat up to high. When the cooker reaches pressure, lower the heat to the minimum needed to maintain pressure. Cook for 25 minutes at high pressure.
6. Open with the natural release method (see Chapter 1).
7. Remove and discard the bay leaf and cinnamon stick. Return the pressure cooker to medium heat, then add honey, salt, pepper, and drained dried plums. Simmer, uncovered, until the liquid is reduced (about 5 minutes).
8. Sprinkle with toasted almonds and sesame seeds and serve.

PER SERVING | Calories: 828 | Fat: 54 g | Protein: 41 g | Sodium: 630 mg | Fiber: 5.5 g | Carbohydrates: 46 g

Braised Quail

You can also make this dish with any small poultry.

INGREDIENTS | SERVES 4

4 whole quails, cleaned and rinsed

1 teaspoon salt

¼ teaspoon pepper

1 tablespoon olive oil

3½ ounces smoked pancetta (or bacon), diced

2 shallots, roughly chopped

1 bunch of thyme, chopped (reserve 1 whole sprig for garnish)

1 bunch of rosemary, chopped (reserve 1 whole sprig for garnish)

1 bay leaf

¾ cup of spumante, champagne, or any sparkling white wine

1. Season quail with salt and pepper. Set aside.
2. Heat olive oil in an uncovered pressure cooker over medium heat. Add the pancetta, shallots, thyme, rosemary, and bay leaf. When the pancetta begins to sizzle and the shallots have softened, move the contents of the pan to one side and put the quails breast-side down in contact with the pan. Turn and brown all sides, then position them breast-side up.
3. Pour in the wine, deglazing the pan and scraping up any brown bits that may be stuck to the bottom and incorporating them in the sauce. Reduce the wine by about ⅓, about 3 minutes. Close and lock the lid.
4. Turn the heat up to high. When the cooker reaches pressure, lower the heat to the minimum needed to maintain pressure. Cook for 7–9 minutes at high pressure.
5. When time is up, open the pressure cooker by releasing pressure.
6. Delicately remove the quail from the pressure cooker and set aside. Strain the cooking liquid and put it back in the cooker over medium-high heat to reduce it to about half.
7. When the sauce has reduced, place the quails back in the pan and continuously spoon the sauce over the quail to warm and glaze them (about 2 minutes).
8. Place the quail on the serving platter and spoon remaining sauce over them. Garnish with reserved herb sprigs.

PER SERVING | Calories: 303 | Fat: 18 g | Protein: 22 g | Sodium: 843 mg | Fiber: 0 g | Carbohydrates: 1.7 g

Rabbit Cacciatore

If you catch a wild rabbit, you will need to marinate it in water and vinegar for about 4 hours. You can add aromatics to the marinade if you like. Supermarket rabbits are much more tender, and their meat does not need to marinate before cooking.

INGREDIENTS | SERVES 6

1 cup black salt-cured olives (Taggiesche, French, or Kalamata)

1 (3-pound) rabbit, cut into pieces

2 tablespoons flour

1 tablespoon olive oil

1 onion, diced

1 carrot, diced

1 celery stalk, diced

1 clove garlic, smashed

½ cup red wine

1 (28-ounce) can whole tomatoes, drained

1 sprig sage

1 sprig rosemary

¼ teaspoon salt

⅛ teaspoon pepper

Good for You, and Good for the Planet

Rabbit meat contains the highest protein per pound of any other commonly eaten meat—21 percent. Beef has 16 percent and pork only 11 percent. Rabbit also contains less fat (4.5 percent, compared to beef at 28 percent and pork at 45 percent). A rabbit can produce 6 pounds of meat on the same amount of food and water it takes a cow to produce just 1 pound of meat. Add rabbit to the menu more often, for your health—and the planet's!

1. Fill a measuring cup with salted black olives, then add water to the 1-cup mark. Set aside.
2. Place the flour and rabbit pieces in a large bag and shake to coat. Heat olive oil in an uncovered pressure cooker over high heat. Brown the meat on all sides and remove to a platter. Keep warm.
3. Add the onion, carrot, and celery to the pressure cooker and sauté until softened (about 5 minutes) and add garlic.
4. Remove the cooker from heat and add wine to the hot pan. Stir and scrape up the browned bits at the bottom of the pan. Add the rabbit, tomatoes, sage, and rosemary.
5. Drain olives, reserving liquid. Set olives aside and add the soaking liquid to the pressure cooker. Return cooker to heat source. Close and lock the lid.
6. Turn the heat up to high. When the cooker reaches pressure, lower the heat to the minimum needed to maintain pressure. Cook for 15–20 minutes at high pressure.
7. Open with the natural release method (see Chapter 1).
8. Discard the herb sprigs and add the olives. Simmer uncovered for about 5 minutes or until sauce is thickened to desired consistency. Taste before seasoning with salt and pepper. Serve.

PER SERVING | Calories: 412 | Fat: 17 g | Protein: 46 g | Sodium: 587 mg | Fiber: 3 g | Carbohydrates: 12 g

CHAPTER 9

Fish and Seafood

Steamed Mussels
159

Steamed Clams
160

Catfish in Creole Sauce
161

Whitefish Fillet with Veggies
162

Fish en Papillote
163

Trout in Parsley Sauce
164

Mediterranean Steamed Fish Fillet
165

Red Snapper in Rice Wine and Miso
166

Fish Burritos
167

Coconut Fish Curry
168

Paprika Catfish with Fresh Tarragon
169

Gulf Grouper with Peppers and Tomatoes
169

Poached Octopus
170

Louisiana Grouper
171

Tomato-Braised Calamari
171

Steamed Mussels

This dish is perfect by itself as an appetizer or, with its steaming juices, as a topper for spaghetti.

INGREDIENTS | SERVES 6

2 pounds mussels, cleaned and debearded
1 tablespoon olive oil
1 white onion, chopped
1 clove garlic, smashed
½ cup dry white wine
½ cup water

Cleaning Mussels

Don't clean fresh mussels until right before cooking. To clean: hold the mussel with the round end toward you and pull on the little "beard," sliding it in the opening toward you as you pull. Then clean the shells by scrubbing with a clean nylon brush or scrubber sponge (with no detergent residue).

1. Place mussels in the steamer basket.
2. Heat olive oil in an uncovered pressure cooker over medium-high heat. Add onion and garlic and sauté until softened (about 5 minutes). Pour the wine and water into the pressure cooker and add the steamer basket. Close and lock the lid.
3. Turn the heat up to high. When the cooker reaches pressure, lower the heat to the minimum needed to maintain pressure. Cook for 1 minute at low pressure.
4. When time is up, open the pressure cooker by releasing pressure.
5. Empty the cooked mussels from the steamer basket into the pressure cooker and mix well. Serve mussels with a generous scoop of cooking liquid.

PER SERVING | Calories: 172 | Fat: 5 g | Protein: 18 g | Sodium: 428 mg | Fiber: 0.3 g | Carbohydrates: 7 g

Steamed Clams

This is another dish that can be served alone, as an appetizer, or on top of spaghetti.

INGREDIENTS | SERVES 6

2 pounds fresh clams, rinsed and purged
1 tablespoon olive oil
1 white onion, chopped
1 clove garlic, smashed
½ cup dry white wine
½ cup water

Closed Clams?

If a stubborn clam refuses to open, discard it. It may either be filled with mud—which will ruin your dish if pried open over it—or it may have died and deteriorated during transport. If a clam dies during transportation, its taste and consistency will be negatively affected.

1. Place clams in the steamer basket.
2. Heat olive oil in an uncovered pressure cooker over medium-high heat. Add onion and garlic and sauté until softened (about 5 minutes). Pour the wine and water into the pressure cooker and add the steamer basket. Close and lock the lid.
3. Turn the heat up to high. When the cooker reaches pressure, lower the heat to the minimum needed to maintain pressure. Cook for 4–6 minutes at high pressure.
4. When time is up, open the pressure cooker by releasing pressure.
5. Empty the cooked clams from the steamer basket into the pressure cooker and mix well. Serve clams with a generous scoop of cooking liquid.

PER SERVING | Calories: 154 | Fat: 3.7 g | Protein: 19 g | Sodium: 85 mg | Fiber: 0.3 g | Carbohydrates: 6 g

Catfish in Creole Sauce

Serve this catfish over cooked rice and have hot sauce available at the table for those who want it.

INGREDIENTS | SERVES 4

1½ pounds catfish fillets

1 (14½-ounce) can diced tomatoes

2 teaspoons dried minced onion

¼ teaspoon onion powder

1 teaspoon dried minced garlic

¼ teaspoon garlic powder

1 teaspoon hot paprika

¼ teaspoon dried tarragon

1 medium green bell pepper, seeded and diced

1 stalk celery, finely diced

¼ teaspoon sugar

½ cup chili sauce

½ teaspoon salt

¼ teaspoon pepper

1. Rinse the catfish in cold water and pat dry between paper towels. Cut into bite-size pieces. Add tomatoes and the rest of ingredients—except fish, salt, and pepper—to the pressure cooker and stir to mix.
2. Gently place the fillet pieces on top of the tomato mixture. Close and lock the lid.
3. Turn the heat up to high. When the cooker reaches pressure, lower the heat to the minimum needed to maintain pressure. Cook for 5 minutes at low pressure (or 2 minutes at high pressure).
4. When time is up, open the pressure cooker by releasing pressure.
5. Stir gently and then taste for seasoning. Add salt and pepper and serve.

PER SERVING | Calories: 225 | Fat: 5 g | Protein: 29 g | Sodium: 978 mg | Fiber: 4 g | Carbohydrates: 13 g

Whitefish Fillet with Veggies

A healthy and quick meal.

INGREDIENTS | SERVES 2

1 cup broccoli florets, cut into small pieces

1 large potato, peeled and thinly diced

1 large carrot, peeled and grated

1 small zucchini, grated

4 ounces fresh mushrooms, sliced

¼ teaspoon dried thyme

¼ teaspoon freshly grated lemon zest

½ pound cod, halibut, sole, or other whitefish

½ cup white wine

½ cup fresh lemon juice

1 teaspoon dried parsley

½ teaspoon salt

¼ teaspoon pepper

1. Place the steamer basket in the pressure cooker. Add the broccoli florets, potato, carrot, zucchini, and mushroom slices in layers to the basket. Sprinkle the vegetables with thyme and lemon zest.
2. Place the fish fillets over the vegetables. Pour the wine and lemon juice over the fish. Sprinkle with parsley, salt, and pepper.
3. Turn the heat up to high. When the cooker reaches pressure, lower the heat to the minimum needed to maintain pressure. Cook for 5–6 minutes at high pressure.
4. When time is up, open the pressure cooker by releasing pressure.
5. Divide the fish and vegetables between two plates and serve.

PER SERVING | Calories: 333 | Fat: 1.7 g | Protein: 27 g | Sodium: 725 mg | Fiber: 8 g | Carbohydrates: 44 g

Quick Vinaigrette

Try this quick vinaigrette with the fish and vegetables. Whisk 1 teaspoon Dijon mustard into ¼ cup strained pan juices and 1 tablespoon fresh lemon juice or white wine vinegar. Slowly whisk in 1–2 tablespoons extra-virgin olive oil. Taste for seasoning, adding more oil if the dressing is too tart or more lemon juice or vinegar if it isn't tart enough. Add salt and freshly ground black pepper to taste.

Fish en Papillote

This recipe will work with any whitefish. Instead of grouper, you can use California sea bass, striped bass, mahi-mahi, black sea bass, red snapper, pompano, lemonfish, or catfish.

INGREDIENTS | SERVES 4

4 grouper fillets

2 teaspoons salt

½ teaspoon pepper

2 tablespoons olive oil

4 sprigs thyme

4 sprigs parsley

1 white onion, thinly sliced into rings

8 thin slices lemon

2 cups water

Double Wrap

Some pressure cooker manufacturers do not recommend putting parchment paper in the pressure cooker because it may obstruct the safety valves, but acidic foods should never come in contact with foil. Instead, place 1 piece of parchment paper over 1 piece of foil, and wrap your food that way. The double wrap means that you get a wonderful parchment packet for presentation, with the safety and security of foil to keep the paper out of harm's way. This double layer slows the cooking down considerably because the super-heated liquid doesn't come in direct contact with the fish.

1. Cut a long piece of parchment paper, lay it over your pressure cooker, and fold it to fit about 1 inch from each side. These parchment creases will be your packet "guidelines." Repeat for all 4 packets.
2. Lay the 4 sheets of creased parchment paper on a flat surface. Layer the ingredients on each sheet in the following order: fish fillet, salt, pepper, olive oil, thyme, parsley, 2–3 onion rings, and 2 lemon slices. Top with a final swirl of olive oil. Fold each paper packet closed. Wrap each packet in a long piece of foil.
3. Pour water into pressure cooker and add the steamer basket. You can cook about 2 fillets at a time in the steamer basket, or if you have a tall pressure cooker, you can make a second layer using another steamer basket or trivet. Just make sure that the packets have space all around them for the steam to come in contact with and heat them. Close and lock the lid.
4. Turn the heat up to high. When the cooker reaches pressure, lower the heat to the minimum needed to maintain pressure. Cook for 12–15 minutes at high pressure.
5. When time is up, turn off the heat and let stand for 5 minutes. Open the pressure cooker by releasing pressure.
6. Open the top and remove the packets. Slide the parchment paper packet out of the tinfoil onto individual plates and carefully open each packet with scissors. Serve.

PER SERVING | Calories: 178 | Fat: 8 g | Protein: 22 g | Sodium: 1243 mg | Fiber: 1 g | Carbohydrates: 4 g

Trout in Parsley Sauce

This recipe is a way to use up lettuce that's no longer crisp enough for a salad but isn't totally past its prime. Using the lettuce to steam the fish keeps it firm and adds a bit of extra flavor to the poaching liquid.

INGREDIENTS | SERVES 4

4 fresh (½-pound each) river trout, rinsed and dried

2⅛ teaspoons salt, divided

4 cups torn lettuce leaves

1 teaspoon white wine vinegar

¾ cup water

½ cup minced, fresh, flat-leaf parsley

1 shallot, peeled and minced

2 tablespoons plain low-fat yogurt

½ teaspoon fresh lemon juice

2 tablespoons sliced almonds, toasted

1. Sprinkle trout with 2 teaspoons salt inside and out. Place 3 cups of the lettuce leaves in the bottom of the pressure cooker. Arrange the trout over the lettuce and cover with the remaining lettuce. Sprinkle with vinegar and water. Close and lock the lid.
2. Turn the heat up to high. When the cooker reaches pressure, lower the heat to the minimum needed to maintain pressure. Cook for 3 minutes at high pressure.
3. When time is up, open the pressure cooker by releasing pressure.
4. Use a spatula to move the fish to a serving plate. Peel and discard the skin from the fish. Remove and discard the heads if desired.
5. To make the parsley sauce, mix together the parsley, shallot, yogurt, lemon juice, and ⅛ teaspoon salt, and sprinkle with toasted almonds. Serve sauce alongside fish.

PER SERVING | Calories: 110 | Fat: 5.4 g | Protein: 13 g | Sodium: 707 mg | Fiber: 1 g | Carbohydrates: 2 g

Mediterranean Steamed Fish Fillet

Do you always eat fish with lemon? Try using sweet cherry tomatoes and vinegary capers instead!
Salty olives and thyme add excitement to an otherwise ho-hum whitefish fillet.

INGREDIENTS | SERVES 4

2 cups water

1 pound cherry tomatoes, halved

1 bunch fresh thyme

4 whitefish fillets

1 clove of garlic, pressed

2 tablespoons olive oil, divided

1 teaspoon salt

1 cup black salt-cured olives
(Taggiesche, French, or Kalamata)

2 tablespoons pickled capers

¼ teaspoon ground black pepper

Insert Choices

For this recipe, you can use a heatproof dish, an unperforated insert, or your steamer basket lined with parchment paper (cut the extra around the edges off so it does not interfere with the inner workings of the pressure cooker or obstruct any of the valves).

1. Prepare the pressure cooker by pouring in 2 cups of water and adding the trivet or steamer basket.
2. Line the bottom of a heatproof dish with half the cherry tomatoes (to keep the fish filet from sticking) and add thyme sprigs (reserve a few for garnish). Place the fish fillets over the cherry tomatoes, sprinkle with remaining tomatoes, garlic, 2 teaspoons olive oil, and salt.
3. Make a foil sling by folding a long piece of foil into three and lower the uncovered heatproof dish into the pressure cooker onto the steamer basket or trivet. Close and lock the lid.
4. Turn the heat up to high. When the cooker reaches pressure, lower the heat to the minimum needed to maintain pressure. Cook for 7–8 minutes at low pressure (or 4–5 minutes at high pressure).
5. When time is up, open the pressure cooker by releasing pressure.
6. Distribute fish onto individual plates and top with the cherry tomatoes that it was cooked with, as well as the olives, capers, thyme sprigs, a crackle of pepper, and the remaining olive oil.

PER SERVING | Calories: 309 | Fat: 12 g | Protein: 42 g | Sodium: 1144 mg | Fiber: 2.5 g | Carbohydrates: 7 g

Red Snapper in Rice Wine and Miso

In this recipe, use a heatproof dish to hold the fish instead of putting it directly in the pressure cooker—where it could easily fall apart during cooking!

INGREDIENTS | SERVES 4

2 cups water

1 tablespoon red miso paste

1 tablespoon rice wine

2 teaspoons fermented black beans

2 teaspoons sesame oil

1 teaspoon dark soy sauce

½ teaspoon Asian chili paste

½ teaspoon sea salt

2 pounds red snapper fillets

1 (2-inch) piece fresh ginger, cut into matchsticks

2 cloves garlic, peeled and minced

4 green onions, halved and cut into 2-inch pieces

Don't Lose Your Head

In some cultures, it's considered a delicacy to cook and serve the entire fish, including the head. If that is something you enjoy, feel free to use the whole fish in this recipe.

1. Prepare the pressure cooker by pouring in 2 cups of water and adding the trivet or steamer basket.
2. In a small bowl, mix the miso, rice wine, black beans, sesame oil, soy sauce, and chili paste, and salt. Cover and rub fish with the mixture. Place half the ginger in a heatproof dish and top with fish fillets. Sprinkle remaining ginger, garlic, and onions on top.
3. Make a foil sling by folding a long piece of foil into three and lower the uncovered heatproof dish into the pressure cooker. Close and lock the lid.
4. Turn the heat up to high. When the cooker reaches pressure, lower the heat to the minimum needed to maintain pressure. Cook for 7–8 minutes at low pressure (or 4–5 minutes at high pressure).
5. When time is up, open the pressure cooker by releasing pressure.
6. Distribute fish onto individual plates and top with the pan sauce.

PER SERVING | Calories: 265 | Fat: 5 g | Protein: 46 g | Sodium: 686 mg | Fiber: 0.6 g | Carbohydrates: 3 g

Fish Burritos

This recipe is also great with any fresh or frozen fish fillet such as whitefish or cod.

INGREDIENTS | SERVES 4

1 tablespoon olive oil

1 yellow onion, chopped

1 green bell pepper, seeded and diced

1½ cups cooked Black Beans and ½ cup of the cooking liquid (see recipe in Chapter 5)

1 (4-ounce) can green chilies, drained

1 teaspoon chili powder

2 whitefish fillets

4 (10-inch) corn tortillas

½ cup tomato salsa

1 cup shredded Monterey jack cheese

1. Heat olive oil in an uncovered pressure cooker over medium heat. Add onion and stir until softened (about 5 minutes). Add bell pepper, beans, bean cooking liquid and chilies and powder to cooker. Mix well.
2. Place fish fillets in steamer basket in the pressure cooker. Close and lock the lid.
3. Turn the heat up to high. When the cooker reaches pressure, lower the heat to the minimum needed to maintain pressure. Cook for 3–4 minutes at high pressure.
4. When time is up, open the pressure cooker by releasing pressure.
5. To prepare, place fish and 1 tablespoon of onion mixture onto each tortilla. Top with salsa and cheese. Roll the filling completely into the tortilla.
6. Serve as is or place burritos on a baking sheet and bake at 350°F for about 10 minutes to melt the cheese and crisp the tortillas.

PER SERVING | Calories: 397 | Fat: 15 g | Protein: 30 g | Sodium: 734 mg | Fiber: 9 g | Carbohydrates: 36 g

Coconut Fish Curry

Spicy, coconutty, and filling . . . this curry can be served by itself as a rich little fish stew or on a fluffy pillow of basmati rice. The trickiest part of this dish is collecting all of the ingredients!

INGREDIENTS | SERVES 6

1 tablespoon vegetable oil

6 fresh curry leaves or bay leaves

2 onions, sliced into strips

2 garlic cloves, minced

1 tablespoon freshly grated ginger

1 tablespoon ground coriander

2 teaspoons ground cumin

½ teaspoon ground turmeric

1 teaspoon cayenne pepper

½ teaspoon ground fenugreek

2 cups unsweetened coconut milk

2 green chilies, sliced into thin strips

1 medium tomato, chopped

1½ pounds fish steaks or fillets, rinsed and cut into bite-size pieces (fresh or frozen and thawed)

2 teaspoons salt

Juice of ½ lemon

1. Heat vegetable oil in an uncovered pressure cooker over medium heat. Drop in the curry or bay leaves and lightly fry them until golden around the edges (about 1 minute). Add the onion, garlic, and ginger and sauté until the onions are soft (about 5 minutes). Add coriander, cumin, turmeric, cayenne pepper, and fenugreek and sauté them together with the onions until they have released their aroma (about 2 minutes).
2. Deglaze the pan with the coconut milk, making sure to scrape anything from the bottom and incorporate it in the sauce. Add the chilies, tomatoes, and fish. Stir delicately to coat the fish well with the mixture. Close and lock the lid.
3. Turn the heat up to high. When the cooker reaches pressure, lower the heat to the minimum needed to maintain pressure. Cook for 4–5 minutes at low pressure (or 2–3 minutes at high pressure).
4. When time is up, open the pressure cooker by releasing pressure.
5. Add salt and lemon juice just before serving.

PER SERVING | Calories: 295 | Fat: 19 g | Protein: 22 g | Sodium: 75 mg | Fiber: 1.7 g | Carbohydrates: 9.7 g

Paprika Catfish with Fresh Tarragon

Serve over the rice of your choice.

INGREDIENTS | SERVES 4

1 (14½-ounce) can diced tomatoes

2 teaspoons dried minced onion

¼ teaspoon onion powder

1 teaspoon dried minced garlic

¼ teaspoon garlic powder

1 teaspoon hot paprika

½ tablespoon chopped fresh tarragon

1 medium green bell pepper, seeded and diced

1 stalk celery, finely diced

1 teaspoon salt

¼ teaspoon pepper

1 pound catfish fillets, rinsed and cut into bite-size pieces

1. Add all ingredients, except fish, to the pressure cooker and stir to mix. Once mixed, top with fish. Close and lock the lid.
2. Turn heat to high. When the cooker reaches pressure, lower the heat to the minimum needed to maintain pressure. Cook for 4–5 minutes at low pressure (2–3 minutes at high pressure).
3. Open the pressure cooker by releasing pressure. Stir and then taste for seasoning. Add more salt and pepper to taste if needed. Serve.

PER SERVING | Calories: 135 | Fat: 3.4 g | Protein: 19 g | Sodium: 792 mg | Fiber: 1.9 g | Carbohydrates: 6.6 g

Gulf Grouper with Peppers and Tomatoes

Grouper is delicious baked, grilled, fried, or steamed, as it is in this recipe. It has a light flavor and texture that goes great with seasonings like lemons and capers.

INGREDIENTS | SERVES 4

1 tablespoon olive oil

1 small onion, peeled and diced

1 stalk celery, diced

1 green bell pepper, seeded and diced

1 (14½-ounce) can diced tomatoes

¼ cup water

1 tablespoon tomato paste

3–4 fresh basil leaves, torn

½ teaspoon chili powder

1½ pounds grouper fillets, rinsed and cut into bite-size pieces

1 teaspoon salt

¼ teaspoon pepper

1. Heat oil in an uncovered pressure cooker over medium heat. Add onion, celery, and bell pepper and sauté for 3 minutes. Stir in tomatoes, water, tomato paste, basil, and chili powder. Gently stir the fish pieces into the sauce. Close and lock the lid.
2. Turn heat to high. When the cooker reaches pressure, lower the heat to the minimum needed to maintain pressure. Cook for 4–5 minutes at low pressure (2–3 minutes at high pressure).
3. Open the pressure cooker by releasing pressure. Stir in salt and pepper and serve.

PER SERVING | Calories: 220 | Fat: 5 g | Protein: 34 g | Sodium: 886 mg | Fiber: 2.2 g | Carbohydrates: 8 g

Poached Octopus

Let the octopus defrost for a day in the refrigerator before using it for this recipe.

INGREDIENTS | SERVES 6

2 pounds potatoes (about 6 medium), washed

4 teaspoons salt, divided

Water for cooking

1 octopus (about 2 pounds), cleaned and rinsed

3 cloves garlic, divided

1 bay leaf

2 teaspoons whole peppercorns

½ cup olive oil

4 tablespoons white wine vinegar

½ teaspoon pepper

1 bunch of parsley, chopped

Tenderize It!

When you buy fresh octopus, you need to either freeze and thaw it or beat it vigorously to tenderize it before cooking. If your fishmonger has fresh octopus, ask him if he will tenderize the octopus for you. Otherwise, spend about half an hour banging on it with a meat tenderizer or just put it in the freezer overnight.

1. Place the potatoes in the pressure cooker with 2 teaspoons salt and enough water to just cover the potatoes halfway. Close and lock the lid.
2. Turn the heat up to high. When the cooker reaches pressure, lower the heat to the minimum needed to maintain pressure. Cook for 10–15 minutes at high pressure.
3. When time is up, open the pressure cooker by releasing pressure.
4. Remove the potatoes with tongs (reserve the cooking water), and peel them as soon as you can handle them. Dice the potatoes into bite-size pieces.
5. Add the octopus to the potato cooking water in the cooker, with more water to cover if needed. Add one whole garlic clove, the bay leaf, and the peppercorns. Close and lock the lid.
6. Crush the remaining garlic cloves and place in a small jar or plastic container. Add olive oil, vinegar, 1 teaspoon salt, and pepper. Close the lid and shake well.
7. Turn the heat up to high. When the cooker reaches pressure, lower the heat to the minimum needed to maintain pressure. Cook for 15–20 minutes at high pressure.
8. Open the pressure cooker by releasing pressure.
9. Check the octopus for tenderness by seeing if a fork will sink easily into the thickest part of the flesh. If not, close the top and bring it to pressure for another minute or two and check again.
10. When the octopus is ready, remove and drain. Chop the head and tentacles into small, bite-size chunks.
11. Right before serving, mix the potatoes with the octopus, cover with the vinaigrette, and sprinkle with parsley.

PER SERVING | Calories: 390 | Fat: 19 g | Protein: 24 g | Sodium: 1826 mg | Fiber: 3.8 g | Carbohydrates: 27 g

Louisiana Grouper

The grouper use their famously large mouths to swallow their prey whole.

INGREDIENTS | SERVES 4

2 tablespoons peanut or vegetable oil

1 onion, peeled and diced

1 stalk celery, diced

1 green bell pepper, seeded and diced

1 (14½-ounce) can diced tomatoes

¼ cup water

1 tablespoon tomato paste

1 teaspoon sugar

⅛ teaspoon dried basil

½ teaspoon chili powder

1 teaspoon salt

¼ teaspoon pepper

4 grouper fillets, cut into bite-size pieces

1. Heat oil in an uncovered pressure cooker over medium heat. Add onion, celery, and peppers. Sauté for 3 minutes. Stir in tomatoes, water, tomato paste, sugar, basil, and chili.
2. Sprinkle with salt and pepper. Gently stir fish into the sauce. Close and lock the lid.
3. Turn the heat up to high. When the cooker reaches pressure, lower the heat to the minimum needed to maintain pressure. Cook for 5–7 minutes at high pressure.
4. Open the pressure cooker by releasing pressure. Remove fish, with slotted spoon and serve.

PER SERVING | Calories: 206 | Fat: 8 g | Protein: 23 g | Sodium: 836 mg | Fiber: 2.4 g | Carbohydrates: 10 g

Tomato-Braised Calamari

Can be served as a main dish on rice or white polenta, or mixed with pasta as a sauce.

INGREDIENTS | SERVES 6

3 tablespoons olive oil, divided

1 clove garlic, smashed

⅛ teaspoon hot pepper flakes

2 anchovies

1½ pounds fresh or frozen calamari, cleaned

½ cup white wine

1 (14½-ounce) can diced tomatoes

1 cup water

1 bunch parsley, chopped, divided

1 teaspoon salt

¼ teaspoon pepper

1. Heat 2 tablespoons oil in an uncovered pressure cooker over low heat. Add garlic, pepper flakes, and anchovies. Cook for 3 minutes, stirring constantly.
2. Add the calamari and sauté about 5 minutes. Add the wine and let it evaporate a bit (about 3 minutes). Add the tomatoes, water, and half the parsley. Close and lock the lid.
3. Turn the heat up to high. When the cooker reaches pressure, lower the heat to the minimum needed to maintain pressure. Cook for 15–20 minutes at high pressure.
4. Open the pressure cooker by releasing pressure. Season with salt and pepper and sprinkle with remaining olive oil and parsley before serving.

PER SERVING | Calories: 193 mg | Fat: 8 g | Protein: 18 g | Sodium: 590 mg | Fiber: 1 g | Carbohydrates: 6.8 g

CHAPTER 10

One-Pot Meals

Veggie Biryani
173

Aloo Gobi
174

JL's Farro, Bean, and Collard
Green Wraps
174

Herb and Quinoa Stuffed
Tomatoes
175

Ricotta-Stuffed Zucchini
176

Hearty Stuffed Peppers
177

Turkish Stuffed Eggplant Boats
178

Jambalaya with Chicken,
Sausage, and Shrimp
179

Beef Pot Roast
180

Turkey and Vegetable Stew
181

Easy Beef Stew
182

African Lamb Stew and
Couscous
183

Fast African Peanut Stew
184

Spanish Chicken and Rice
185

Cuban Black Beans
and Rice
186

Italian Chickpea and
Barley Stew
187

New Orleans–Style
Black Beans and Rice
187

Red Beans and Rice
188

Mushroom Chicken with
Potatoes
189

Turkey with Mixed Vegetables
and Potatoes
190

Herbed Chicken Stew with
Dumplings
191

Ginger Soy Pork Chops with
Broccoli and Rice
192

Cajun-Style Chicken
with Rice
193

Quick "Paella"
194

Veggie Biryani

This Indian rice dish will serve 2 as a vegetarian main course or 4 as a side dish.

INGREDIENTS | SERVES 4

1 tablespoon vegetable oil

2 teaspoons turmeric

2 teaspoons garam masala

⅛ teaspoon cayenne pepper

1 onion, peeled and sliced

1 teaspoon minced garlic

1 teaspoon minced ginger

4 ounces fresh mushrooms, sliced

1 small green bell pepper, seeded and diced

1 cup basmati rice, rinsed and drained

½ cup small cauliflower florets

1 carrot, diced

1½ cups Vegetable Stock (see recipe in Chapter 4)

½ cup frozen peas, thawed

½ teaspoon salt

1. Heat oil in an uncovered pressure cooker over medium heat. Add the turmeric, garam masala, cayenne pepper, and onion. Cook, stirring, until the onion begins to turn golden (about 8–10 minutes). Add the remaining ingredients and mix well. Close and lock the lid.
2. Turn the heat up to high. When the cooker reaches pressure, lower the heat to the minimum needed to maintain pressure. Cook for 4–5 minutes at high pressure.
3. Open with the natural release method (see Chapter 1).
4. Serve with an optional dollop of yogurt.

PER SERVING | Calories: 256 | Fat: 4 g | Protein: 6 g | Sodium: 524 mg | Fiber: 3.6 g | Carbohydrates: 48 g

Indian via Persia

Biryani is derived from the Persian word "birian." In Farsi, birian means "fried before cooking," and although we use vegetable oil, it is typically made with ghee (clarified butter). The route Biryani took to get to India is not clear. It could have either been brought by Arabian traders from across the sea or to Northern India through Afghanistan.

Aloo Gobi

Aloo gobi is a vegetarian Indian dish made from potatoes and cauliflower.

INGREDIENTS | SERVES 4

1 tablespoon vegetable oil

1 teaspoon cumin seeds

1 clove garlic, minced

1 teaspoon minced ginger

1 teaspoon turmeric

1 teaspoon garam masala

1 teaspoon salt

2 cups peeled and cubed potatoes

1 cup water

2 cups bite-size pieces of cauliflower

1. Heat oil in an uncovered pressure cooker over medium heat. Add cumin seeds, garlic, and ginger. Sauté together for 1 minute and add turmeric, garam masala, and salt. Stir in the potatoes and water. Finally add the cauliflower on top, but do not stir. Close and lock the lid.
2. Turn the heat up to high. When the cooker reaches pressure, lower the heat to the minimum needed to maintain pressure. Cook for 5 minutes at high pressure.
3. Open the pressure cooker by releasing pressure. Stir all ingredients together and serve.

PER SERVING | Calories: 100 | Fat: 3.8 g | Protein: 2.4 g | Sodium: 612 mg | Fiber: 3 g | Carbohydrates: 15 g

JL's Farro, Bean, and Collard Green Wraps

This recipe was shared by JL Fields from www.jlgoesvegan.com.
I asked for her permission to include my very lightly modified version of her recipe because it shows how creative, delicious, and filling a vegan one-pot meal can be!

INGREDIENTS | SERVES 4

2 tablespoons olive oil

1 cup semi-perlato farro

1 onion, diced

3 cloves garlic, minced

½ teaspoon thyme

½ teaspoon dried basil

1 cup dry black-eyed peas

2½ cups water

1 tablespoon Bragg's Liquid Aminos

½ teaspoon hot sauce

4 collard green leaves, washed and dried

1. Heat olive oil in an uncovered pressure cooker over medium heat. Add the farro and onion and sauté together until the onion is soft (about 5 minutes). Add garlic, thyme, basil, black-eyed peas, and water. Close and lock the lid.
2. Turn the heat up to high. When the cooker reaches pressure, lower the heat to the minimum needed to maintain pressure. Cook for 10 minutes at high pressure.
3. Open with the natural release method (see Chapter 1).
4. Stir in the Bragg's Liquid Aminos and hot sauce and serve by spooning the mixture onto collard green leaves.

PER SERVING | Calories: 397 | Fat: 8 g | Protein: 15 g | Sodium: 260 mg | Fiber: 13 g | Carbohydrates: 68 g

Herb and Quinoa Stuffed Tomatoes

This healthy treat is a great way to "disguise" quinoa for those who think they don't like it!

INGREDIENTS | SERVES 4

1 cup water
4 large tomatoes
1 cup cooked quinoa
1 stalk celery, chopped
1 tablespoon minced garlic
2 tablespoons chopped, fresh oregano
2 tablespoons chopped, fresh parsley
½ teaspoon salt
¼ teaspoon pepper

1. Place water in the pressure cooker and add the steamer basket.
2. Remove the core from each tomato and discard. Scoop out the seeds, leaving the walls of the tomato intact.
3. In a small bowl, stir together the quinoa, celery, garlic, oregano, parsley, salt, and pepper. Divide evenly among the four tomatoes. Place the filled tomatoes in a single layer on the steamer basket. Close and lock the lid.
4. Turn the heat up to high. When the cooker reaches pressure, lower the heat to the minimum needed to maintain pressure. Cook for 5–7 minutes at high pressure.
5. When time is up, open the pressure cooker by releasing pressure. Gently lift out the steamer basket and, using tongs or two spoons, place each tomato (they will be very delicate) on individual plates.

PER SERVING | Calories: 93 | Fat: 1 g | Protein: 4 g | Sodium: 318 mg | Fiber: 3.7 g | Carbohydrates: 18 g

Ricotta-Stuffed Zucchini

This recipe lets nothing go to waste and everything is cooked together:
zucchini, stuffing, and the tomato zucchini sauce, which is also the steaming liquid.

INGREDIENTS | SERVES 6

3 large, thick zucchini

2 tablespoons olive oil, divided

2 garlic cloves, pressed

½ teaspoon salt

¼ teaspoon pepper

1 cup fresh ricotta

½ cup unseasoned bread crumbs

1 bunch thyme, woody stems removed and leaves chopped

1 bunch oregano, woody stems removed and leaves chopped

1 medium onion, chopped

1 (14½-ounce) can chopped tomatoes

1 bunch basil, chopped

½ cup water

1. Slice the zucchini in 1½-inch thick rounds. Scoop out the insides of each round to ¾ the depth (about 1-inch deep) to make little cups. Reserve zucchini flesh and set aside.
2. Heat 1 tablespoon olive oil in an uncovered pressure cooker over medium heat. Add the reserved zucchini flesh, garlic, salt, and pepper. Cook until zucchini is softened (about 8 minutes), remove from pressure cooker, and set aside in a mixing bowl. Add ricotta, bread crumbs, thyme, and oregano to bowl and mix well.
3. Stuff the zucchini cups with the zucchini-ricotta mixture.
4. Return the pressure cooker to medium heat. Add another tablespoon of olive oil and sauté the onions until softened (about 5 minutes). Add the tomatoes, basil, and water.
5. Lower the steamer basket into the pressure cooker over the sauce. Carefully place the stuffed zucchini cups in the basket. Close and lock the lid.
6. Turn the heat up to high. When the cooker reaches pressure, lower the heat to the minimum needed to maintain pressure. Cook for 5 minutes at high pressure.
7. When time is up, open the pressure cooker by releasing pressure.
8. Using tongs, carefully remove the zucchini cups to a serving platter. Pour tomato sauce over zucchini cups and serve.

PER SERVING | Calories: 169 | Fat: 8.6 g | Protein: 8 g | Sodium: 419 mg | Fiber: 2.5 g | Carbohydrates: 16 g

Hearty Stuffed Peppers

For even more protein, substitute the rice for quinoa.

INGREDIENTS | SERVES 4

4 medium green bell peppers

1 pound lean ground beef

1 cup cooked rice of your choice

1 large egg

3 cloves garlic, peeled and minced

1 yellow onion, peeled and diced

1 teaspoon salt

¼ teaspoon pepper

⅛ teaspoon allspice

½ cup Chicken Stock (see recipe in Chapter 4)

½ cup tomato sauce

Stuff it!

Peppers are not the only vegetables you can stuff: you can stuff tomatoes, onions, zucchini (cups or boats) and even eggplant!

1. Cut the tops off the green peppers. Remove and discard the seeds and set aside. Dice any of the green pepper that you can salvage from around the stem and mix well with ground beef, rice, egg, garlic, onion, salt, pepper, and allspice.
2. Evenly divide the meat mixture between the green peppers. Place the steamer basket in the pressure cooker and pour the stock into the cooker. Place the peppers in the steamer basket and pour the tomato sauce over the peppers. Close and lock the lid.
3. Turn the heat up to high. When the cooker reaches pressure, lower the heat to the minimum needed to maintain pressure. Cook for 15 minutes at high pressure.
4. Open the pressure cooker by releasing pressure. Move the peppers to plates using tongs and serve.

PER SERVING | Calories: 288 | Fat: 7.6 g | Protein: 29 g | Sodium: 889 mg | Fiber: 3 g | Carbohydrates: 25 g

Turkish Stuffed Eggplant Boats

This Turkish dish is called Karniyarik, and all of the ingredients are fried separately, then baked. Here we only lightly brown some of the ingredients and do the rest of the cooking with steam. If you have a low, wide pressure cooker, you can easily double this recipe to fit in your extra-wide steamer basket!

INGREDIENTS | SERVES 6

3 thin, long eggplants

1 tablespoon vegetable oil

4 ounces ground beef

1 small onion, chopped

2 sprigs parsley (stems and leaves divided), chopped

2 cloves garlic, minced

1 large tomato, chopped and drained

1 teaspoon salt

1 teaspoon pepper

3 banana peppers, sliced into strips

1 cup water

1. Poke each eggplant with a fork all around, then slice in half lengthwise.
2. Heat oil in an uncovered pressure cooker over medium heat. Place each eggplant half cut-side down in the pressure cooker and cook until lightly browned, about 5 minutes. Remove and set aside.
3. Add the beef, onion, and parsley stems to the cooker and sauté until onions have softened and meat has begun to brown (about 5–7 minutes). Add the garlic, tomato, salt, and pepper. Mix thoroughly and turn off the heat.
4. Slice the eggplant halves in the middle with a shallow cut that does not reach the ends or bottom. Arrange halves in the steamer basket and stuff them with the meat mixture. Lay banana pepper strips over the stuffed eggplant halves.
5. Add 1 cup of water to the pressure cooker and lower the steamer basket. Close and lock the lid.
6. Turn the heat up to high. When the cooker reaches pressure, lower the heat to the minimum needed to maintain pressure. Cook for 10 minutes at high pressure.
7. When time is up, open the pressure cooker by releasing pressure.
8. Carefully remove the eggplant boats using a long spatula and tongs. Sprinkle with parsley leaves before serving.

PER SERVING | Calories: 161 | Fat: 4.7 g | Protein: 7 g | Sodium: 414 mg | Fiber: 10 g | Carbohydrates: 18 g

Jambalaya with Chicken, Sausage, and Shrimp

Jambalaya was originally created as a flavorful way to enjoy leftovers.
The origins of this classic dish's name is not clear, but it's commonly accepted
that the name is a union of the French jambon (ham) and African aya (rice).

INGREDIENTS | SERVES 6

1 tablespoon peanut oil
1 large carrot, peeled and grated
1 stalk celery, finely diced
1 large green bell pepper, seeded and chopped
1 yellow onion, peeled and diced
2 green onions, chopped
½ pound pork steak, cut into bite-size-pieces
½ pound boneless, skinless chicken thighs, cut into bite-size-pieces
¼ pound smoked sausage, thinly sliced
2 cloves garlic, minced
¼ pound cooked ham, diced
1 (14½-ounce) can diced tomatoes, drained
1 cup chicken broth
½ tablespoon chopped parsley
½ teaspoon thyme
¼ teaspoon hot sauce
2 tablespoons Worcestershire sauce
½ pound shrimp, peeled and deveined
1 teaspoon salt
½ teaspoon pepper
3 cups cooked brown rice

1. Heat oil in an uncovered pressure cooker over medium heat. Add the carrots, celery, and green bell pepper and sauté for 3–5 minutes or until soft. Add the yellow and green onions and sauté until transparent (about 3 minutes).
2. Raise the heat to high and add the pork, chicken, and sausage and stir-fry for 5 minutes. Then add the garlic, ham, tomatoes, broth, parsley, thyme, hot sauce, and Worcestershire sauce. Close and lock the lid.
3. Turn the heat up to high. When the cooker reaches pressure, lower the heat to the minimum needed to maintain pressure. Cook for 5–8 minutes at high pressure.
4. When time is up, open the pressure cooker by releasing pressure.
5. Mix in the shrimp, then close and lock the lid. Leave the shrimp in the cooker for about 5 minutes without turning on the heat.
6. Taste for seasoning and add salt and pepper. Mix with cooked brown rice to serve.

PER SERVING | Calories: 373 | Fat: 10 g | Protein: 34 g | Sodium: 1193 mg | Fiber: 3.8 g | Carbohydrates: 34 g

Substitute or Leave Out

The beauty of Jambalaya is that the recipe is incredibly flexible. Don't have some of the ingredients? Leave them out. Have too much of a certain veggie in your fridge? Add it in. It's really a great option for when you have a little bit of everything in your refrigerator, but not enough of one thing to make a specific dish.

Beef Pot Roast

This is an elegant one-pot meal that ticks all the boxes: meat, vegetables, and a starch.

INGREDIENTS | SERVES 6

1 tablespoon olive oil
1 (4-pound) beef roast
1 cup Beef Stock (see recipe in Chapter 4)
1 teaspoon salt
1 teaspoon pepper
2 sprigs fresh thyme
2 pounds potatoes, roughly cubed
1 pound thick carrots, peeled (not cut)
1 cup red wine
2 tablespoons unsalted butter
1 bunch parsley, chopped

Size Matters

The size, density, and thickness of a food will dictate how long it will take to cook in the pressure cooker. Use this information to your advantage when crafting a one-pot meal. For example, carrots (which only need 2 minutes at high pressure) and potatoes (which need 10 minutes at high pressure) can cook together in just 5 minutes if you adjust the size of the pieces. Whole thick carrots take a little more time, and potatoes cut into large cubes need a little less time to pressure cook.

1. Heat olive oil in an uncovered pressure cooker over medium heat. Sear the roast well on all sides. Deglaze the pressure cooker with stock and sprinkle the roast with salt and pepper. Add thyme. Close and lock the lid.
2. Turn the heat up to high. When the cooker reaches pressure, lower the heat to the minimum needed to maintain pressure. Cook for 25–30 minutes at high pressure.
3. When time is up, open the pressure cooker by releasing pressure.
4. Add the potatoes and place the whole carrots on top. Close and lock the lid.
5. Turn the heat up to high. When the cooker reaches pressure, lower the heat to the minimum needed to maintain pressure. Cook for 5 minutes at high pressure.
6. When time is up, open the pressure cooker by releasing pressure.
7. Remove the carrots, slice them, and place them on the serving platter. Pull out the roast and place it on a plate tented with aluminum foil to rest. Remove the potatoes with a slotted spoon and place on the serving platter.
8. Strain the remaining liquid in the cooker and add wine and butter. Simmer, uncovered, over medium-high heat until the liquid is reduced to about half.
9. Slice roast and serve on platter with carrots and potatoes. Sprinkle with fresh parsley and top with some of the pan sauce. Serve the rest of the au jus sauce in a gravy boat.

PER SERVING | Calories: 866 | Fat: 49 g | Protein: 63 g | Sodium: 687 mg | Fiber: 5.7 g | Carbohydrates: 32 g

Turkey and Vegetable Stew

This recipe is a quick and healthy one-pot meal.

INGREDIENTS | SERVES 4

1 tablespoon vegetable oil

1 pound skinless, boneless turkey breast, cut into bite-size pieces

2 pounds potatoes, peeled and cut in ¼-inch dice

2 medium zucchini, sliced ½-inch thick

1 medium eggplant, peeled and diced

1 medium onion, peeled and diced

1 medium green bell pepper, seeded and diced

½ pound mushrooms, sliced

1 (28-ounce) can diced tomatoes, undrained

3 tablespoons tomato paste

2 cloves garlic, peeled and minced

2 teaspoons dried basil

¼ teaspoon dried red pepper flakes

1 teaspoon salt

½ teaspoon pepper

½ cup grated Parmigiano-Reggiano cheese

1. Heat oil in an uncovered pressure cooker over medium heat and brown the turkey on all sides. Add the potatoes, zucchini, eggplant, onion, bell pepper, mushrooms, undrained tomatoes, tomato paste, garlic, basil, red pepper flakes, salt, and pepper. Close and lock the lid.
2. Turn the heat up to high. When the cooker reaches pressure, lower the heat to the minimum needed to maintain pressure. Cook for 5 minutes at high pressure.
3. Open with the natural release method (see Chapter 1).
4. Serve topped with a generous amount of Parmigiano-Reggiano cheese.

PER SERVING | Calories: 463 | Fat: 9 g | Protein: 42 g | Sodium: 1129 mg | Fiber: 11 g | Carbohydrates: 57 g

Easy Beef Stew

This is a quick and easy way to turn leftover roast beef into a hearty stew.
Serve with crackers or dinner rolls and you have an easy, complete, comfort food meal.

INGREDIENTS | SERVES 8

2 cups cooked roast beef, cut into bite-size pieces

1 onion, chopped

1 (28-ounce can) whole stewed tomatoes

¼ teaspoon onion powder

¼ teaspoon celery seeds

⅛ teaspoon paprika

2 tablespoons sea salt

1 teaspoon white pepper

1 tablespoon Worcestershire sauce

2 cups Beef Stock (see recipe in Chapter 4)

1 (24-ounce) bag frozen vegetables

2 pounds potatoes, roughly chopped

1 tablespoon all-purpose flour

1. Add all of the ingredients, except for the flour, into the pressure cooker. Close and lock the lid.
2. Turn the heat up to high. When the cooker reaches pressure, lower the heat to the minimum needed to maintain pressure. Cook for 10–15 minutes at high pressure.
3. Open with the natural release method (see Chapter 1).
4. Sprinkle in the flour and stir well. Simmer uncovered for 5 minutes, or until desired thickness is reached, and serve.

PER SERVING | Calories: 214 | Fat: 4.5 g | Protein: 16 g | Sodium: 2097 mg | Fiber: 6 g | Carbohydrates: 27 g

Are Frozen Veggies Better than Fresh?

In some cases, yes. Not only are frozen vegetables picked at their peak of ripeness, they are usually frozen within hours of being picked. Most supermarket fresh vegetables are picked unripe to survive the ride to the distributor and then to the store. Farmers' market veggies are always the freshest, sometimes picked in the wee hours of the morning before being brought to market.

African Lamb Stew and Couscous

Few things fill the kitchen with a more appetizing aroma than cinnamon simmering in orange juice. Your family will rush to the table for this dish.

INGREDIENTS | SERVES 6

1 tablespoon olive oil

2 pounds boneless lamb shoulder, cut into bite-size pieces

1 large onion, peeled and roughly diced

2 cloves garlic, peeled and minced

⅓ cup raisins

⅓ cup blanched whole almonds

1 tablespoon minced, fresh ginger

½ teaspoon ground cinnamon

¾ cup Vegetable Stock (see recipe in Chapter 4)

¼ cup fresh orange juice

⅓ cup fresh mint leaves

1 teaspoon salt

¼ teaspoon pepper

1 cup couscous, uncooked

1 cup hot water

1. Heat olive oil in an uncovered pressure cooker over medium heat. Brown the lamb pieces, working in batches if need. Add the onion and garlic and sauté with the meat for about 3 minutes. Add raisins, almonds, ginger, cinnamon, stock, juice, mint, salt, and pepper. Close and lock the lid.
2. Turn the heat up to high. When the cooker reaches pressure, lower the heat to the minimum needed to maintain pressure. Cook for 20–25 minutes at high pressure.
3. Just before releasing pressure, combine the couscous and water in a heatproof bowl that will fit into the pressure cooker.
4. When time is up, open the pressure cooker by releasing pressure.
5. Quickly lower the bowl into the pressure cooker, then close and lock the lid. Let the couscous cook in the residual heat and steam of the pressure cooker for about 5 minutes.
6. Serve together.

PER SERVING | Calories: 568 | Fat: 33 g | Protein: 31 g | Sodium: 562 mg | Fiber: 3.3 g | Carbohydrates: 34 g

Fast African Peanut Stew

This is an American adaptation of a traditional spicy African stew from Ghana, which is usually served with fufu—a giant, gelatinous starch dumpling.

INGREDIENTS | SERVES 6

1 tablespoon peanut oil

1 onion, cut into strips

1 tablespoon grated, fresh ginger

1 tablespoon minced garlic

⅛ teaspoon hot pepper flakes

1 cup roasted and shelled peanuts, lightly crushed

1 pound skinless, boneless chicken tenders, or breasts cut into chunks

1 teaspoon salt

½ teaspoon freshly ground black pepper

2 cups Vegetable Stock (see recipe in Chapter 4)

1 pound sweet potatoes, cut into large cubes

1 (28-ounce) can whole stewed tomatoes

1 pound collard greens, chopped

¼ cup peanut butter, chunky or smooth

1. Heat oil in an uncovered pressure cooker over medium heat. Sauté the onions until soft (about 5 minutes). Add the ginger and garlic and sauté for 1 additional minute. Add the remaining ingredients, except for peanut butter, and stir. Close and lock the lid.
2. Turn the heat up to high. When the cooker reaches pressure, lower the heat to the minimum needed to maintain pressure. Cook for 5–8 minutes at high pressure.
3. Open with the natural release method (see Chapter 1).
4. Using a potato masher, lightly mash half of the sweet potatoes and stir in peanut butter. Mix well and serve.

PER SERVING | Calories: 518 | Fat: 31 g | Protein: 23 g | Sodium: 630 mg | Fiber: 8.8 g | Carbohydrates: 39 g

Spanish Chicken and Rice

Adapt the heat level of this Spanish Chicken and Rice recipe by choosing between mild, medium, or hot chili powder, according to your tastes. In addition, you can substitute jalapeño pepper for some or all of the green pepper.

INGREDIENTS | SERVES 4

1 tablespoon vegetable oil

1 pound boneless chicken breast, cut into bite-size pieces

1 large green pepper, seeded and diced

1 teaspoon chili powder

1 teaspoon smoked paprika

¼ teaspoon dried thyme

⅛ teaspoon dried oregano

¼ teaspoon freshly ground black pepper

⅛ teaspoon cayenne pepper

1 medium white onion, peeled and diced

2 cloves garlic, peeled and minced

2 cups chicken broth

1 cup long-grain rice, uncooked

½ cup pitted and halved black olives

1. Heat oil in an uncovered pressure cooker over medium heat. Sauté the chicken, green pepper, chili powder, paprika, thyme, oregano, black pepper, cayenne pepper, and onion for about 5 minutes, or until the chicken is lightly browned. Then add the garlic, broth, and rice. Close and lock the lid.

2. Turn the heat up to high. When the cooker reaches pressure, lower the heat to the minimum needed to maintain pressure. Cook for 3 minutes at high pressure.

3. Open with the natural release method (see Chapter 1).

4. Mix in the olives and fluff rice with a fork before serving.

PER SERVING | Calories: 588 | Fat: 25 g | Protein: 23 g | Sodium: 1086 mg | Fiber: 4 g | Carbohydrates: 66 g

Cuban Black Beans and Rice

Cuban cuisine is the combination of African, Caribbean, and Spanish cuisines.

INGREDIENTS | SERVES 6

3 tablespoons olive or vegetable oil

1 medium green bell pepper, seeded and diced

1 stalk celery, finely diced

1 carrot, peeled and grated

1 onion, diced

2 cloves garlic, minced

1 cup medium- or long-grain white rice

1 cup dried black beans, soaked overnight

2 cups Vegetable Stock (see recipe in Chapter 4)

2 teaspoons paprika

½ teaspoon cumin

¼ teaspoon chili powder

1 bay leaf

1 teaspoon salt

¼ teaspoon black pepper

1. Heat oil in an uncovered pressure cooker over medium heat. Sauté green bell pepper, celery, carrots, and onions until the onions are soft (about 5 minutes). Add the garlic and rice and stir everything together until the rice begins to toast. Then add the beans, stock, paprika, cumin, chili powder, and bay leaf. Close and lock the lid.
2. Turn the heat up to high. When the cooker reaches pressure, lower the heat to the minimum needed to maintain pressure. Cook for 3–5 minutes at high pressure.
3. Open with the natural release method (see Chapter 1).
4. Stir and add salt and pepper to taste. Remove bay leaf before serving.

PER SERVING | Calories: 253 | Fat: 1.5 g | Protein: 10 g | Sodium: 632 mg | Fiber: 7 g | Carbohydrates: 50 g

The Bay Leaf

Bay leaves come from the bay laurel plant and are most commonly used to season soups and stews. When used whole, they should be removed from a dish before serving.

Italian Chickpea and Barley Stew

As a stew, this dish should have a thick consistency and not be runny or have too much liquid like a soup.

INGREDIENTS | SERVES 4

1 cup dry chickpeas, soaked
1 cup pearl barley
1 clove garlic, pressed
2 tablespoons olive oil, divided
2 carrots, diced
2 celery stalks, diced
1 large white onion, diced
4 cups water
2 teaspoons salt
1 teaspoon white pepper

1. Add all of the ingredients to the pressure cooker, except for the salt, pepper, and 1 tablespoon olive oil. Close and lock the lid.
2. Turn the heat up to high. When the cooker reaches pressure, lower the heat to the minimum needed to maintain pressure. Cook for 15 minutes at high pressure.
3. Open with the natural release method (see Chapter 1).
4. Stir in salt and pepper and serve with a swirl of the remaining olive oil.

PER SERVING | Calories: 336 | Fat: 8.5 g | Protein: 9 g | Sodium: 1235 mg | Fiber: 12 g | Carbohydrates: 57 g

New Orleans–Style Black Beans and Rice

This dish is also great with crabmeat or, for a truly New Orleans–style dish, use crawfish.

INGREDIENTS | SERVES 4

1 tablespoon olive oil
1 cup brown rice
1 yellow onion, chopped
3 cloves garlic, minced
3 cups water
1 (14-ounce) can diced tomatoes, drained
1 cup dry black beans, soaked
½ teaspoon cumin
⅛ teaspoon cayenne pepper
8 ounces frozen bay shrimp, thawed and coarsely chopped
1 teaspoon salt
¼ teaspoon pepper

1. Heat olive oil in an uncovered pressure cooker over medium heat. Sauté the rice, onion, and garlic for about 3 minutes. Add water, tomatoes, beans, cumin, cayenne pepper, and shrimp. Close and lock the lid.
2. Turn the heat up to high. When the cooker reaches pressure, lower the heat to the minimum needed to maintain pressure. Cook for 18–20 minutes at high pressure.
3. Open with the natural release method (see Chapter 1).
4. Stir in salt and pepper and serve.

PER SERVING | Calories: 229 | Fat: 5 g | Protein: 17 g | Sodium: 1002 mg | Fiber: 5.8 g | Carbohydrates: 28 g

Red Beans and Rice

Red beans and rice is a New Orleans staple that is traditionally served on Mondays—
a customary use of leftovers from their traditional Sunday pork roast.
For an extra kick, bring this to the table with a bottle of hot sauce.

INGREDIENTS | SERVES 6

1 tablespoon vegetable oil

1 large green bell pepper, seeded and diced

1 medium onion, peeled and diced

4 stalks celery, finely diced

½ pound smoked sausage, diced

1 bay leaf

1 teaspoon white pepper

1 teaspoon thyme

1 teaspoon garlic powder

¼ teaspoon cayenne pepper

1 ham hock (about 1 pound)

1 cup dry red beans, soaked overnight

1 cup brown rice

2 cups Vegetable Stock (see recipe in Chapter 4)

1 teaspoon salt

2 teaspoons hot sauce

1. Heat oil in an uncovered pressure cooker over medium heat. Sauté the pepper, onion, celery, and smoked sausage until the onions have softened (about 5 minutes). Add the rest of the ingredients except for salt and hot sauce. Close and lock the lid.
2. Turn the heat up to high. When the cooker reaches pressure, lower the heat to the minimum needed to maintain pressure. Cook for 18–20 minutes at high pressure.
3. Open with the natural release method (see Chapter 1).
4. Remove the bone of the ham hock and the bay leaf. Fluff the rice with a fork and taste for seasoning (the smoked sausage and ham are already salty, so you may not need additional salt).
5. Stir in hot sauce or top individual servings with a few drops.

PER SERVING | Calories: 307 | Fat: 12 g | Protein: 24 g | Sodium: 1610 mg | Fiber: 4 g | Carbohydrates: 24 g

Red Beans Rule!

Red beans are a powerhouse of vitamins and minerals. A one cup serving can provide 66 percent of your daily requirement for fiber, 29 percent of iron, and 12 percent of calcium!

Mushroom Chicken with Potatoes

This is a wonderful one-pot meal for the whole family. Serve with fresh grilled vegetables or a simple salad of sliced romaine with your favorite dressing.

INGREDIENTS | SERVES 6

1 tablespoon olive oil

4 tablespoons butter, divided

2 large onions, peeled and diced

1 pound mushrooms, sliced thinly

4 boneless, skinless chicken breasts, cut into bite-size pieces

4 medium potatoes, peeled and sliced

1 pound carrots, peeled and sliced into thick rounds

½ cup Chicken Stock (see recipe in Chapter 4)

2 teaspoons salt

1 teaspoon white pepper

½ cup water

2½ cups whole milk

4 tablespoons flour

1. Heat olive oil and 1 tablespoon butter in an uncovered pressure cooker over medium heat. Sauté the onions until soft (about 5 minutes). Add the mushrooms and sauté for about 3 more minutes. Add the chicken, potatoes, carrots, stock, salt, pepper, and water. Mix well. Close and lock the lid.
2. Turn the heat up to high. When the cooker reaches pressure, lower the heat to the minimum needed to maintain pressure. Cook for 5–7 minutes at high pressure.
3. When time is up, open the pressure cooker by releasing pressure.
4. Add the milk, flour, and remaining butter and mix well. Simmer uncovered, stirring frequently, until the contents have reached the desired consistency, and serve.

PER SERVING | Calories: 587 | Fat: 28 g | Protein: 24 g | Sodium: 1246 mg | Fiber: 8 g | Carbohydrates: 60 g

Turkey with Mixed Vegetables and Potatoes

For a real casserole feel, pour this recipe into a casserole dish and slide it under the broiler for a few minutes to give it a brown top.

INGREDIENTS | SERVES 6

1 tablespoon vegetable oil

¾ pound skinless, boneless turkey breast, cut into bite-size pieces

2 medium zucchini, sliced into thick rounds

1 eggplant, peeled and diced

1 onion, peeled and diced

1 green bell pepper, seeded and diced

1 pound potatoes, roughly diced

5 tomatoes, diced, or 1 (28-ounce) can diced tomatoes

3 tablespoons tomato paste

2 cloves garlic, peeled and minced

2 teaspoons fresh chopped basil

1 teaspoon salt

¼ teaspoon white pepper

4 tablespoons Pecorino Romano cheese, grated

1. Heat oil in an uncovered pressure cooker over medium heat. Sauté the turkey until it begins to brown. Add the zucchini, eggplant, onion, bell pepper, potatoes, tomatoes, paste, garlic, and basil. Stir well. Close and lock the lid.
2. Turn the heat up to high. When the cooker reaches pressure, lower the heat to the minimum needed to maintain pressure. Cook for 5–7 minutes at high pressure.
3. When time is up, open the pressure cooker by releasing pressure.
4. Taste for seasoning and add salt and pepper. Serve topped with grated cheese.

PER SERVING | Calories: 216 | Fat: 4 g | Protein: 19 g | Sodium: 566 mg | Fiber: 8 g | Carbohydrates: 27 g

Herbed Chicken Stew with Dumplings

Nothing says comfort food like chicken and dumplings. You can stretch this recipe to 6 or 8 main dish servings if you serve the stew over another favorite comfort food companion: mashed potatoes.

INGREDIENTS | SERVES 4

2¼ cups flour, divided
1 tablespoon baking powder
1 teaspoon salt, divided
6 tablespoons unsalted butter, divided
1 large egg, beaten
¾ cup buttermilk
¼ teaspoon freshly ground black pepper
8 bone-in chicken thighs, skin removed
1 tablespoon vegetable oil
2 stalks celery, finely diced
1 large onion, peeled and diced
1 teaspoon dried thyme
1 pound carrots, cut into 1-inch rounds
2½ cups Chicken Stock (see recipe in Chapter 4)
½ cup dry white wine
1 bay leaf

1. Make dumpling batter: Add 2 cups flour, baking powder, and ½ teaspoon salt to a mixing bowl. Stir to combine, then use a pastry blender or two forks to cut in 5 tablespoons butter. Stir in egg and buttermilk until the mixture comes together. Set aside.
2. Add the ¼ cup flour, ½ teaspoon salt, pepper, and chicken to a large zip-closure plastic bag. Shake to coat.
3. Heat oil and 1 tablespoon butter in an uncovered pressure cooker over medium heat. Brown the chicken pieces for 3 minutes on each side, working in batches if needed. Set the chicken aside.
4. Add the celery, onion, and thyme and cook until the onion is softened (about 5 miuntes). Stir in the carrots, stock, wine, and bay leaf. Return the browned chicken thighs (and their juices) to the pressure cooker. Close and lock the lid.
5. Turn the heat up to high. When the cooker reaches pressure, lower the heat to the minimum needed to maintain pressure. Cook for 8–10 minutes at high pressure.
6. When time is up, open the pressure cooker by releasing pressure.
7. Remove and discard the bay leaf. Let liquid simmer, uncovered. Drop heaping teaspoons of the dumpling batter into the simmering stew.
8. Cover loosely to allow a small amount of the steam to escape and cook for 10–15 minutes or until the dumplings are puffy and cooked through. Serve.

PER SERVING | Calories: 784 | Fat: 30 g | Protein: 43 g | Sodium: 1324 mg | Fiber: 6 g | Carbohydrates: 78 g

Ginger Soy Pork Chops with Broccoli and Rice

An easy and unexpected one-pot meal.

INGREDIENTS | SERVES 4

4 boneless pork chops
2 tablespoons soy sauce
½ cup unsweetened pineapple juice
1 tablespoon apple cider vinegar
1 teaspoon raw sugar
1 tablespoon fresh ginger root, minced
2 cups frozen broccoli florets
1 cup uncooked long-grain white rice, rinsed and strained
1½ cups Chicken Stock (see recipe in Chapter 4)

1. Place pork chops in a zip-closure bag and add soy sauce, pineapple juice, cider vinegar, sugar, and ginger. Seal bag and refrigerate for up to 2 hours. Empty contents of the bag into the pressure cooker. Close and lock the lid.
2. Turn the heat up to high. When the cooker reaches pressure, lower the heat to the minimum needed to maintain pressure. Cook for 6–8 minutes at high pressure.
3. When time is up, open the pressure cooker by releasing pressure. Add broccoli, rice, and stock. Close and lock the lid.
4. Turn the heat up to high. When the cooker reaches pressure, lower the heat to the minimum needed to maintain pressure. Cook for 3 minutes at low pressure.
5. Open with the natural release method (see Chapter 1).
6. Serve immediately.

PER SERVING | Calories: 479 | Fat: 8 g | Protein: 49 g | Sodium: 681 mg | Fiber: 2.4 g | Carbohydrates: 49 g

Cajun-Style Chicken with Rice

Serve with steamed broccoli, sautéed green beans, or grilled artichoke hearts.

INGREDIENTS | SERVES 6

1 tablespoon vegetable oil

1 white onion, peeled and diced

1 large green bell pepper, seeded and diced

1½ pounds boneless, skinless chicken breasts, cut into bite-size pieces

4 cloves garlic, peeled and minced

1 teaspoon rosemary

1 teaspoon thyme

1 teaspoon paprika

¼ teaspoon dried red pepper flakes

½ cup white wine

1 (28-ounce) can diced tomatoes

½ cup Chicken Stock (see recipe in Chapter 4)

2 cups thawed and sliced frozen okra

1 cup frozen whole kernel corn, thawed

2 large carrots, peeled and sliced

1 cup long-grain white rice, rinsed and drained

½ cup chopped fresh cilantro, packed

1 bay leaf

1 teaspoon salt

¼ teaspoon pepper

1. Heat oil in an uncovered pressure cooker over medium heat. Sauté the onion, bell pepper, and chicken until lightly browned (7–8 minutes). Add the garlic, rosemary, thyme, paprika, and red pepper flakes. Sauté for 2 more minutes.
2. Pour in the wine, and deglaze the pan, scraping up any bits stuck to the bottom of the pan. Add the remaining ingredients and stir to mix. Close and lock the lid.
3. Turn the heat up to high. When the cooker reaches pressure, lower the heat to the minimum needed to maintain pressure. Cook for 4 minutes at high pressure.
4. Open with the natural release method (see Chapter 1).
5. Remove and discard the bay leaf. Fluff the rice with a fork. Taste for seasoning and adjust if necessary. Serve.

PER SERVING | Calories: 533 | Fat: 21 g | Protein: 22 g | Sodium: 1137 mg | Fiber: 6 g | Carbohydrates: 62 g

Quick "Paella"

The Spanish paella is naturally a one-pot meal. In Spain, where pressure cookers are very popular, there is a Paella just for the pressure cooker called Paella Express.

INGREDIENTS | SERVES 6

1 tablespoon olive oil

3 slices bacon, diced

2 large yellow onions, sliced

1 small green bell pepper, seeded and sliced

3 boneless, skinless chicken thighs, cut into bite-size pieces

3 boneless, skinless chicken breasts, cut into bite-size pieces

4 cloves garlic, minced

2 cups long-grain white rice

4½ cups Chicken Stock (see recipe in Chapter 4)

3 tablespoons tomato paste

3 tablespoons fresh lemon juice

2 tablespoons chopped parsley

1 teaspoon salt

½ teaspoon sweet paprika

¼ teaspoon red pepper flakes, crushed

2 teaspoons dried oregano

1 cup frozen peas

¼ pound bay scallops

¼ pound uncooked, cleaned shrimp

1 lemon, sliced

1 cup gourmet black olives, pitted

1. Heat olive oil in an uncovered pressure cooker over medium heat. Sauté the bacon until crisp. Add the onions and bell pepper and sauté until the onions become translucent (about 3 minutes). Add the chicken thighs and breasts, garlic, rice, stock, tomato paste, lemon juice, parsley, salt, paprika, pepper flakes, oregano, and peas. Stir well. Close and lock the lid.
2. Turn the heat up to high. When the cooker reaches pressure, lower the heat to the minimum needed to maintain pressure. Cook for 8 minutes at high pressure.
3. When time is up, open the pressure cooker by releasing pressure.
4. Quickly stir in the scallops and shrimp. Close and lock the lid. Count 10 minutes cooking time using the residual heat of the pressure cooker (no additional heat).
5. Serve garnished with lemon slices and olives.

PER SERVING | Calories: 704 | Fat: 25 g | Protein: 37 g | Sodium: 1127 mg | Fiber: 5 g | Carbohydrates: 80 g

Paella Types

Other than Paella Express, there are several versions of paella for your pressure cooker. They are: Paella valenciana, from Valencia made with chicken, pork, and sometimes rabbit; Paella de marisco, seafood paella with prawns, mussels, and squid; Paella mixita, a free-form paella that can contain both seafood and meats (as the name implies, it's mixed).

CHAPTER 11

Pasta Sauces

Basic Tomato Sauce
196

Fresh Tomato Sauce
196

Mixed Pepper Sauce
197

Spicy Eggplant Sauce
198

Light Mushroom Cream Sauce
199

Quick Sausage Ragu
200

Bolognese Meat Sauce
201

Basic Tomato Sauce

This is an Italian classic, also called marinara sauce. Though there is no fish involved in the sauce, it would be a perfect base for a seafood sauce. Serve with any pasta shape, though this is perfectly suited for spaghetti. This recipe makes enough for a 1-pound package of pasta.

INGREDIENTS | SERVES 6

1 tablespoon olive oil

2 garlic cloves, pressed

1 (14½-ounce) can chopped tomatoes

1 cup tomato purée

¼ teaspoon salt

⅛ teaspoon pepper

1 sprig basil

Umami Boost

Give this sauce a little extra umami by adding two anchovies while sautéing the garlic. When the anchovies have melted into the oil, continue with the recipe (omitting the salt).

1. Heat olive oil in an uncovered pressure cooker over medium heat. Sauté the garlic until golden (about 1 minute). Add the tomatoes, salt, pepper, and basil. Close and lock the lid.
2. Turn the heat up to high. When the cooker reaches pressure, lower the heat to the minimum needed to maintain pressure. Cook for 5 minutes at high pressure.
3. Open with the natural release method (see Chapter 1).
4. Remove the stem from the sprig of basil before serving.

PER SERVING | Calories: 48 | Fat: 2 g | Protein: 1.2 g | Sodium: 361 mg | Fiber: 1.4 g | Carbohydrates: 6.7 g

Fresh Tomato Sauce

When tomatoes are in season and are naturally sweet and ripe, this is an excellent sauce to make. It takes a little longer than the canned, because the liquids will need to reduce significantly. It's perfect with homemade pasta.

INGREDIENTS | SERVES 6

1 tablespoon olive oil

2 garlic cloves, smashed

8 Roma-type tomatoes, chopped and drained

¼ teaspoon salt

⅛ teaspoon pepper

1 sprig basil

1. Heat olive oil in an uncovered pressure cooker over medium heat. Sauté the garlic until golden (about 1 minute). Add the tomatoes, salt, pepper, and basil. Close and lock the lid.
2. Turn the heat up to high. When the cooker reaches pressure, lower the heat to the minimum needed to maintain pressure. Cook for 5 minutes at high pressure.
3. Open the pressure cooker by releasing pressure. Remove the stem from the sprig of basil and simmer uncovered over medium-low heat for about 1 minute or until sauce consistency is reached.

PER SERVING | Calories: 50 | Fat: 2.5 g | Protein: 1.5 g | Sodium: 106 mg | Fiber: 2 g | Carbohydrates: 6.5 g

Mixed Pepper Sauce

Serve this sauce with ricotta-filled pasta, like ravioli. You can also serve this as a side dish by doubling the recipe. Do not purée the vegetables at the end and remove with slotted spoon to a serving dish immediately and top with a teaspoon or two of olive oil.

INGREDIENTS | SERVES 6

1 tablespoon olive oil

2 red peppers, thinly sliced into strips

2 yellow peppers, thinly sliced into strips

1 green pepper, thinly sliced into strips

1 red onion, thinly sliced

4 Roma-type tomatoes, puréed (or 1 cup canned chopped tomatoes)

1 garlic clove, pressed

1 bunch fresh parsley, chopped

1. Heat olive oil in an uncovered pressure cooker over medium heat. Add peppers and onion. Stir infrequently until one side is lightly browned (about 5 minutes). Add the tomatoes and their liquid. Close and lock the lid.
2. Turn the heat up to high. When the cooker reaches pressure, lower the heat to the minimum needed to maintain pressure. Cook for 3–5 minutes at high pressure.
3. When time is up, open the pressure cooker by releasing pressure.
4. Add the garlic and parsley and purée using an immersion blender.

PER SERVING | Calories: 65 | Fat: 2.6 g | Protein: 1.8 g | Sodium: 9 mg | Fiber: 2.3 g | Carbohydrates: 10 g

Spicy Eggplant Sauce

This sauce, made in double the quantity, can also be served as a side dish!
Serve on any short pasta like farfalle, penne, or fusilli.

INGREDIENTS | SERVES 6

1 tablespoon olive oil

¼ teaspoon hot pepper flakes

2 anchovies

1 clove, garlic, smashed

2 large eggplants, diced

1 teaspoon salt

¼ teaspoon pepper

⅔ cup water

1 sprig of fresh oregano

Even Heat

Infusing olive oil with hot pepper flakes at the beginning of a recipe (like this one) helps to evenly distribute the heat through the whole dish, versus little pops of heat whenever your diner happens to bite on a flake.

1. In the cold pressure cooker, add the oil, pepper flakes, anchovies, and garlic. Turn on low heat to infuse the oil with these flavors until the garlic begins to sizzle and the anchovies fall apart, about 3 minutes.
2. Separate the diced eggplant into two piles. Turn the heat up to medium and add half of the eggplant into the pressure cooker, uncovered. Add salt and pepper to taste.
3. Stir the eggplant around, lightly browning it on most sides for about 5 minutes. Add the remaining eggplant. Mix everything well, add water, and rest the oregano sprig on top. Close and lock the lid.
4. Turn the heat up to high. When the cooker reaches pressure, lower the heat to the minimum needed to maintain pressure. Cook for 3–5 minutes at high pressure.
5. When time is up, open the pressure cooker by releasing pressure.
6. Discard the herb sprigs and pour the contents on freshly strained pasta, or if using as a side dish, remove the eggplant to a serving dish immediately to stop it from cooking further and falling apart.

PER SERVING | Calories: 45 | Fat: 2.5 g | Protein: 1.5 g | Sodium: 443 mg | Fiber: 3 g | Carbohydrates: 5 g

Light Mushroom Cream Sauce

This is a very rich and strong-flavored sauce that is best used on homemade pasta or rich egg pasta.

INGREDIENTS | SERVES 6

1 tablespoon olive oil

2 tablespoons butter, divided

1 pound button mushrooms, roughly sliced

1 bunch parsley, stems and leaves divided and chopped

1 cup vegetable broth

2 ounces dried porcini mushrooms, crumbled

½ teaspoon salt

¼ teaspoon white pepper

1 tablespoon flour

1 cup whole milk

¼ teaspoon nutmeg

More Flavor with Less

Combine cheaper button mushrooms with fresh or dried gourmet mushrooms to increase flavor without increasing the cost. If porcini are not available, substitute with cremini, portobello, and even oyster mushrooms!

1. Heat olive oil and 1 tablespoon butter in an uncovered pressure cooker over medium heat. Sauté button mushrooms and parsley stems, stirring infrequently until mushrooms are lightly browned (about 8–10 minutes). Add the broth, porcini mushrooms, salt, and pepper. Mix well. Close and lock the lid.
2. Turn the heat up to high. When the cooker reaches pressure, lower the heat to the minimum needed to maintain pressure. Cook for 5 minutes at high pressure.
3. When time is up, open the pressure cooker by releasing pressure.
4. Mix in flour, milk, and nutmeg. Purée sauce using an immersion blender.
5. Simmer sauce on low heat until desired consistency is reached.
6. Sprinkle with parsley leaves before serving.

PER SERVING | Calories: 129 | Fat: 7 g | Protein: 4.5 g | Sodium: 311 mg | Fiber: 2 g | Carbohydrates: 12 g

Quick Sausage Ragu

A small pressure pan is best, but not required, for making this recipe. If you purchased a pressure cooker set, you can make the sauce in the small pressure pan and boil water for the pasta in the larger base.

INGREDIENTS | SERVES 6

8 ounces Italian sausage, removed from casing

1 red onion, chopped

1 clove garlic, pressed

3 sprigs of fresh oregano, chopped

¼ teaspoon salt

⅛ teaspoon pepper

1 (14½-ounce can) chopped tomatoes

Ragu Don'ts

A ragu is an Italian tomato-based meat sauce. It can contain one or several cuts of meat. This includes beef, pork, veal, goat, lamb, rabbit, boar, or other wild and domesticated meats . . . but never chicken or turkey!

1. In the cold pressure cooker, add the crumbled Italian sausage, then set the heat to low to slowly melt and render the fat. Stir the sausage to break it up and then add the onion and raise the heat to medium-high. Sauté for 5 minutes or until the onion begins to soften. Add garlic, oregano, salt, pepper, and tomatoes. Stir well, scraping the bottom to remove and incorporate any browned bits that may have gotten stuck. Close and lock the lid.
2. Turn the heat up to high. When the cooker reaches pressure, lower the heat to the minimum needed to maintain pressure. Cook for 5–6 minutes at high pressure.
3. Open with the natural release method (see Chapter 1).
4. Pour over freshly strained pasta, mix, and serve.

PER SERVING | Calories: 75 | Fat: 3 g | Protein: 6.5 g | Sodium: 315 mg | Fiber: 1 g | Carbohydrates: 5 g

Bolognese Meat Sauce

This is the pressure cooker version of the original sauce as filed in the official recipe archive of the Commerce Department in Bologna, Italy. You will still need to caramelize and evaporate liquids as in the original sauce, but the overall simmering is reduced to just minutes. Serve over egg pasta or as the star ingredient in a lasagna.

INGREDIENTS | SERVES 6

4 ounces pancetta, cubed

1 onion, chopped

1 carrot, chopped

1 celery stalk chopped

11 ounces ground beef

½ cup of Sangiovese, or other dry red wine

5 tablespoons tomato paste

1 cup Beef Stock (see recipe in Chapter 4)

½ teaspoon salt

¼ teaspoon pepper

1 tablespoon heavy cream

Faster Bolognese

You can make this recipe more quickly by sautéing everything together on high heat before adding the tomatoes and using half of the wine indicated. It will be good, but it won't be as good as the "real" Bolognese!

1. In the cold pressure cooker, place the pancetta in a flat layer and turn on the lowest possible heat to render the fat. When the pancetta begins to sizzle, raise heat to medium-high and add the onion, carrot, and celery. Sauté until the onions have softened (about 5 minutes). If the ingredients begin to stick, you can add a tablespoon of water.

2. Add ground beef and brown well, stirring occasionally until all of the liquid is evaporated and the fat begins to sizzle (about 20–30 minutes).

3. Add the wine, scraping the bits stuck to the bottom and sides of the pan, and evaporate it completely (about 7 minutes). In the meantime, mix the tomato paste with the beef stock, salt, and pepper. Add stock mixture to the pan and stir well, scraping the bottom of the pan. Close and lock the lid.

4. Turn the heat up to high. When the cooker reaches pressure, lower the heat to the minimum needed to maintain pressure. Cook for 18–20 minutes at high pressure.

5. Open with the natural release method (see Chapter 1).

6. Stir in the cream and serve.

PER SERVING | Calories: 229 | Fat: 14 g | Protein: 14 g | Sodium: 583 mg | Fiber: 1.2 g | Carbohydrates: 6.5 g

CHAPTER 12

Pasta, Rice, and Grains

Penne in Ragu
204

All-American Mac & Cheese
205

Italian Mac & Cheese
206

Fusilli in Spinach Pesto
207

Spicy Tomato Pasta
208

Basic Pasta
209

Jasmine Rice
210

Basmati Rice
210

White Long-Grain Rice
211

South African Yellow Rice
211

Cranberry Pecan Rice
212

Coconut Rice
212

Mexican Burrito Rice
213

Veggie Rice Pilaf
214

Three-Grain Rice Pilaf
214

Arborio Rice
215

Italian Rice Salad
215

Basic White Risotto
216

Zucchini Risotto
217

Tomato Risotto
218

Brown Rice
219

Peppery Brown Rice Risotto
219

Brown Rice with Peanuts
220

Roasted Corn and Brown Rice
221

Wild Rice
222

Lemon Brown and Wild Rice
222

Amaranth
223

Whole Barley
223

Pearl Barley
224

Barley and Gorgonzola Risotto
224

Summer Barley Caprese Salad
225

Barley and Tuna Salad
225

Buckwheat
226

Bulgur
226

Bulgur Stuffing
227

Cracked Wheat and Chickpea
Pilaf with Lemon
227

Pearled Farro
228

Farro and Dried Porcini
Mushroom Pilaf
228

Steel-Cut Oats
229

Irish Oatmeal and Fruit
229

Polenta
230

Three Cheese Polenta
231

Fresh Herb Polenta
231

Quinoa
232

Quinoa and Artichoke Hearts
Salad
232

Wheat Berries
233

Wheat Berry Salad
233

Penne in Ragu

If you don't have penne, use fusilli, ziti, or rigatoni. If you're using an electric pressure cooker, you may need to shave off a minute or two from the pressure cooking time to achieve al dente results.

INGREDIENTS | SERVES 6

1 tablespoon butter
1 onion, finely chopped
1 carrot, finely chopped
1 celery stalk, finely chopped
10 ounces ground beef
2½ teaspoons salt, divided
½ teaspoon ground black pepper
⅓ cup red wine
1 pound penne pasta
2 cups tomato purée
Water for cooking

Cheesy Penne Casserole

You can turn this pasta dish into a casserole easily. As soon as you open the pressure cooker, pour half the contents into a buttered, ovensafe casserole dish and sprinkle with 6 ounces diced or shredded mozzarella cheese. Then pour on the rest of the pasta and sprinkle another 6 ounces of cheese and 2 tablespoons of butter on top. Grill under the broiler for about 5 minutes or until the cheese is bubbly and golden.

1. Heat butter in an uncovered pressure cooker over medium heat. Sauté the onion, carrot, and celery in the butter until the onion is soft (about 5 minutes).
2. Turn the heat to high and add the ground beef, ½ teaspoon salt, and pepper. Use a wooden spoon to break up the beef and brown it on all sides (about 10 minutes). The meat should be almost fully cooked.
3. Add wine and deglaze the pan. Continue cooking until the liquid in the pan evaporates fully (about 1 minute).
4. Pour in the pasta, tomato purée, 2 teaspoons salt, and enough water to just cover the pasta. Stir everything together and flatten the pasta out in an even layer. Close and lock the lid.
5. Turn the heat up to high. When the cooker reaches pressure, lower the heat to the minimum needed to maintain pressure. Cook for 4 minutes at low pressure (1–2 minutes at high pressure).
6. When time is up, open the pressure cooker by releasing pressure.
7. Stir the contents and let the pasta sit for about 1 minute before serving.

PER SERVING | Calories: 432 | Fat: 7 g | Protein: 20 g | Sodium: 1267 mg | Fiber: 4.5 g | Carbohydrates: 66 g

All-American Mac & Cheese

You can speed up the cooking process by stirring the milk, cream, and cheeses into the macaroni over very low heat until the cheese is melted. Also, instead of baking for 30 minutes, you can simply place the casserole under the broiler for about 5 minutes to brown the bread crumb topping.

INGREDIENTS | SERVES 6

1 tablespoon vegetable oil

1 onion, peeled and diced

1 clove garlic, peeled and minced

2 cups elbow macaroni

3 cups Chicken Stock (see recipe in Chapter 4)

1 teaspoon salt

⅛ teaspoon white pepper

½ cup whole milk

½ cup heavy cream

4 ounces Cheddar cheese, grated

4 ounces mozzarella cheese, grated

4 ounces Colby cheese, grated

¼ cup dried bread crumbs

2 tablespoons butter, melted

Heavy Cream Substitute

Whole milk or low-fat yogurt is a lighter substitute for heavy cream. Yogurt tops out at 4 percent fat, while heavy cream contains a whopping 40 percent! The yogurt gives the flavor a boost, too.

1. Heat oil in an uncovered pressure cooker over medium heat. Sauté the onion until it is soft (about 5 minutes). Add garlic and macaroni and stir to coat it in the oil. Stir in the stock, salt, and pepper. Close and lock the lid.
2. Turn the heat up to high. When the cooker reaches pressure, lower the heat to the minimum needed to maintain pressure. Cook for 6 minutes at high pressure.
3. When time is up, open the pressure cooker by releasing pressure.
4. Preheat the oven to 350°F. Drain the macaroni. Transfer to a 9" × 13" ovenproof baking dish. Stir in the milk, cream, and cheeses. Mix the bread crumbs together with the melted butter and sprinkle over the top of the macaroni and cheese. Bake for 30 minutes or until the cheeses are melted and the bread crumbs are golden brown.
5. Remove from the oven and let rest for 5 minutes before serving.

PER SERVING | Calories: 541 | Fat: 32 g | Protein: 23 g | Sodium: 937 mg | Fiber: 1.5 g | Carbohydrates: 38 g

Italian Mac & Cheese

Called Cacio e Pepe, *or Cheese and Pepper, this cheesy pasta has a delicate taste that becomes hot and spicy thanks to the liberal use of pepper. I've limited the use in this recipe for heat-sensitive readers, but you can double or triple the quantities to taste.*

INGREDIENTS | SERVES 6

1 tablespoon olive oil

1 pound elbow macaroni, penne, or other short, tubular pasta

2 teaspoons sea salt

Water for cooking

1 pound sheep's milk or cow's milk ricotta

1 teaspoon black pepper

½ cup grated Pecorino Romano cheese

1 sprig basil, finely chopped

1. In a preheated pressure cooker, add the olive oil, pasta, salt, and enough water to just cover the pasta. Stir everything together and flatten the pasta out in an even layer. Close and lock the lid.
2. Turn the heat up to high. When the cooker reaches pressure, lower the heat to the minimum needed to maintain pressure. Cook for 4 minutes at low pressure (1–2 minutes at high pressure). If you're using an electric pressure cooker, you may need to shave off a minute or two from the pressure cooking time to achieve al dente results.
3. When time is up, open the pressure cooker by releasing pressure.
4. Pour out about half of the cooking water from the pressure cooker. Quickly mix in the ricotta cheese and pepper.
5. Top each dish with Pecorino Romano and basil before serving.

PER SERVING | Calories: 436 | Fat: 11 g | Protein: 21 g | Sodium: 999 mg | Fiber: 2.5 g | Carbohydrates: 60 g

Fusilli in Spinach Pesto

This is not real pesto because it uses spinach instead of basil. The spinach releases its juice in the cooking water, which is then absorbed by the pasta, turning it slightly green and making it more nutritious!

INGREDIENTS | SERVES 6

1 tablespoon olive oil
1 pound spinach, chopped
4 cloves garlic, finely chopped, divided
1 pound fusilli pasta
2 teaspoons salt
Water for cooking
¼ cup pine nuts, whole or chopped
1 tablespoon good-quality olive oil

1. Heat olive oil in an uncovered pressure cooker over medium heat. Sauté the spinach, stirring frequently, until most of the moisture has evaporated (about 8 minutes). Add half of the garlic and mix in well. Next add the pasta, salt, and enough water to cover the pasta. Stir everything together and flatten the pasta out in an even layer. Cover and lock the lid.
2. Turn the heat up to high. When the cooker reaches pressure, lower the heat to the minimum needed to maintain pressure. Cook for 4 minutes at low pressure (1–2 minutes at high pressure). If you're using an electric pressure cooker, you may need to shave off a minute or two from the pressure cooking time to achieve al dente results.
3. When time is up, open the pressure cooker by releasing pressure.
4. Mix in the rest of the garlic and let the pasta sit for about a minute. Top each bowl with a sprinkling of pine nuts and a small swirl of your best olive oil.

PER SERVING | Calories: 395 | Fat: 11 g | Protein: 13 g | Sodium: 858 mg | Fiber: 5 g | Carbohydrates: 60 g

Spicy Tomato Pasta

This spicy sauce is also known as all'arrabbiata in Italy. Since the pasta absorbs most of the sauce, the intense tomato flavor and spice is distributed evenly and turns the pasta slightly red!

INGREDIENTS | SERVES 6

1 tablespoon olive oil
2 cloves garlic, pressed
1 teaspoon hot pepper flakes
¼ teaspoon oregano
1 pound farfalle pasta
2 cups tomato purée
2 teaspoons salt
Water for cooking
1 tablespoon good-quality olive oil

Pressure Cooker Pasta

Any short- or medium-cut, hard, semolina pasta can be pressure cooked. Nests of dried egg fettuccine can also be pressure cooked, but they should be strained since they require more water to cook than they will absorb. Frozen or dried stuffed pasta, like ravioli or tortellini, may work, if used in a pressure cooker recipe written expressly for them.

1. In a cold pressure cooker, add olive oil, garlic, pepper flakes, and oregano. Heat uncovered, slowly, over low heat. Allow the ingredients to infuse the oil until the garlic cloves sizzle and turn lightly golden, about 1 minute.
2. Pour in the pasta, tomato purée, salt, and just enough water to cover the pasta. Stir everything together and flatten the pasta out in an even layer. Close and lock the lid.
3. Turn the heat up to high. When the cooker reaches pressure, lower the heat to the minimum needed to maintain pressure. Cook for 6 minutes at low pressure (2–3 minutes at high pressure). If you're using an electric pressure cooker, you may need to shave off a minute or two from the pressure cooking time to achieve al dente results.
4. When time is up, open the pressure cooker by releasing pressure.
5. Stir the contents and finish with a swirl of your best olive oil before serving.

PER SERVING | Calories: 350 | Fat: 5.8 g | Protein: 11 g | Sodium: 1025 mg | Fiber: 4 g | Carbohydrates: 63 g

Basic Pasta

This is a basic pressure cooker pasta technique. Use this when you're using fresh pasta sauces like sun-dried tomato or basil pesto. Don't omit the oil; it reduces the foaming of the pasta.

INGREDIENTS | SERVES 6

1 tablespoon olive oil
1 pound short pasta
2 teaspoons salt
Water for cooking

Not Every Pasta Shape Will Work

Don't use your pressure cooker for any pasta that requires 7 minutes or less of cooking time. Very small pasta intended for soups—like stelline, quadratini, or orzetto—could clog the safety mechanisms of your pressure cooker. However, they can be added into an open pressure cooker after preparing a sauce or soup. Orecchiette have a tendency to fall into little stacks and will turn into a solid mass in the pressure cooker; fresh pasta will fall apart if pressure cooked; and potato gnocchi need to be visible as they cook (they're done when they float to the top of the cooking liquid), so they're not a good choice for a pressure cooker either. You should not break spaghetti in half to fit in your pressure cooker—it will be too short to wind around the fork making it difficult to eat. Breaking it in half is considered bad luck.

1. In a preheated pressure cooker, add oil, pasta, salt, and enough water to cover the pasta. Close and lock the lid.
2. Turn the heat up to high. When the cooker reaches pressure, lower the heat to the minimum needed to maintain pressure. Cook for 5 minutes at low pressure (2–3 minutes at high pressure). If you're using an electric pressure cooker, you may need to shave off a minute or two from the pressure cooking time to achieve al dente results.
3. When time is up, open the pressure cooker by releasing pressure.
4. Strain the pasta and serve with your favorite sauce.

PER SERVING | Calories: 296 | Fat: 3 g | Protein: 9 g | Sodium: 782 mg | Fiber: 2 g | Carbohydrates: 55 g

Jasmine Rice

Following the Thai tradition, jasmine rice should always be rinsed.

INGREDIENTS | SERVES 6

2 cups jasmine rice, rinsed
2½ cups water
1 tablespoon vegetable oil

How to Rinse Rice

Put the rice in a fine strainer. Run cold water over the rice until the water coming out of the strainer is no longer white and milky. The rice is rinsed when the water looks clear.

1. Add the rice, water, and oil to the pressure cooker. Close and lock the lid.
2. Turn the heat up to high. When the cooker reaches pressure, lower the heat to the minimum needed to maintain pressure. Cook for 1 minute at high pressure.
3. Open with the natural release method (see Chapter 1).
4. Fluff with a fork and serve.

PER SERVING | Calories: 246 | Fat: 2.6 g | Protein: 4.3 g | Sodium: 6 mg | Fiber: 1 g | Carbohydrates: 48 g

Basmati Rice

For nonsoaked basmati rice, use 2 cups of water per cup of rice.

INGREDIENTS | SERVES 6

2 cups basmati rice, rinsed and soaked
3 cups water
1 tablespoon vegetable oil

How to Soak Rice

Rinse rice under cold water in a strainer, then lower the strainer into a larger bowl full of water. Soak for 15–20 minutes. When it's ready to use, lift and lightly shake the strainer to remove excess water.

1. Add rice, water, and oil to the pressure cooker. Close and lock the lid.
2. Turn the heat up to high. When the cooker reaches pressure, lower the heat to the minimum needed to maintain pressure. Cook for 3 minutes at high pressure.
3. Open with the natural release method (see Chapter 1).
4. Fluff with a fork and serve.

PER SERVING | Calories: 225 | Fat: 2.5 g | Protein: 4 g | Sodium: 9 mg | Fiber: 1 g | Carbohydrates: 49 g

White Long-Grain Rice

This dish can function as a base for any of the dishes from the veggie chapter!

INGREDIENTS | SERVES 6

2 cups long-grain white rice, rinsed

3 cups water

1 tablespoon vegetable oil

Why Rinse?

Rice coming from the East may be picked and dried in less than ideal conditions—sometimes on reed mats on the street. It's always best to rinse rice to get rid of the ambient dust that may have landed on it while drying. The act of rinsing rice removes any starch that may have developed during transport from the grains rubbing each other.

1. Add the rice, water, and oil to the pressure cooker. Close and lock the lid.
2. Turn the heat up to high. When the cooker reaches pressure, lower the heat to the minimum needed to maintain pressure. Cook for 5 minutes at high pressure.
3. Open with the natural release method (see Chapter 1).
4. Fluff with a fork and serve.

PER SERVING | Calories: 245 | Fat: 2.5 g | Protein: 4 g | Sodium: 6 mg | Fiber: 1 g | Carbohydrates: 49 g

South African Yellow Rice

This sweet rice is best accompanied by fresh tropical fruit or a spicy chutney.

INGREDIENTS | SERVES 6

¾ cup raisins

2 cups white long-grain rice, rinsed

1 teaspoon turmeric

¼ teaspoon salt

3 cups water

2 sticks cinnamon

1 tablespoon butter

¼ teaspoon powdered cinnamon

¼ teaspoon sugar

1. Cover raisins in hot water and soak for 15 minutes. Drain and set aside.
2. Add the rice, turmeric, salt, water, cinnamon sticks, butter, and raisins to the pressure cooker. Close and lock the lid.
3. Turn the heat up to high. When the cooker reaches pressure, lower the heat to the minimum needed to maintain pressure. Cook for 5 minutes at high pressure.
4. Open with the natural release method (see Chapter 1).
5. Remove and discard cinnamon sticks. Fluff with a fork and sprinkle with cinnamon and sugar before serving.

PER SERVING | Calories: 298 | Fat: 2 g | Protein: 5 g | Sodium: 107 mg | Fiber: 1.5 g | Carbohydrates: 64 g

Cranberry Pecan Rice

Pecans add extra protein, cranberries a little tang. A very exciting side dish!

INGREDIENTS | SERVES 6

½ cup dried cranberries

2 cups white long-grain rice, rinsed

1 cup pecans, roughly chopped

3 cups water

1 tablespoon vegetable oil

1. Cover cranberries in hot water and soak for 15 minutes, then rinse and drain. Add the rice, pecans, water, vegetable oil, and cranberries to the pressure cooker. Close and lock the lid.
2. Turn the heat up to high. When the cooker reaches pressure, lower the heat to the minimum needed to maintain pressure. Cook for 5 minutes at high pressure.
3. Open with the natural release method (see Chapter 1).
4. Fluff with a fork and serve.

PER SERVING | Calories: 399 | Fat: 15 g | Protein: 6 g | Sodium: 7 mg | Fiber: 3 g | Carbohydrates: 60 g

Coconut Rice

The combination of coconut, currants, and spices transforms this rice into a succulent dish. It is especially good served with a curry entrée.

INGREDIENTS | SERVES 6

1 tablespoon butter

2 cups extra long-grain white rice, rinsed and drained

½ cup flaked or grated unsweetened coconut

3 cups water

¼ cup currants

½ teaspoon ground cinnamon

1 teaspoon anise seeds

⅛ teaspoon ground cloves

½ teaspoon salt

1. Heat butter in an uncovered pressure cooker over medium heat. Sauté the rice, stirring well to coat it in the butter. Add the coconut, water, currants, cinnamon, anise seeds, cloves, and salt. Close and lock the lid.
2. Turn the heat up to high. When the cooker reaches pressure, lower the heat to the minimum needed to maintain pressure. Cook for 3 minutes at high pressure.
3. Open with the natural release method (see Chapter 1).
4. Fluff with a fork and serve.

PER SERVING | Calories: 272 | Fat: 6 g | Protein: 5 g | Sodium: 206 mg | Fiber: 2.8 g | Carbohydrates: 49 g

Mexican Burrito Rice

This rice is also known as Spanish rice, though it's not actually from Spain.

INGREDIENTS | SERVES 6

1 tablespoon vegetable oil

1 onion, chopped

2 cups medium- or long-grain white rice, rinsed

1 cup chopped tomatoes and their juice

2½ cups water

2 teaspoons salt

1 teaspoon oregano

⅛ teaspoon cayenne pepper

1. Heat oil in an uncovered pressure cooker over medium heat. Sauté onion until it begins to soften (about 5 minutes). Add the rice and sauté until the first few grains begin to brown (about 3 minutes). Add the tomatoes, water, salt, oregano, and cayenne pepper. Mix well and be sure to scrape the bottom of the pan to unstick any rice. Close and lock the lid.
2. Turn the heat up to high. When the cooker reaches high pressure, lower the heat to the minimum needed to maintain pressure. Pressure cook for 5–7 minutes at high pressure.
3. Open with the natural release method (see Chapter 1).
4. Fluff with a fork and serve.

PER SERVING | Calories: 265 | Fat: 3 g | Protein: 5.5 g | Sodium: 791 mg | Fiber: 2 g | Carbohydrates: 53 g

Veggie Rice Pilaf

You can replace most of the vegetables with frozen mixed vegetables for a more convenient last-minute rice.

INGREDIENTS | SERVES 6

1 tablespoon vegetable oil

1 onion, chopped

1 carrot, chopped

2 cups medium- or long-grain white rice, rinsed and drained

1 cup peas, fresh or frozen

2½ cups Chicken Stock (see recipe in Chapter 4)

1 teaspoon salt

1. Heat oil in an uncovered pressure cooker over medium heat. Add onion and carrot, and sauté until the onions begin to soften (about 5 minutes). Add the rice and sauté until the first few grains begin to brown (about 3 minutes). Add peas, stock, and salt. Mix well and be sure to scrape the bottom of the pan to unstick any rice. Close and lock the lid.
2. Turn the heat up to high. When the cooker reaches high pressure, lower the heat to the minimum needed to maintain pressure. Pressure cook for 5–7 minutes at high pressure.
3. Open with the natural release method (see Chapter 1).
4. Fluff with a fork and serve.

PER SERVING | Calories: 298 | Fat: 3.5 g | Protein: 8 g | Sodium: 548 mg | Fiber: 3 g | Carbohydrates: 59 g

Three-Grain Rice Pilaf

Millet is a good source of protein and B vitamins.

INGREDIENTS | SERVES 6

1 tablespoon olive oil

1 scallion, sliced

1 cup jasmine rice

½ cup millet

½ cup quinoa

2½ cups Vegetable Stock (see recipe in Chapter 4)

1 teaspoon salt

¼ teaspoon pepper

1. Heat olive oil in an uncovered pressure cooker over medium heat. Sauté the scallion for 2–3 minutes. Add rice, millet, and quinoa and sauté for another 2 minutes. Add the stock. Close and lock the lid.
2. Turn the heat up to high. When the cooker reaches pressure, lower the heat to the minimum needed to maintain pressure. Cook for 2 minutes at high pressure.
3. Open with the natural release method (see Chapter 1).
4. Season with salt and pepper and fluff with a fork before serving.

PER SERVING | Calories: 253 | Fat: 4 g | Protein: 6 g | Sodium: 625 mg | Fiber: 2.8 g | Carbohydrates: 47 g

Arborio Rice

This is a basic recipe to substitute for boiled rice. It can be used in rice salads or for stuffing vegetables.

INGREDIENTS | SERVES 6

2 cups arborio rice, not rinsed

3 cups water

1 tablespoon vegetable oil

No-Rinse Rice

Italian rice is never rinsed because you want to save the starches and nutrients for a creamy result. The rice is dried using machinery, coated with extra nutrients—including the amino acid L-lysinea, calcium, iron, and vitamins A, B1, B2, C, and D—and vacuum-packed in plastic bricks. Don't rinse these extra nutrients away!

1. Add rice, water, and oil to the pressure cooker. Close and lock the lid.
2. Turn the heat up to high. When the cooker reaches pressure, lower the heat to the minimum needed to maintain pressure. Cook for 5 minutes at high pressure.
3. Open with the natural release method (see Chapter 1).
4. Fluff with a fork and use in your favorite recipe.

PER SERVING | Calories: 258 | Fat: 2.6 g | Protein: 4 g | Sodium: 5 mg | Fiber: 1.8 g | Carbohydrates: 52 g

Italian Rice Salad

A refreshing summer treat.

INGREDIENTS | SERVES 12

4 cups cooked Arborio Rice (see recipe in this chapter), rinsed in cold water to stop cooking

2 medium tomatoes, chopped

3 hard-boiled eggs (2 chopped and 1 wedged for decoration)

1 cup chopped olives (black or green)

1 bunch basil, chopped

4 ounces ham, cubed

12 ounces mozzarella, cubed

3 tablespoons capers, rinsed

2 tablespoons olive oil

1 teaspoon salt

1. In a large bowl, mix the rice and all of the remaining ingredients. Serve at room temperature or chilled.

PER SERVING | Calories: 235 | Fat: 11 g | Protein: 12 g | Sodium: 648 mg | Fiber: 0.5 g | Carbohydrates: 20 g

Basic White Risotto

This risotto is perfect as a side dish, or as a pillow under fish, meat, or veggies.

INGREDIENTS | SERVES 6

1 tablespoon olive oil

1 onion, finely chopped

¼ teaspoon salt

2 cups arborio rice

¼ cup white wine

4 cups Vegetable Stock (see recipe in Chapter 4)

1 tablespoon butter

2 tablespoons grated Parmigiano-Reggiano cheese

Out of Wine?

Risotto requires you to use an acid to give the dish a bit of tang. Traditionally, wine is used for this purpose, but suitable substitutes include white wine vinegar, white balsamic vinegar, tomato juice, or unsweetened citrus juice.

1. Heat olive oil in an uncovered pressure cooker over medium heat. Add onion and salt and sauté until softened (about 5 minutes). Add the rice and toast the grains (about 3 minutes).
2. Deglaze the pan with wine and wait until it is fully absorbed into the rice or evaporated. Add the stock, stirring and scraping the bottom to dislodge any rice that may have attached itself to the bottom of the cooker. Close and lock the lid.
3. Turn the heat up to high. When the cooker reaches pressure, lower the heat to the minimum needed to maintain pressure. Cook for 7–9 minutes at high pressure.
4. When time is up, open the pressure cooker by releasing pressure.
5. Stir in the butter and cheese and serve.

PER SERVING | Calories: 307 | Fat: 5 g | Protein: 5.3 g | Sodium: 498 mg | Fiber: 2 g | Carbohydrates: 56 g

Zucchini Risotto

Whenever you make a risotto with very "wet" veggies, you either need to evaporate most of their liquid before pressure cooking or decrease the liquid for the whole recipe accordingly.

INGREDIENTS | SERVES 6

2 tablespoons extra-virgin olive oil, divided

1 onion, finely chopped

2 medium zucchini, diced

¼ teaspoon salt

2 cups arborio rice

¼ cup lemon juice

3½ cups Vegetable Stock (see recipe in Chapter 4)

2 tablespoons grated Pecorino Romano cheese

1 sprig basil, finely chopped

1. Heat 1 tablespoon olive oil in an uncovered pressure cooker over medium heat. Add onion, zucchini, and salt and sauté together until the zucchini are golden (about 8–10 minutes). Add the rice and toast the grains (about 3 minutes).
2. Deglaze the pan with lemon juice and wait until it is fully absorbed into the rice or evaporated. Add the stock, stirring and scraping the bottom to dislodge any rice that may have attached itself to the bottom of the cooker. Close and lock the lid.
3. Turn the heat up to high. When the cooker reaches pressure, lower the heat to the minimum needed to maintain pressure. Cook for 7–9 minutes at high pressure.
4. When time is up, open the pressure cooker by releasing pressure.
5. Stir in 1 tablespoon olive oil, cheese, and basil before serving.

PER SERVING | Calories: 309 | Fat: 5.5 g | Protein: 5.7 g | Sodium: 459 mg | Fiber: 2.8 g | Carbohydrates: 58 g

Tomato Risotto

This classic recipe can be made with fresh or canned tomatoes. Using canned tomatoes makes it an easy meal that can be tossed together with pantry ingredients.

INGREDIENTS | SERVES 6

1 tablespoon olive oil

3 garlic cloves, finely chopped

¼ teaspoon salt

2 cups arborio rice

2 cups chopped tomatoes

2½ cups Vegetable Stock (see recipe in Chapter 4)

1 tablespoon butter

2 tablespoons grated Parmigiano-Reggiano cheese

1. Heat olive oil in an uncovered pressure cooker over medium heat. Add the garlic and salt and sauté until the garlic begins to turn golden (about 1 minute). Add the rice and toast the grains (about 3 minutes).
2. Deglaze the pan with the tomatoes and vegetable stock, stirring and scraping the bottom to dislodge any rice that may have attached itself to the bottom of the cooker. Close and lock the lid.
3. Turn the heat up to high. When the cooker reaches pressure, lower the heat to the minimum needed to maintain pressure. Cook for 7–9 minutes at high pressure.
4. When time is up, open the pressure cooker by releasing pressure.
5. Stir in the butter and cheese and serve.

PER SERVING | Calories: 299 | Fat: 5 g | Protein: 6 g | Sodium: 363 mg | Fiber: 2.5 g | Carbohydrates: 56 g

Brown Rice

You can make this health food staple even more quickly thanks to the magic of pressure cooking.

INGREDIENTS | SERVES 6

2 cups brown rice, rinsed

2¾ cups water

1 tablespoon vegetable oil

Soaking Reduces Time, But . . .

According to Jill Nussinow, also known as The Veggie Queen (www.theveggiequeen.com), brown rice that has been soaked pressure cooks faster than dry brown rice. However, calculating the cooking time becomes tricky. Since pressure cooking the rice is so fast, anyway, she recommends skipping the soaking step.

1. Add rice, water, and oil to the pressure cooker. Close and lock the lid.
2. Turn the heat up to high. When the cooker reaches pressure, lower the heat to the minimum needed to maintain pressure. Cook for 20–22 minutes at high pressure.
3. Open with the natural release method (see Chapter 1).
4. Fluff with a fork and serve.

PER SERVING | Calories: 92 | Fat: 2.8 g | Protein: 1.5 g | Sodium: 4 mg | Fiber: 1 g | Carbohydrates: 15 g

Peppery Brown Rice Risotto

The white grape juice concentrate gives the rice a touch of sweetness. If you'd rather keep it completely savory, omit the white grape juice concentrate and instead use ¼ cup white wine and 2½ cups water.

INGREDIENTS | SERVES 6

1 tablespoon butter

2 medium leeks, chopped

1 small fennel bulb, trimmed and chopped

2 cups short-grain brown rice, rinsed and drained

2¾ cups water

1 tablespoon frozen white grape juice concentrate

½ cup grated Fontina cheese

1 teaspoon salt

1½ teaspoons freshly ground black pepper

1. Heat butter in an uncovered pressure cooker over medium heat. Sauté leeks and fennel until the leeks begin to wilt (about 2 minutes). Add the rice and toast the grains (about 3 minutes), then add the water and juice. Close and lock the lid.
2. Turn the heat up to high. When the cooker reaches pressure, lower the heat to the minimum needed to maintain pressure. Cook for 18–20 minutes at high pressure.
3. Open with the natural release method (see Chapter 1).
4. Fluff the rice with a fork. Stir in the cheese, salt, and pepper before serving.

PER SERVING | Calories: 154 | Fat: 5 g | Protein: 5 g | Sodium: 486 mg | Fiber: 2.5 g | Carbohydrates: 22 g

Brown Rice with Peanuts

Peanuts harmonize with the nutty flavor of brown rice to make a very special dish.

INGREDIENTS | SERVES 6

1 tablespoon peanut oil
1 onion, chopped
2 cups brown rice
¼ teaspoon cumin
1 cup salted and roasted peanuts
2¾ cups water
1 tablespoon lemon juice
1 green onion, chopped

To Rinse or Not to Rinse . . .

There is no particular need to rinse brown rice since it is still in the grain and starch has not yet built up on the surface from rubbing the white rice grains together during processing, handling, and transportation. Whether you want to include the extra step is up to you!

1. Heat oil in an uncovered pressure cooker over medium heat. Sauté onions until they begin to soften (about 5 minutes). Add the rice and toast the grains (about 3 minutes), then add the cumin, peanuts, and water. Close and lock the lid.
2. Turn the heat up to high. When the cooker reaches pressure, lower the heat to the minimum needed to maintain pressure. Cook for 18–20 minutes at high pressure.
3. Open with the natural release method (see Chapter 1).
4. Sprinkle with lemon juice and fluff the rice with a fork. Top with green onion before serving.

PER SERVING | Calories: 238 | Fat: 14 g | Protein: 8 g | Sodium: 109 mg | Fiber: 3.5 g | Carbohydrates: 20 g

Roasted Corn and Brown Rice

*You can add ½ cup roughly chopped shrimp, diced chicken,
or ground sausage to this wonderfully simple dish.*

INGREDIENTS | SERVES 6

2 cups corn kernels, fresh or frozen

1 tablespoon olive oil

1 yellow onion, chopped

3 cloves garlic, chopped

1 cup long-grain brown rice

2 cups Vegetable Stock (see recipe in Chapter 4)

½ teaspoon salt

¼ teaspoon pepper

2 green onions, chopped

1 (3-ounce) package cream cheese, cut into cubes

Roasting Veggies

Roasting vegetables gives them a richer flavor that permeates the entire dish. Use roasted vegetables for simple salads, in soups, on pizzas, or for almost any recipe with vegetables.

1. Preheat oven to 400°F. Place corn on parchment-lined baking sheet and place in oven for 20 minutes. Let cool and set aside.

2. Heat olive oil in an uncovered pressure cooker over medium heat. Sauté onion, garlic, and rice until the onion begins to soften (about 5 minutes). Add corn, stock, salt, and pepper. Close and lock the lid.

3. Turn the heat up to high. When the cooker reaches pressure, lower the heat to the minimum needed to maintain pressure. Cook for 18–20 minutes at high pressure.

4. Open with the natural release method (see Chapter 1).

5. Sprinkle with green onion and cream cheese cubes before serving.

PER SERVING | Calories: 161 | Fat: 8 g | Protein: 3 g | Sodium: 600 mg | Fiber: 2 g | Carbohydrates: 21 g

Wild Rice

Wild rice is actually a type of grass, not rice, that grows in marshlands. Most wild rice has a nutty flavor, but it varies slightly depending on the type.

INGREDIENTS | SERVES 6

2 cups wild rice, rinsed

5 cups water

1 tablespoon vegetable oil

1. Add the rice, water, and oil to the pressure cooker. Close and lock the lid.
2. Turn the heat up to high. When the cooker reaches pressure, lower the heat to the minimum needed to maintain pressure. Cook for 22–25 minutes at high pressure.
3. Open with the natural release method (see Chapter 1).
4. Fluff with a fork and serve.

PER SERVING | Calories: 210 | Fat: 2.8 g | Protein: 8 g | Sodium: 9 mg | Fiber: 3 g | Carbohydrates: 39 g

Lemon Brown and Wild Rice

Lemon brings a bright note and counterpoint to this naturally nutty-tasting combination.

INGREDIENTS | SERVES 6

1 cup wild rice, rinsed

1 cup brown rice, rinsed

4 cups water

Juice and zest of 1 lemon

1 teaspoon salt

1 tablespoon vegetable oil

1. Add wild and brown rice, water, lemon zest, salt, and oil to the pressure cooker. Close and lock the lid.
2. Turn the heat up to high. When the cooker reaches pressure, lower the heat to the minimum needed to maintain pressure. Cook for 22–25 minutes at high pressure.
3. Open with the natural release method (see Chapter 1).
4. Fluff with a fork and sprinkle with lemon juice before serving.

PER SERVING | Calories: 151 | Fat: 3 g | Protein: 4.5 g | Sodium: 395 mg | Fiber: 2 g | Carbohydrates: 27 g

Amaranth

Amaranth has been cultivated in the Americas for about 8,000 years. It was a staple food (like corn) of the Aztecs, ancient Mexican peoples.

INGREDIENTS | SERVES 6

2 cups amaranth

4 cups water

1 tablespoon vegetable oil

1. Add amaranth, water, and oil to the pressure cooker. Close and lock the lid.
2. Turn the heat up to high. When the cooker reaches pressure, lower the heat to the minimum needed to maintain pressure. Cook for 3 minutes at high pressure.
3. Open with the natural release method (see Chapter 1).
4. Stir well before serving.

PER SERVING | Calories: 230 | Fat: 3 g | Protein: 8 g | Sodium: 10 mg | Fiber: 5 g | Carbohydrates: 45 g

Whole Barley

According to www.wholegrainscouncil.org, barley has the highest amount of fiber of all the whole grains, with 17–30 percent of fiber, depending on the variety! Compare that with brown rice, which contains 3.5 percent fiber, corn with 7 percent, oats with 10 percent, and wheat 12 percent!

INGREDIENTS | SERVES 6

1½ cups whole barley, rinsed and soaked

4½ cups water

1 tablespoon vegetable oil

Soaking Barley

Rinse barley under cold water in a strainer. Then lower the strainer into a larger bowl full of water. Soak for 15–20 minutes. When it's ready to use, lift and lightly shake the strainer to remove excess water.

1. Add barley, water, and oil to the pressure cooker. Close and lock the lid.
2. Turn the heat up to high. When the cooker reaches pressure, lower the heat to the minimum needed to maintain pressure. Cook for 30–35 minutes at high pressure.
3. Open with the natural release method (see Chapter 1).
4. Fluff with a fork and serve.

PER SERVING | Calories: 201 | Fat: 3 g | Protein: 5 g | Sodium: 10 mg | Fiber: 8 g | Carbohydrates: 40 g

Pearl Barley

Pearl barley is whole barley that has had part of its outer hull removed.
It's less nutritious than whole, but much faster to cook.

INGREDIENTS | SERVES 6

1½ cups pearl barley, rinsed

3¾ cups water

1 tablespoon vegetable oil

1. Add barely, water, and oil to the pressure cooker. Close and lock the lid.
2. Turn the heat up to high. When the cooker reaches pressure, lower the heat to the minimum needed to maintain pressure. Cook for 18–20 minutes at high pressure.
3. Open with the natural release method (see Chapter 1).
4. Fluff with a fork and serve.

PER SERVING | Calories: 196 | Fat: 2.5 g | Protein: 5 g | Sodium: 9 mg | Fiber: 7 g | Carbohydrates: 38 g

Barley and Gorgonzola Risotto

Although not gluten-free, barley's round, always al dente grains make it a perfect substitute for rice in risotto. Do not add additional salt without tasting, as Gorgonzola can be quite salty.

INGREDIENTS | SERVES 6

1 tablespoon olive oil

1 sprig sage, chopped

1 onion, chopped

1 cup pearl barley

¼ cup dry white wine

3½ cups Vegetable Stock (see recipe in Chapter 4)

6 ounces sharp Gorgonzola cheese, cubed

2 tablespoons grated Parmigiano-Reggiano cheese

Orzotto

In Italy, barley is called orzo and a barley risotto is called orzotto.

1. Heat oil in an uncovered pressure cooker over medium heat. Add sage and onion and sauté about 5 minutes. Add barley and toast the grains (about 3 minutes).
2. Deglaze the pan with wine and wait until it is fully absorbed into the rice or evaporated. Then add the stock, stirring and scraping the bottom to dislodge any barley that may have attached itself to the bottom of the cooker. Close and lock the lid.
3. Turn the heat up to high. When the cooker reaches pressure, lower the heat to the minimum needed to maintain pressure. Cook for 18–20 minutes at high pressure.
4. Open the pressure cooker by releasing pressure. Stir in the cheeses.

PER SERVING | Calories: 272 | Fat: 11 g | Protein: 10 g | Sodium: 863 mg | Fiber: 5.5 g | Carbohydrates: 30 g

Summer Barley Caprese Salad

An easy summer salad!

INGREDIENTS | SERVES 6

1 recipe Pearl Barley (see recipe in this chapter)

3 ripe tomatoes, chopped

8 ounces mozzarella cheese, diced

1 bunch fresh basil, chopped

2 tablespoons extra-virgin olive oil

1 teaspoon sea salt

½ teaspoon black pepper

1. Mix all of the ingredients and serve at room temperature or chilled.

PER SERVING | Calories: 360 | Fat: 14 g | Protein: 15 g | Sodium: 597 mg | Fiber: 8.5 g | Carbohydrates: 42 g

Barley and Tuna Salad

During summer in Italy, when appetites are light, this salad is often eaten as a one-pot meal.

INGREDIENTS | SERVES 6

1 recipe Pearl Barley (see recipe in this chapter)

8 ounces high-quality canned tuna in olive oil, drained

3 tablespoons capers, drained

1 bunch fresh parsley, chopped

1 teaspoon sea salt

½ teaspoon black pepper

1. Mix all of the ingredients and serve at room temperature or chilled.

PER SERVING | Calories: 271 | Fat: 6 g | Protein: 16 g | Sodium: 657 mg | Fiber: 8 g | Carbohydrates: 39 g

Buckwheat

Natural buckwheat often looks light green. When toasted, buckwheat groats are often brown and called kasha.

INGREDIENTS | SERVES 6

2 cups buckwheat
3½ cups water
1 tablespoon vegetable oil

1. Add buckwheat, water, and oil to the pressure cooker. Close and lock the lid.
2. Turn the heat up to high. When the cooker reaches pressure, lower the heat to the minimum needed to maintain pressure. Cook for 3 minutes at high pressure.
3. Open with the natural release method (see Chapter 1).
4. Fluff with a fork and serve.

PER SERVING | Calories: 209 | Fat: 3.5 g | Protein: 6.5 g | Sodium: 10 mg | Fiber: 5.6 g | Carbohydrates: 40 g

Bulgur

Bulgur is the result of passing whole wheat berries between two rollers to crack them, a process that reduces their cooking time considerably.

INGREDIENTS | SERVES 6

1 cup bulgur
3 cups water
1 tablespoon vegetable oil

1. Add bulgur, water, and oil to the pressure cooker. Close and lock the lid.
2. Turn the heat up to high. When the cooker reaches pressure, lower the heat to the minimum needed to maintain pressure. Cook for 8–10 minutes at high pressure.
3. Open with the natural release method (see Chapter 1).
4. Fluff with a fork and serve.

PER SERVING | Calories: 99 | Fat: 2.5 g | Protein: 3 g | Sodium: 7.5 mg | Fiber: 4 g | Carbohydrates: 17 g

Bulgur Stuffing

Bulgur is a healthier alternative to white bread in stuffing.

INGREDIENTS | SERVES 6

2 tablespoons butter

½ onion, diced

½ cup diced celery

½ cup chopped mushrooms

½ teaspoon dried thyme

½ teaspoon dried sage

½ teaspoon salt

¾ teaspoon black pepper

1 cup bulgur

3 cups Vegetable Stock (see recipe in Chapter 4)

Tasty Substitutions

Turn this dish into a cranberry stuffing by adding dried cranberries and chopped pecan pieces instead of the mushrooms and celery.

1. Heat butter in an uncovered pressure cooker over medium heat. Sauté onion and celery until soft (about 5 minutes). Add the mushrooms, thyme, sage, salt, and pepper, and sauté for an additional 2 minutes. Add the bulgur and stock to the pressure cooker. Close and lock the lid.
2. Turn the heat up to high. When the cooker reaches pressure, lower the heat to the minimum needed to maintain pressure. Cook for 9 minutes at high pressure.
3. Open with the natural release method (see Chapter 1).
4. Stir well and serve.

PER SERVING | Calories: 127 | Fat: 4 g | Protein: 3.4 g | Sodium: 484 mg | Fiber: 4.7 g | Carbohydrates: 20 g

Cracked Wheat and Chickpea Pilaf with Lemon

The two major ingredients in this dish sometimes go by other names: cracked wheat is just uncooked bulgur, while chickpeas are often referred to as garbanzo beans. No matter what you call them, when mixed together they create a tasty and satisfying meal.

INGREDIENTS | SERVES 6

1 tablespoon vegetable oil

1 onion, chopped

1 cup bulgur

3 cups Vegetable Stock (see recipe in Chapter 4)

1 cup dry chickpeas, soaked overnight and drained

1 bunch parsley, finely chopped (leaves and stems)

Juice of 1 lemon

1 teaspoon salt

1. Heat oil in an uncovered pressure cooker over medium heat. Sauté onion until softened (about 5 minutes). Add the bulgur and cover the grains in oil. Next add the stock and chickpeas. Close and lock the lid.
2. Turn the heat up to high. When the cooker reaches pressure, lower the heat to the minimum needed to maintain pressure. Cook for 13 minutes at high pressure.
3. Open with the natural release method (see Chapter 1).
4. Sprinkle with parsley, lemon juice, and salt. Mix well and serve.

PER SERVING | Calories: 157 | Fat: 3.3 g | Protein: 5.5 g | Sodium: 674 mg | Fiber: 6.6 g | Carbohydrates: 28 g

Pearled Farro

Like pearl barley, pearled farro is a whole grain that has had only part of the outer shell removed to hasten cooking time.

INGREDIENTS | SERVES 6

2 cups pearled farro

4 cups water

1 tablespoon vegetable oil

1. Add farro, water, and oil to the pressure cooker. Close and lock the lid.
2. Turn the heat up to high. When the cooker reaches pressure, lower the heat to the minimum needed to maintain pressure. Cook for 7–9 minutes at high pressure.
3. Open with the natural release method (see Chapter 1).
4. Fluff with a fork and serve.

PER SERVING ⅓ CUP | Calories: 113 | Fat: 1 g | Protein: 4 g | Sodium: 0 mg | Fiber: 3 g | Carbohydrates: 23 g

Farro and Dried Porcini Mushroom Pilaf

In Italy, a risotto made from farro is called farrotto. Farrotto is very rich in taste and is nutritious as well. There is no need to pre-soak the porcini; they rehydrate quickly in the pressure cooker.

INGREDIENTS | SERVES 6

1 tablespoon olive oil

1 onion, chopped

1 teaspoon chopped, fresh sage

1 teaspoon chopped, fresh thyme

1½ cups pearled farro

¼ cup red wine

3 cups Vegetable Stock (see recipe in Chapter 4)

1 cup crushed, dried porcini mushrooms

1. Heat olive oil in an uncovered pressure cooker over medium heat. Add onion, sage, and thyme and sauté until softened (about 5 minutes). Add the farro and toast the grains (about 3 minutes).
2. Deglaze the pan with wine and wait until it is fully absorbed into the rice or evaporated. Add the stock and porcini, stirring and scraping the bottom to dislodge any farro that may have attached itself to the bottom of the cooker. Close and lock the lid.
3. Turn the heat up to high. When the cooker reaches pressure, lower the heat to the minimum needed to maintain pressure. Cook for 7–9 minutes at high pressure.
4. Open the pressure cooker by releasing pressure. Serve with a sprinkling of your favorite cheese, if desired.

PER SERVING | Calories: 200 | Fat: 4 g | Protein: 5 g | Sodium: 278 mg | Fiber: 3.5 g | Carbohydrates: 31 g

Steel-Cut Oats

Steel-cut oats are whole grain groats that have been cut into only two or three pieces. They are high in B vitamins, calcium, protein, and fiber, and are sometimes referred to as Irish oatmeal.

INGREDIENTS | SERVES 2

4 cups water, divided

1 cup steel-cut oats, toasted

1 tablespoon butter

⅛ teaspoon salt

Toasting Steel-Cut Oats

Preheat the oven to 300°F. Place the steel-cut oats on a baking sheet. Bake for 20 minutes. Store toasted steel-cut oats in a covered container in a cool place. Toasting steel-cut oats will enhance the flavor and allow them to cook in half the time.

1. Place 1 cup water in the pressure cooker and add the steamer basket.
2. In a metal bowl that will fit inside the pressure cooker, add the oats, butter, salt, and 3 cups water.
3. Lower the uncovered bowl into the pressure cooker using a foil sling. Close and lock the lid.
4. Turn the heat up to high. When the cooker reaches pressure, lower the heat to the minimum needed to maintain pressure. Cook for 3–5 minutes at high pressure.
5. Open with the natural release method (see Chapter 1).
6. Spoon the cooked oats into bowls and season as you would regular oatmeal.

PER SERVING | Calories: 204 | Fat: 8 g | Protein: 5 g | Sodium: 150 mg | Fiber: 4 g | Carbohydrates: 27 g

Irish Oatmeal and Fruit

This recipe is very flexible and is open to an infinite amount of substitutions. Replace dried cranberries with raisins or snipped dried apricots. You can also replace the maple syrup with brown sugar. You can add a handful of chopped nuts such as walnuts or pecans and finish with a twirl of milk, half-and-half, or heavy cream!

INGREDIENTS | SERVES 2

3 cups water, divided

1 cup toasted steel-cut oats

2 teaspoons butter

1 cup apple juice

1 tablespoon dried cranberries

1 tablespoon maple syrup

¼ teaspoon ground cinnamon

⅛ teaspoon salt

1. Place 1 cup water in the pressure cooker and add the steamer basket.
2. In a metal bowl that will fit inside the pressure cooker, add the oats, butter, apple juice, cranberries, maple syrup, cinnamon, salt, and 2 cups water.
3. Lower the bowl into the pressure cooker using a foil sling. Close and lock the lid.
4. Turn the heat up to high. When the cooker reaches pressure, lower the heat to the minimum needed to maintain pressure. Cook for 3–5 minutes at high pressure.
5. Open with the natural release method (see Chapter 1).
6. Spoon the cooked oats into bowls and serve.

PER SERVING | Calories: 283 | Fat: 6 g | Protein: 5.5 g | Sodium: 9 mg | Fiber: 5 g | Carbohydrates: 51 g

Polenta

*Rustic ground polenta can cook as quickly as instant polenta,
but it will have a deeper flavor and more creaminess.*

INGREDIENTS | SERVES 8

8 cups water

2 teaspoons salt

2 tablespoons olive oil

2 cups polenta (not instant polenta)

Scorch It!

You can make perfect polenta in the pressure cooker, but it will scorch and burn a bit on the base. This is completely normal and even harks back to the flavor of classic polenta prepared in a copper cauldron over an open fire.

1. Add water, salt, and olive oil to uncovered pressure cooker. On high heat, bring the water to a boil. Drizzle in the polenta while stirring clockwise to prevent lumps from forming. As soon as all has been added, quickly close and lock the lid.

2. Keep the heat on high. When the cooker reaches pressure, lower the heat to the minimum needed to maintain pressure. Cook for 7–9 minutes at high pressure.

3. When time is up, open the pressure cooker by releasing pressure.

4. Pour polenta out of the pressure cooker into individual bowls or serving dish (the polenta sets quickly so move fast!).

PER SERVING | Calories: 176 | Fat: 4 g | Protein: 3 g | Sodium: 582 mg | Fiber: 1 g | Carbohydrates: 31 g

Three Cheese Polenta

This polenta is less firm than the classic dish. It is very creamy and rich.

INGREDIENTS | SERVES 8

8 cups Vegetable Stock (see recipe in Chapter 4)

2 tablespoons butter

2 cups polenta (not instant polenta)

3 ounces grated Parmigiano-Reggiano cheese

3 ounces diced Emmental (Swiss) cheese

3 ounces fresh goat cheese, diced

1. Add stock and butter to uncovered pressure cooker. Over high heat, bring the water to a boil. Drizzle in the polenta while stirring clockwise to prevent lumps from forming. As soon as all has been added, quickly close and lock the lid.
2. Keep the heat on high. When the cooker reaches pressure, lower the heat to the minimum needed to maintain pressure. Cook for 7–9 minutes at high pressure.
3. Open the pressure cooker by releasing pressure.
4. Mix in the three cheeses, then pour polenta into a serving dish.

PER SERVING | Calories: 316 | Fat: 13 g | Protein: 13 g | Sodium: 760 mg | Fiber: 1.6 g | Carbohydrates: 35 g

Fresh Herb Polenta

This side dish is an aromatic counterpoint to boiled or steamed meats.

INGREDIENTS | SERVES 8

8 cups water

2 teaspoons salt

2 tablespoons olive oil

2 cups polenta (not instant polenta)

1 bunch parsley, chopped

1 bunch sage, chopped

1 bunch thyme, chopped

1. Add water, salt, and olive oil to uncovered pressure cooker. Over high heat, bring the water to a boil. Drizzle in the polenta while stirring clockwise to prevent lumps from forming. As soon as all the polenta has been added, quickly close and lock the lid.
2. Keep the heat on high. When the cooker reaches pressure, lower the heat to the minimum needed to maintain pressure. Cook for 7–9 minutes at high pressure.
3. Open the pressure cooker by releasing pressure.
4. Stir in parsley, sage, and thyme. Immediately pour the polenta out of the pressure cooker and into individual bowls or serving dish.

PER SERVING | Calories: 176 | Fat: 4 g | Protein: 3 g | Sodium: 582 mg | Fiber: 1.5 g | Carbohydrates: 31 g

Quinoa

Quinoa is not exactly a grain; it's a seed. It already cooks quickly on its own, in 20 minutes, but cooking it under pressure makes the whole procedure quick and painless.

INGREDIENTS | SERVES 6

2 cups quinoa
3 cups water
⅛ teaspoon salt

Always Rinse Quinoa Well

Quinoa has a naturally produced residue, saponin, that keeps insects from consuming it. It is not very tasty to humans, either. Rinse the quinoa very well under running water to remove all of the residue prior to cooking.

1. Add all of the ingredients to the pressure cooker. Close and lock the lid.
2. Turn the heat up to high. When the cooker reaches pressure, lower the heat to the minimum needed to maintain pressure. Cook for 1 minute at high pressure.
3. Open with the natural release method (see Chapter 1).
4. Fluff with a fork and serve.

PER SERVING | Calories: 208 | Fat: 3 g | Protein: 8 g | Sodium: 55 mg | Fiber: 4 g | Carbohydrates: 36 g

Quinoa and Artichoke Hearts Salad

Use either, black, white, or rainbow quinoa for this. The black version has more impact.

INGREDIENTS | SERVES 8

1 recipe Quinoa (see recipe above)
Juice and zest of 2 limes
1 bunch cilantro (or parsley), roughly chopped
2 large Roma tomatoes, finely diced
2 yellow bell peppers, finely diced
1 large cucumber, seeded and finely diced

1. In a mixing bowl mix the quinoa with the rest of the ingredients. Serve at room temperature or chilled.

PER SERVING | Calories: 168 | Fat: 2.5 g | Protein: 6.5 g | Sodium: 5 mg | Fiber: 4 g | Carbohydrates: 30 g

Wheat Berries

Wheat berries are the entire kernel of the wheat and can be used for both savory and sweet dishes—even as a breakfast porridge!

INGREDIENTS | SERVES 6

2 cups wheat berries

3 cups water

2 tablespoons vegetable oil

1. Add the wheat berries, water, and oil to the pressure cooker. Close and lock the lid.
2. Turn the heat up to high. When the cooker reaches pressure, lower the heat to the minimum needed to maintain pressure. Cook for 30–40 minutes at high pressure.
3. Open with the natural release method (see Chapter 1).
4. Fluff with a fork and serve.

PER SERVING | Calories: 113 | Fat: 5 g | Protein: 1.5 g | Sodium: 4 mg | Fiber: 1 g | Carbohydrates: 15 g

Wheat Berry Salad

Wheat berries make excellent salads. They remain "al dente" and give the salad a nice texture.

INGREDIENTS | SERVES 8

1½ teaspoons Dijon mustard

1 teaspoon sugar

1 teaspoon sea salt

½ teaspoon freshly ground black pepper

¼ cup white wine vinegar

½ cup extra-virgin olive oil

½ small red onion, peeled and diced

1 recipe Wheat Berries (see recipe in this chapter)

1⅓ cups frozen corn, thawed

1 medium zucchini, peeled, grated, and drained

2 stalks celery, finely diced

1 red bell pepper, seeded and diced

4 green onions, diced

¼ cup diced, sun-dried tomatoes

¼ cup fresh Italian flat-leaf parsley, chopped

1. Make the dressing by puréeing the mustard, sugar, salt, pepper, vinegar, olive oil, and red onion in a food processor or blender. Stir ½ cup dressing into the cooled wheat berries.
2. Toss the seasoned wheat berries with remaining ingredients. Taste for seasoning and add additional salt, pepper, or dressing if needed. Cover and refrigerate leftover dressing for up to 3 days.

PER SERVING | Calories: 244 | Fat: 14 g | Protein: 5 g | Sodium: 320 mg | Fiber: 5 g | Carbohydrates: 26 g

CHAPTER 13

Condiments and Preserves

Fresh Cranberry Sauce
235

Barbecue Sauce with Smoked
Paprika and Molasses
236

Sweet Onion Relish
237

Mango Chutney
238

Tomato Chutney with Fresh
Ginger Root
239

Green Tomato Chutney
240

Dried Plum Sauce
240

Rainbow Bell Pepper Marmalade
241

Dried Apricot Preserves
242

Blueberry Jam
243

Strawberry Jam
244

Fresh Apricot Jam
245

Blackberry Jam
246

Peach Jam
247

Wild Berry Black Currant Jam
248

Mixed-Citrus Marmalade
249

Lemon Marmalade
250

Peach-Apricot Preserves with
Toasted Almonds
251

Vanilla-Spice Pear Butter
252

Cinnamon Apple Butter
253

Lemon Curd
254

Fresh Cranberry Sauce

You can make this cranberry sauce several days in advance, store it in the refrigerator, and then bring it back to temperature on the stove. For additional flavor, stir in some orange liqueur, bourbon, or brandy.

INGREDIENTS | SERVES 6

1 (12-ounce) bag fresh cranberries

1 cup sugar

½ cup water

⅛ teaspoon salt

1 tablespoon frozen orange juice concentrate

¼ teaspoon cinnamon

⅛ teaspoon ground cloves

Dried Cranberries

Cranberries are about 80 percent water, so you can make this recipe with 4 ounces of dried cranberries and 1 cup of water in place of the fresh ones.

1. Rinse and drain the cranberries. Remove and discard any stems or blemished cranberries. Add the cranberries to the pressure cooker along with the sugar, water, and salt. Close and lock the lid.

2. Turn the heat up to high. When the cooker reaches pressure, lower the heat to the minimum needed to maintain pressure. Cook for 8–10 minutes at high pressure.

3. Open with the natural release method (see Chapter 1).

4. Add the orange juice concentrate and stir well, breaking the cranberries apart with a spoon or mashing them slightly with a potato masher.

5. Stir in cinnamon and cloves. Serve warm or chilled.

PER SERVING (½ CUP) | Calories: 160 | Fat: 0 g | Protein: 0.3 g | Sodium: 51 mg | Fiber: 2.5 g | Carbohydrates: 41 g

Barbecue Sauce with Smoked Paprika and Molasses

Pan-toasting the smoked paprika before you add the other ingredients will intensify its smoky flavor.

INGREDIENTS | YIELDS 5 CUPS

2 tablespoons smoked paprika

2 (6-ounce) cans tomato paste

¾ cup white vinegar

4 tablespoons brown sugar

5 teaspoons garlic powder

2 tablespoons onion powder

1 teaspoon salt

1 teaspoon molasses

2½ cups water

2 teaspoons cayenne pepper

1½ teaspoons celery seed

1 teaspoon celery salt

1 teaspoon ground cumin

2 teaspoons mustard powder

1 teaspoon black pepper

¼ teaspoon ground ginger

½ teaspoon ground allspice

¼ teaspoon dried thyme

1. Add the smoked paprika to the pressure cooker. Lightly toast it over medium heat until it begins to release its smoky fragrance, about 1 minute. Stir in the remaining ingredients. Close and lock the lid.
2. Turn the heat up to high. When the cooker reaches pressure, lower the heat to the minimum needed to maintain pressure. Cook for 8–10 minutes at high pressure.
3. Open with the natural release method (see Chapter 1).
4. Allow sauce to cool, then refrigerate in a covered container for up to a week, or freeze until needed.

PER SERVING (1 TABLESPOON) | Calories: 20 | Fat: 0.2 g | Protein: 0.5 g | Sodium: 189 mg | Fiber: 0.5 g | Carbohydrates: 4 g

Ketchup Base

You can use ketchup as a jumping off point for making barbecue sauce, but this recipe lets you make it from scratch so that you can carefully control all of the ingredients.

Sweet Onion Relish

Use sweet onions like Vidalia, Candy, First Edition, Maui, or Walla Walla for this relish.

INGREDIENTS | YIELDS 4 CUPS

4 medium sweet onions

2¾ cups water, divided

¾ cup golden raisins

1 cup honey

1 tablespoon cider vinegar

⅛ teaspoon salt

1. Peel and thinly slice onions using a mandoline slicer. Put them in the pressure cooker and pour in about 2 cups water to cover. Bring to a boil over high heat and drain immediately, discarding the water.
2. Return onions to pressure cooker and stir in raisins, honey, vinegar, and salt until honey is evenly distributed throughout onion slices. Pour in ¾ cups of water. Close and lock the lid.
3. Turn the heat up to high. When the cooker reaches pressure, lower the heat to the minimum needed to maintain pressure. Cook for 5 minutes at high pressure.
4. When time is up, open the pressure cooker by releasing pressure.
5. Reduce the liquid in the uncovered cooker over low heat until the contents reach "relish" consistency (about 5 minutes).
6. Serve warm or store in a covered container in the refrigerator for up to 4 weeks.

PER SERVING (2 TABLESPOONS) | Calories: 47 | Fat: 0 g | Protein: 0.3 g | Sodium: 11 mg | Fiber: 0.4 g | Carbohydrates: 13 g

Mango Chutney

*This versatile chutney is good with Indian foods, greens and grains,
meats and poultry, and even over ice cream.*

INGREDIENTS | YIELDS 2 CUPS

2 almost ripe mangoes, peeled, pitted, and diced

2 small serrano or jalapeño peppers, minced

1 large clove garlic, minced

2 teaspoons grated, fresh ginger

6 unsweetened dried plums, coarsely chopped

¾ cup dark brown sugar, firmly packed

¾ cup raw sugar, or turbinado sugar

1 cup white wine vinegar

2 teaspoons mustard powder

⅛ teaspoon salt

1. Place all ingredients in the pressure cooker and stir to combine. Close and lock the lid.
2. Turn the heat up to high. When the cooker reaches pressure, lower the heat to the minimum needed to maintain pressure. Cook for 5 minutes at high pressure.
3. Open with the natural release method (see Chapter 1).
4. Remove the lid, return the pan to medium heat, and bring to a boil. Boil briskly for 10 minutes, stirring often. Cool thoroughly.
5. Cover and refrigerate overnight before using. Store covered in the refrigerator for up to 6 weeks.

PER SERVING (1 TABLESPOON) | Calories: 52 | Fat: 0 g | Protein: 0.1 g | Sodium: 15 mg | Fiber: 0.5 g | Carbohydrates: 13 g

Tomato Chutney with Fresh Ginger Root

For a delicious appetizer, you can spread this chutney over Indian chapati bread, flatbread, or pizza crust. Top with goat cheese and bake.

INGREDIENTS | YIELDS 2 PINTS

4 pounds ripe tomatoes, peeled
1 (1-inch) piece fresh ginger root
3 cloves garlic
1¾ cups white sugar
1 cup red wine vinegar
2 onions, diced
¼ cup golden raisins
¾ teaspoon ground cinnamon
½ teaspoon ground coriander
¼ teaspoon ground cloves
¼ teaspoon ground nutmeg
¼ teaspoon ground ginger
1 teaspoon chili powder
⅛ teaspoon paprika
1 tablespoon curry paste

1. Purée the tomatoes and ginger in a blender or food processor. Transfer purée to pressure cooker and stir in remaining ingredients. Close and lock the lid.
2. Turn the heat up to high. When the cooker reaches pressure, lower the heat to the minimum needed to maintain pressure. Cook for 5–7 minutes at high pressure.
3. When time is up, open the pressure cooker by releasing pressure.
4. Refrigerate in a covered container until ready to use. Serve chilled or at room temperature.

PER SERVING (2 TABLESPOONS) | Calories: 61 | Fat: 0.1 g | Protein: 0.6 g | Sodium: 5 mg | Fiber: 1 g | Carbohydrates: 15 g

Peeling Fresh Tomatoes

Add enough water to a saucepan to cover the tomatoes and bring to a boil over medium-high heat. Use a slotted spoon to submerge the tomatoes in the boiling water for 1 minute, or until their skins begin to crack and peel. Use the slotted spoon to remove the tomatoes from the water, then plunge them into ice water. The peels will slip right off.

Green Tomato Chutney

If you prefer spicy chutney, you can substitute an Anaheim and 4 small red chili or jalapeño peppers for the red bell peppers.

INGREDIENTS | YIELDS 5 CUPS

2 pounds green tomatoes, stems removed, diced

1 white onion, peeled, quartered lengthwise, thinly sliced

2 red bell peppers, seeded and diced

¼ cup currants

2 tablespoons grated, fresh ginger

¾ cup dark brown sugar, firmly packed

¾ cup white wine vinegar

⅛ teaspoon sea salt

1. Put all ingredients in the pressure cooker and stir to mix. Close and lock the lid.
2. Turn the heat up to high. When the cooker reaches pressure, lower the heat to the minimum needed to maintain pressure. Cook for 5–7 minutes at high pressure.
3. When time is up, open the pressure cooker by releasing pressure.
4. Cool and refrigerate overnight before serving. Store in a covered container in the refrigerator for up to 2 months.

PER SERVING (1 TABLESPOON) | Calories: 12 | Fat: 0 g | Protein: 0.2 g | Sodium: 6 mg | Fiber: 0.2 g | Carbohydrates: 3 g

Dried Plum Sauce

This Chinese sauce can be served as a dipping sauce for egg rolls and pot stickers. It's even better as a condiment when served with duck or other strongly flavored meats, or even in place of a barbecue sauce.

INGREDIENTS | SERVES 12

7 ounces dried plums, pitted

1 tablespoon brown sugar

⅛ onion, sliced

1 teaspoon minced or grated ginger

1 teaspoon fresh red chile, minced

1 clove garlic, minced

⅔ cup water

2 tablespoons rice wine vinegar

1. Add all ingredients except vinegar to pressure cooker, then close and lock the lid.
2. Turn the heat up to high. When the cooker reaches pressure, lower the heat to the minimum needed to maintain pressure. Cook for 5–7 minutes at high pressure.
3. Open the pressure cooker by releasing pressure.
4. Add the vinegar and purée the contents of the pressure cooker using an immersion blender.
5. On low heat, stir frequently until the contents have reached sauce consistency (about 5 minutes).

PER SERVING (1 TABLESPOON) | Calories: 45 | Fat: 0 g | Protein: 0.5 g | Sodium: 1 mg | Fiber: 1.5 g | Carbohydrates: 12 g

Fresh Plums?

You really need to start with the strong, concentrated flavor of dried plums to hit the right notes with this recipe.

Rainbow Bell Pepper Marmalade

Serve Rainbow Bell Pepper Marmalade as a relish for meat or on top of cream cheese on crackers.

INGREDIENTS | YIELDS 2 CUPS

1 large green bell pepper
1 large red bell pepper
1 large yellow bell pepper
1 large purple or orange bell pepper
1 small yellow, white, or sweet onion
3¾ cups water, divided
2 cups granulated sugar
⅛ teaspoon salt
2 tablespoons balsamic vinegar

1. Wash, quarter, and seed the bell peppers. Cut into thin slices or dice them. Peel, quarter, and thinly slice the onion. Add the peppers and onion to the pressure cooker.
2. Add enough water to the pressure cooker to cover the peppers and onion (approximately 3 cups). Bring to a boil over high heat. Drain immediately and discard the water.
3. Return the peppers and onion to the pressure cooker. Stir in the sugar, salt, vinegar, and ¾ cup of fresh water. Close and lock the lid.
4. Turn the heat up to high. When the cooker reaches pressure, lower the heat to the minimum needed to maintain pressure. Cook for 5 minutes at high pressure.
5. When time is up, open the pressure cooker by releasing pressure.
6. Simmer briskly over medium-high heat for 6 minutes or until the mixture is thickened. Once cooled, store in a covered container in the refrigerator overnight before using.

PER SERVING (1 TABLESPOON) | Calories: 55 | Fat: 0 g | Protein: 0.2 g | Sodium: 11 mg | Fiber: 0.4 g | Carbohydrates: 13 g

Dried Apricot Preserves

Starting with already dried apricots helps to make a quick and intensely flavored jam.

INGREDIENTS | YIELDS 7 CUPS

5 black peppercorns

5 cardamom pods

2 (3-inch) cinnamon sticks

2 star anise

4 cups chopped, dried apricots

2 cups water

½ cup lemon juice

4 cups granulated sugar

Determining the Gel Point

Test a small amount of preserves by spooning it onto an ice-cold plate. It's reached the gel point when it's as thick as you desire. A softer set is ideal for use in sauces, but if you prefer a firm, jam-like consistency, you may need to continue to boil the mixture for up to 20 minutes.

1. Wrap the peppercorns, cardamom pods, cinnamon sticks, and star anise in cheesecloth and secure with a string. Add to the pressure cooker along with the apricots, water, and lemon juice. Close and lock the lid.
2. Turn the heat up to high. When the cooker reaches pressure, lower the heat to the minimum needed to maintain pressure. Cook for 8–10 minutes at high pressure.
3. Open with the natural release method (see Chapter 1).
4. Uncover the pressure cooker. Remove and discard the cheesecloth spice bag and stir in the sugar. Return the pressure cooker to the heat source and bring to a rapid boil over medium-high heat. Boil uncovered for about 5 minutes or until the apricot mixture reaches the gel point.
5. Skim off and discard any foam. Ladle into hot, sterilized, glass containers or jars, leaving ½ inch of headspace. Seal the containers or jars. Cool and refrigerate for a week or freeze.

PER SERVING (1 TABLESPOON) | Calories: 39 | Fat: 0 g | Protein: 0.2 g | Sodium: 1 mg | Fiber: 0.3 g | Carbohydrates: 10 g

Blueberry Jam

You can substitute a 6-ounce bottle of pectin for the dry pectin.

INGREDIENTS | YIELDS 4 CUPS

4 cups blueberries

4 cups granulated sugar

1 cup orange juice

1 teaspoon orange zest

⅛ teaspoon freshly ground nutmeg

⅛ teaspoon salt

1 (1¾-ounce) package dry pectin

The Half Full Rule

Never fill the pressure cooker more than half full when making preserves, chutneys, or other fruit dishes. Most fruits can generate a lot of foam and it can interfere with the safety mechanisms of the pressure cooker.

1. Add the blueberries, sugar, orange juice, orange zest, nutmeg, and salt to the pressure cooker. Stir to combine. Close and lock the lid.
2. Turn the heat up to high. When the cooker reaches pressure, lower the heat to the minimum needed to maintain pressure. Cook for 3 minutes at high pressure.
3. Open with the natural release method (see Chapter 1).
4. Process the contents of the cooker through a food mill or press it through a fine mesh strainer to separate the pulp from the skins.
5. Return the pulp to the pressure cooker. Place over medium-high heat, stir in the pectin, and bring mixture to a rolling boil, stirring constantly. Continue to boil and stir for 1 minute.
6. Skim off and discard any foam. Ladle into hot, sterilized, glass containers or jars, leaving ½ inch of headspace. Seal the containers or jars.
7. Cool and refrigerate for a week or freeze.

PER SERVING (1 TABLESPOON) | Calories: 55 | Fat: 0 g | Protein: 0 g | Sodium: 5 mg | Fiber: 0.2 g | Carbohydrates: 14 g

Strawberry Jam

In addition to the usual uses for fruit spread, this jam can be used as the perfect addition to plain yogurt or as an ice cream topping.

INGREDIENTS | **YIELDS 4 CUPS**

4 cups strawberries

3 cups granulated sugar

¼ cup fresh lemon juice

1. Rinse and hull the strawberries, then quarter or halve them. Add to the pressure cooker. Stir in the sugar. Set aside for 1 hour or until the strawberries are juicy.
2. Use a potato masher to crush the fruit and mix it with the sugar until all of it is dissolved into the fruit juices. Stir in the lemon juice. Close and lock the lid.
3. Turn the heat up to high. When the cooker reaches pressure, lower the heat to the minimum needed to maintain pressure. Cook for 5–7 minutes at high pressure.
4. Open with the natural release method (see Chapter 1).
5. Remove the lid. Return to heat source and bring to a full boil over medium-high heat. Boil for 3 minutes or until jam reaches the desired gel state.
6. Skim off and discard any foam. Ladle into hot, sterilized, glass containers or jars, leaving ½ inch of headspace. Seal the containers or jars. Cool and refrigerate for a week or freeze.

PER SERVING (1 TABLESPOON) | Calories: 39 | Fat: 0 g | Protein: 0 g | Sodium: 0.3 mg | Fiber: 0.2 g | Carbohydrates: 10 g

Fresh Apricot Jam

Adjust sugar to taste.

INGREDIENTS | YIELDS 6 CUPS

6 cups halved apricots

6 cups sugar

Juice and zest of 1 orange

1. In a food processor, purée apricots in batches if necessary. Pour into pressure cooker.
2. Add sugar, orange juice, and orange zest and let stand for 30 minutes. Bring to a boil, stirring until sugar is dissolved. Close and lock the lid.
3. Turn the heat up to high. When the cooker reaches pressure, lower the heat to the minimum needed to maintain pressure. Cook for 6–8 minutes at high pressure.
4. Open with the natural release method (see Chapter 1).
5. Remove the lid and purée the contents using an immersion bender. Return to medium heat and bring to a full boil, stirring constantly for 3 minutes or until jam reaches the desired gel state.
6. Skim off and discard any foam. Ladle into hot, sterilized, glass containers or jars, leaving ½ inch of headspace. Seal the containers or jars. Cool and refrigerate for a week or freeze.

PER SERVING (1 TABLESPOON) | Calories: 39 | Fat: 0 g | Protein: 0 g | Sodium: 0.3 mg | Fiber: 0.2 g | Carbohydrates: 10 g

Blackberry Jam

This will result in a rustic, "crunchy" jam. For a smooth jam, remove the gritty blackberry seeds by passing the jam through the fine strainer of a food mill after cooking.

INGREDIENTS | YIELDS 6 CUPS

4 cups blackberries

4 cups granulated sugar

1 cup orange juice

1 teaspoon lemon juice

⅛ teaspoon salt

1 (1¾–ounce) package dry pectin

1. Add the blackberries, sugar, orange juice, lemon juice, and salt to the pressure cooker. Stir to combine. Close and lock the lid.
2. Turn the heat up to high. When the cooker reaches pressure, lower the heat to the minimum needed to maintain pressure. Cook for 1 minute at high pressure.
3. Open with the natural release method (see Chapter 1).
4. Remove the lid and purée the contents using an immersion bender. Return to medium heat, add pectin and bring to a full boil, stirring constantly for 3 minutes or until jam reaches the desired gel state.
5. Skim off and discard any foam. Ladle into hot, sterilized, glass containers or jars, leaving ½ inch of headspace. Seal the containers or jars. Cool and refrigerate for a week or freeze.

PER SERVING (1 TABLESPOON) | Calories: 36 | Fat: 0 g | Protein: 0.1 g | Sodium: 3 mg | Fiber: 0.3 g | Carbohydrates: 9 g

Peach Jam

In most states, peach season is during summer. Using in-season fruit will result in the best flavor for homemade jams.

INGREDIENTS | YIELDS 6 CUPS

4 cups peeled and chopped peaches

4 cups granulated sugar

1 teaspoon lemon juice

1 (1¾-ounce) package dry pectin

1. Add the peaches, sugar, and lemon juice to the pressure cooker. Close and lock the lid.
2. Turn the heat up to high. When the cooker reaches pressure, lower the heat to the minimum needed to maintain pressure. Cook for 1 minute at high pressure.
3. Open with the natural release method (see Chapter 1).
4. Remove the lid and purée the contents using an immersion bender. Return to medium heat and bring to a full boil, add pectin stirring constantly for 3 minutes or until jam reaches the desired gel state.
5. Skim off and discard any foam. Ladle into hot, sterilized, glass containers or jars, leaving ½ inch of headspace. Seal the containers or jars. Cool and refrigerate for a week or freeze.

PER SERVING (1 TABLESPOON) | Calories: 35 | Fat: 0 g | Protein: 0 g | Sodium: 0 mg | Fiber: 0 g | Carbohydrates: 9 g

Wild Berry Black Currant Jam

This richly flavored jam is a delightful addition to holiday stuffing and can be used as a filling in pies, cobblers, or dolloped over vanilla bean ice cream. If you can't find currants, you can substitute raisins.

INGREDIENTS | YIELDS 3 CUPS

3 cups cranberries

3 cups hulled and diced strawberries

1 cup blueberries

¼ cup diced rhubarb stalk

¼ cup dried black currants

Zest and juice of 1 lemon

3 cups granulated sugar

2 tablespoons water

⅛ teaspoon sea salt

Rhubarb

Rhubarb is an herbaceous, perennial plant whose leaves are actually toxic. When cooking, only use the stalks. They are great not only in jams, but in other culinary delights such as pies, cobblers, and sauces.

1. Add the cranberries, strawberries, blueberries, rhubarb stalk, currants, lemon zest, and orange juice to the pressure cooker. Stir in the sugar. Set aside for 1 hour, until the fruit is juicy.
2. Stir in the water and sea salt. Close and lock the lid.
3. Turn the heat up to high. When the cooker reaches pressure, lower the heat to the minimum needed to maintain pressure. Cook for 8–10 minutes at high pressure.
4. Open with the natural release method (see Chapter 1).
5. Remove the lid and purée the contents using an immersion bender. Return to medium heat and bring to a full boil, stirring constantly for 3 minutes or until jam reaches the desired gel state.
6. Skim off and discard any foam. Ladle into hot, sterilized, glass containers or jars, leaving ½ inch of headspace. Seal the containers or jars. Cool and refrigerate for a week or freeze.

PER SERVING (1 TABLESPOON) | Calories: 56 | Fat: 0 g | Protein: 0.1 g | Sodium: 6.5 mg | Fiber: 0.5 g | Carbohydrates: 15 g

Mixed-Citrus Marmalade

The fruit in this marmalade is an unexpectedly delicious combination.

INGREDIENTS | YIELDS 6 CUPS

1 grapefruit
2 mandarins
1 orange
2 lemons
1 lime
1 cup water
About 4 pounds sugar

1. Slice citrus thinly using a mandoline. Remove seeds from slices and set aside. Stack slices and cut stacks of slices into quarters.
2. Put your pressure cooker on a large food scale and reset scale to zero. Add sliced fruit and any accumulated juice to the pressure cooker. Record the weight of the fruit. Add water, then close and lock the lid.
3. Turn the heat up to high. When the cooker reaches pressure, lower the heat to the minimum needed to maintain pressure. Cook for 10 minutes at high pressure.
4. Open with the natural release method (see Chapter 1).
5. Put all of the seeds in a tea ball or gauze packet.
6. Calculate how much sugar to add by doubling the weight of the fruit. Pour the sugar in the uncovered pressure cooker over medium heat. Add the seed packet and stir constantly until the contents begin to boil. Boil everything together for about 5 minutes.
7. Discard seeds and ladle marmalade into hot, sterilized, glass containers or jars, leaving ½ inch of headspace. Seal the containers or jars. Cool and refrigerate for a week or freeze.

PER SERVING (1 TABLESPOON) | Calories: 75 | Fat: 0 g | Protein: 0 g | Sodium: 0.3 mg | Fiber: 0.1 g | Carbohydrates: 19.5 g

Lemon Marmalade

Adjust the sugar to taste. I prefer twice as much in weight for bitter fruits and half as much in weight for sweeter fruits. Either way, you can add a bit of sugar and sneak a taste once it has melted before adding more!

INGREDIENTS | YIELDS 6 CUPS

2 pounds organic lemons
1 cup water
About 4 pounds sugar

1. Slice lemons thinly using a mandoline. Remove seeds from slices and set aside. Stack slices and cut stacks of slices into quarters.
2. Put your pressure cooker on a large food scale and reset scale to zero. Add sliced fruit and any accumulated juice to the pressure cooker. Record the weight of the fruit. Add water, then close and lock the lid.
3. Turn the heat up to high. When the cooker reaches pressure, lower the heat to the minimum needed to maintain pressure. Cook for 10 minutes at high pressure.
4. Open with the natural release method (see Chapter 1).
5. Put all of the seeds in a tea ball or gauze packet.
6. Calculate how much sugar to add by doubling the weight of the fruit. Pour the sugar into the uncovered pressure cooker over medium heat. Add the seed packet and stir constantly until the contents begin to boil. Boil everything together for about 5 minutes.
7. Discard seeds and ladle into hot, sterilized, glass containers or jars, leaving ½ inch of headspace. Seal the containers or jars. Cool and refrigerate for a week or freeze.

PER SERVING (1 TABLESPOON) | Calories: 74 | Fat: 0 g | Protein: 0 g | Sodium: 0.4 mg | Fiber: 0.3 g | Carbohydrates: 20 g

Peach-Apricot Preserves with Toasted Almonds

Toasting the almonds is an important step that enhances the rich flavor of these preserves.

INGREDIENTS | YIELDS 6 CUPS

6 fresh ripe peaches

1 cup water

1 (8-ounce) package dried apricots, diced

½ cup toasted almonds

1¼ cups orange juice

¼ cup lemon juice

4½ cups granulated sugar

2 whole cloves

1 (3-inch) cinnamon stick

⅛ teaspoon sea salt

1 (1¾-ounce) package dry pectin

Toasting Nuts

Toasting brings out the natural oils of the nut and gives the outside a richer, deeper flavor that blends into your recipes. To toast on a stovetop, place nuts in a heavy skillet over low to medium-low heat. Shake the pan occasionally to toss the nuts and toast until fragrant (about 8–10 minutes) and lightly browned. To toast in an oven, heat oven to 250°F. Distribute nuts evenly on a parchment paper–lined baking sheet. Place in oven for about 15 minutes or until fragrant.

1. Use a toothpick to poke holes in the peaches. Place peaches in the pressure cooker and pour the water over them. Close and lock the lid.
2. Turn the heat up to high. When the cooker reaches pressure, lower the heat to the minimum needed to maintain pressure. Cook for 3 minutes at high pressure.
3. When time is up, open the pressure cooker by releasing pressure.
4. Use a slotted spoon to move the peaches to a large bowl of ice water or to a bowl under cold running water. Peel the peaches, then cut them into small pieces, discarding the pits.
5. Add the peaches, apricots, almonds, orange juice, lemon juice, sugar, cloves, cinnamon stick, and salt to the water remaining in the pressure cooker. Stir to combine. Close and lock the lid.
6. Turn the heat up to high. When the cooker reaches pressure, lower the heat to the minimum needed to maintain pressure. Cook for 3 minutes at high pressure.
7. When time is up, open the pressure cooker by releasing pressure.
8. Remove and discard the cloves and cinnamon stick. Stir the pectin into the fruit mixture. Return to heat source and bring to a rolling boil, over medium-high heat, stirring constantly.
9. Skim off and discard any foam. Ladle into hot, sterilized, glass containers or jars, leaving ½ inch of head space. Seal the containers or jars. Cool, then refrigerate for up to 5 weeks or freeze for up to 8 months.

PER SERVING (1 TABLESPOON) | Calories: 50 | Fat: 0.2 g | Protein: 0.2 g | Sodium: 4 mg | Fiber: 0.5 g | Carbohydrates: 15 g

Vanilla-Spice Pear Butter

Place vanilla bean pods in granulated sugar to make vanilla sugar.
Use this sugar when making cakes, pies, and cookies for an extra flavorful twist.

INGREDIENTS | YIELDS 2 CUPS

6 medium Bartlett pears

¼ cup dry white wine, such as Sauvignon Blanc

Zest and juice of 1 lemon

¾ cup sugar

2 orange slices

1 lemon slice

2 whole cloves

1 vanilla bean, split lengthwise

1 cinnamon stick

¼ teaspoon ground cardamom

⅛ teaspoon salt

1. Rinse, peel, and core the pears, then dice them into 1-inch pieces. Add the pears, wine, zest, and lemon juice to the pressure cooker. Close and lock the lid.
2. Turn the heat up to high. When the cooker reaches pressure, lower the heat to the minimum needed to maintain pressure. Cook for 5 minutes at high pressure.
3. Open with the natural release method (see Chapter 1).
4. Purée the contents of the cooker using an immersion blender. Add the sugar. Stir and cook over low heat until sugar dissolves, about 3 minutes.
5. Stir in the remaining ingredients. Increase the heat to medium and boil gently, cooking and stirring for about 30 minutes or until mixture thickens and mounds slightly on spoon.
6. Remove and discard the orange and lemon slices, cloves, and cinnamon stick. Remove the vanilla pod; use the back of a knife to scrape away any vanilla seeds still clinging to the pod and stir them into the pear butter.
7. Cool and refrigerate covered for up to 10 days or freeze for up to 4 months.

PER SERVING (2 TABLESPOONS) | Calories: 78 | Fat: 0 g | Protein: 0.5 g | Sodium: 19 mg | Fiber: 2 g | Carbohydrates: 20 g

Cinnamon Apple Butter

To make red-hot apple butter, stir 3–4 tablespoons of Red Hots cinnamon candy into the apple butter after simmering for 30 minutes.

INGREDIENTS | YIELDS 2 CUPS

¾ cup apple juice or cider

6 medium apples, cored and sliced

1 teaspoon ground cinnamon

½ teaspoon ground allspice

⅛ teaspoon ground cloves

¾ cups sugar

1. Add all of the ingredients to the pressure cooker, except for the sugar. Close and lock the lid.
2. Turn the heat up to high. When the cooker reaches pressure, lower the heat to the minimum needed to maintain pressure. Cook for 1 minute at high pressure.
3. Open with the natural release method (see Chapter 1).
4. Purée the contents of the pressure cooker with an immersion blender and return to low heat. Stir in the sugar and simmer uncovered for about 1 hour, stirring frequently to prevent the contents from sticking and burning.
5. Cool and refrigerate covered for up to 10 days or freeze for up to 4 months.

PER SERVING (2 TABLESPOONS) | Calories: 71 | Fat: 0 g | Protein: 0 g | Sodium: 1 mg | Fiber: 1 g | Carbohydrates: 18 g

Lemon Curd

This tart lemon dish is most commonly spread on toast. It can also be used to fill baked tart shells.

INGREDIENTS | SERVES 6

1⅓ cups sugar

3 large eggs

1 egg yolk

¼ cup butter, softened

¼ cup fresh lemon juice

1 teaspoon grated lemon zest

2 cups water

1. Add the sugar to a blender or food processor. Process to create superfine sugar. Add the eggs, egg yolk, butter, lemon juice, and lemon zest. Process until well mixed.
2. Prepare a 3-cup heatproof casserole dish that will sit on the rack of the pressure cooker by treating it with nonstick spray or coating the inside with butter.
3. Strain the mixture from the blender or food processor into the dish. Cover tightly with aluminum foil.
4. Prepare the pressure cooker by inserting the trivet, or steamer basket, and filling it with 2 cups of water. Make a foil sling by folding a long piece of foil into three and lower the casserole dish into the pressure cooker. Close and lock the lid.
5. Turn the heat up to high. When the cooker reaches pressure, lower the heat to the minimum needed to maintain pressure. Cook for 8–10 minutes at high pressure.
6. When time is up, open the pressure cooker by releasing pressure.
7. Being careful not to get any moisture clinging to the foil into the lemon curd, remove the foil. Use a small whisk or a fork to whisk the lemon curd.
8. Lemon curd can be served warm, but it will be somewhat runny. Cool, then refrigerate covered for at least 4 hours to thicken the curd.
9. Spoon onto fruit cups, pastries, or blind-baked tart shell.

PER SERVING (2 TABLESPOONS) | Calories: 288 | Fat: 10 g | Protein: 4 g | Sodium: 39 mg | Fiber: 0 g | Carbohydrates: 45 g

CHAPTER 14

Fruits and Desserts

Dried Fruit Compote
256

Only-Apples Sauce
256

Cranberry Applesauce
257

Stuffed Apples
258

Amaretti-Stuffed Apricots
259

Pears Poached in Wine
260

Pear Clafoutis
261

Golden Fruit Compote
262

Fresh Figs Poached in Wine
262

Spiced Peaches
263

Dried Apricots and Plums
263

Brown Betty Apple Dessert
264

Plum Pudding with Brandy Sauce
265

French Cherry Clafoutis
266

Date Pudding
267

Piña Colada Bread Pudding
268

Lemon Poppy Seed Cake
269

Maple Dessert Bread
270

Lemon Pot de Crème
271

Chocolate Berry Pudding
272

Molten Chocolate Mug Cake
273

Tapioca Pudding
274

Cinnamon Brown Rice Pudding with Raisins
275

Creamy Coconut Rice Pudding
275

Jennadene's Ricotta Cake
276

Banana Cream Custard
277

Crema Catalana
278

Crème Caramel
279

Crème Brûlée
280

Vanilla Pot de Crème
281

Dried Fruit Compote

You might not expect dried fruit to be tart, but dried apricots and plums add a nice tang to this recipe. You can make this with your favorite mix of fruit, but don't leave out the plums and apricots!

INGREDIENTS | SERVES 8

1 cup water

1 vanilla bean, halved lengthwise

¾ cup light-colored honey (like acacia)

½ cup dried apricots

½ cup dried plums, pitted

2 cups mixed dried fruits of your choice: raisins, cherries, cranberries, figs, mangoes, dates, pineapple, or ginger

Top It!

You can top this compote with nuts or a dollop of plain yogurt or whipped cream. Or use the compote as a topping for coffee cake or ice cream.

1. Add all of the ingredients to the pressure cooker. Close and lock the lid.
2. Turn the heat up to high. When the cooker reaches pressure, lower the heat to the minimum needed to maintain pressure. Cook for 5 minutes at high pressure.
3. Open with the natural release method (see Chapter 1).
4. Discard the vanilla pod before serving.

PER SERVING | Calories: 250 | Fat: 0 g | Protein: 2 g | Sodium: 7 mg | Fiber: 3 g | Carbohydrates: 66 g

Only-Apples Sauce

This recipe works with any apple or mix of apples.

INGREDIENTS | SERVES 6

6 apples, cored and sliced

¾ cup lemon juice

Keep Skins On!

Apples contain special phytonutrients that give them unique and potent antioxidant and anti-inflammatory qualities. But did you know that the peel contains six times the antioxidant power of the pulp? Whenever possible, eat apples with their skins.

1. Add apples and lemon juice to the pressure cooker. Close and lock the lid.
2. Turn the heat up to high. When the cooker reaches pressure, lower the heat to the minimum needed to maintain pressure. Cook for 1 minute at high pressure.
3. Open with the natural release method (see Chapter 1).
4. Purée the contents of the pressure cooker with an immersion blender and serve warm, or store tightly covered in the refrigerator for up to a week.

PER SERVING | Calories: 53 | Fat: 0.2 g | Protein: 0.5 g | Sodium: 6 mg | Fiber: 3 g | Carbohydrates: 22 g

Cranberry Applesauce

This applesauce is delicious on its own or as a sauce over cooked pork.

INGREDIENTS | SERVES 4

2 medium tart apples, cored and diced
2 medium sweet apples, cored and diced
½ cup cranberries
Zest and juice from 1 large orange
¼ cup dark brown sugar
¼ cup granulated cane sugar
1 tablespoon unsalted butter
2 teaspoons ground cinnamon
½ teaspoon ground cloves
⅛ teaspoon freshly ground black pepper
⅛ teaspoon salt
1 tablespoon fresh lemon juice

1. Add all of the ingredients to the pressure cooker. Close and lock the lid.
2. Turn the heat up to high. When the cooker reaches pressure, lower the heat to the minimum needed to maintain pressure. Cook for 1 minute at high pressure.
3. Open with the natural release method (see Chapter 1).
4. Purée the contents of the pressure cooker with an immersion blender and serve warm, or store tightly covered in the refrigerator for up to a week.

PER SERVING | Calories: 234 | Fat: 3 g | Protein: 1 g | Sodium: 79 mg | Fiber: 4.5 g | Carbohydrates: 54 g

Apple Slicer and Dicer

An apple slicer slices and cores the apples all at once. To dice apples, simply make about three horizontal cuts, stopping at the core, before using the apple slicer. Instant apple dices!

Stuffed Apples

You can replace the sugar with maple syrup or brown sugar if desired.
Serve as a dessert with a scoop of vanilla or caramel swirl ice cream.

INGREDIENTS | SERVES 4

½ cup apple juice
¼ cup golden raisins
¼ cup toasted and chopped walnuts
2 tablespoons sugar
½ teaspoon grated orange zest
½ teaspoon ground cinnamon
4 cooking apples
4 teaspoons butter
1 cup water

Cooking Apples

Cooking apples are large, tart apples. Their firm flesh holds up well when cooking and won't turn into applesauce. Popular varieties of cooking apples include Granny Smith, Pink Lady, and McIntosh. Some apples are both eating and cooking apples, so if you're not sure what kind to use, ask your grocer.

1. In a sauce pan, bring the apple juice to a boil and pour over the raisins. Soak the raisins in a large bowl for 30 minutes.
2. Drain, reserving the apple juice. Add the nuts, sugar, orange rind, and cinnamon to the raisins and stir to mix.
3. Rinse and dry the apples. Cut off the top of each apple. Peel the cut portion and chop it, then stir the diced apple pieces into the raisin mixture. Hollow out and core the apples by cutting to, but not through, the apple bottoms—turning them into cups.
4. Place each apple on a piece of aluminum foil that is large enough to wrap the apple completely. Fill the apple centers with the raisin mixture.
5. Top each with a teaspoon of the butter. Wrap the foil around each apple, folding the foil over at the top and pinching it firmly together.
6. Insert the trivet or steamer basket into the pressure cooker and fill the pressure cooker with 1 cup of water. Place the apples in the basket. Close and lock the lid.
7. Turn the heat up to high. When the cooker reaches pressure, lower the heat to the minimum needed to maintain pressure. Cook for 8–10 minutes at high pressure.
8. When time is up, open the pressure cooker by releasing pressure.
9. Carefully lift the apples out of the pressure cooker. Unwrap and transfer to serving plates. Serve hot, at room temperature, or chilled.

PER SERVING | Calories: 225 | Fat: 8 g | Protein: 2 g |
Sodium: 3 mg | Fiber: 3.5 g | Carbohydrates: 38 g

Amaretti-Stuffed Apricots

Sweet, tart, crunchy, and elegant, these apricots take more time to describe than to cook. They are steamed in red wine and dessert is served in just 4 minutes! Serve with whipped cream or vanilla ice cream.

INGREDIENTS | SERVES 6

3 apricots, mature but lightly firm

1 cup crumbled, amaretti cookies (about 8 cookies)

2 tablespoons almonds

1 teaspoon lemon zest

2 tablespoons butter, melted

1 cup red wine

4 tablespoons sugar

1. Wash the apricots well, slice them in half, and remove the pit. Make the hole a little deeper with the large end of a melon baller.
2. Crumble the cookies and almonds in a chopper, then stir in the lemon zest and butter.
3. Place wine and sugar in the pressure cooker and add the steamer basket. Fill the apricots with the cookie crumble filling and place carefully in the steamer basket. Close and lock the lid.
4. Turn the heat up to high. When the cooker reaches pressure, lower the heat to the minimum needed to maintain pressure. Cook for 3 minutes at high pressure.
5. When time is up, open the pressure cooker by releasing pressure.
6. Carefully remove the apricots with tongs. If you like, you can reduce the red wine in the pan (uncovered) and use it as a syrupy sauce.
7. Serve at room temperature or chilled.

PER SERVING | Calories: 215 | Fat: 10 g | Protein: 1.5 g | Sodium: 44 mg | Fiber: 0 g | Carbohydrates: 23 g

Pears Poached in Wine

Sweet and tart at the same time, no dessert is more stunning than wine-poached pears. Just peel, poach, and serve! They look lovely decorated with fresh herbs—try sage, mint, oregano, or basil.

INGREDIENTS | SERVES 6

6 firm pears, peeled
1 bottle dry red wine
1 bay leaf
4 cloves
1 cinnamon stick, or 1 teaspoon cinnamon powder
1 (1-inch) piece fresh ginger, or 1 teaspoon ginger powder
1⅓ cups sugar

Cooking Pears

You'll want to use firm, slightly unripe pears for this dish. Otherwise they will melt down into a pear purée. Some of the varieties that are most recommended for cooking are Green Anjou, Bosc, and Forelle.

1. Peel the pears, leaving the stem attached. Pour the bottle of wine in the pressure cooker.
2. Add the bay leaf, cloves, cinnamon, ginger, and sugar. Mix well to dissolve the sugar.
3. Carefully place the pears in the pressure cooker. Close and lock the lid.
4. Turn the heat up to high. When the cooker reaches pressure, lower the heat to the minimum needed to maintain pressure. Cook for 5 minutes at high pressure.
5. When time is up, open the pressure cooker by releasing pressure.
6. Remove the pears carefully using tongs, pulling them by their stems, or scoop them out carefully with a soup ladle.
7. Set the pears aside and put the pressure cooker back on the heat source, and simmer, uncovered, to reduce the cooking liquid by about half. Strain syrup and drizzle over pears. Serve either at room temperature or chilled.

PER SERVING | Calories: 283 | Fat: 0 g | Protein: 1 g | Sodium: 3 mg | Fiber: 5 g | Carbohydrates: 69 g

Pear Clafoutis

This French dessert, traditionally made with cherries, can also be made with pears or apples.

INGREDIENTS | SERVES 6

Butter or oil (to hold wax paper in place)

1 tablespoon raw sugar

3 cooking pears, cored and sliced into thin wedges

2 eggs

½ cup granulated sugar

1 tablespoon vanilla extract

¾ cup flour

1 cup whole milk

2 cups water

1. Butter a heatproof dish and line it with wax paper. Sprinkle the dish with an even layer of raw sugar, then artfully place the pear slices on the bottom (which will become the top). Not all will fit. Slice the remaining pear wedges in half and set aside.
2. In a mixing bowl, add the eggs, granulated sugar, and vanilla and whisk well. Add the flour and milk. Pour the mixture into the dish, then evenly distribute the remaining pears over the batter. Cover tightly with foil.
3. Prepare the pressure cooker by filling it with water and inserting the trivet or steamer basket. Make a foil sling and lower the covered dish into the pressure cooker and onto the steamer or trivet. Close and lock the lid.
4. Turn the heat up to high. When the cooker reaches pressure, lower the heat to the minimum needed to maintain pressure. Cook for 15–20 minutes at high pressure.
5. When time is up, open the pressure cooker by releasing pressure.
6. Check to see if the dessert is done by inserting a toothpick into its center. The dessert is done if the toothpick comes out clean. If it still needs more cooking time, close and lock the lid again and let the residual heat of the pan keep cooking it for an additional 5 minutes.
7. When it is ready, remove the dish from the pressure cooker, let it cool, and flip onto a serving dish. Serve warm or chilled.

PER SERVING | Calories: 233 | Fat: 3 g | Protein: 5 g | Sodium: 42 mg | Fiber: 3 g | Carbohydrates: 46 g

Golden Fruit Compote

This recipe can be served warm or room-temperature. If you add sugar to the dried fruit compote, be sure to do so before the fruit has cooled so that it can dissolve into the warm fruit.

INGREDIENTS | SERVES 6

1 (8-ounce) package dried apricots, cut into quarters

1 (8-ounce) package dried peaches, cut into quarters

1 cup golden raisins

1½ cups orange juice

1 cinnamon stick

4 whole cloves

1. Add all ingredients to pressure cooker. Close and lock the lid.
2. Turn the heat up to high. When the cooker reaches pressure, lower the heat to the minimum needed to maintain pressure. Cook for 3–5 minutes at high pressure.
3. Open with the natural release method (see Chapter 1).
4. Remove and discard the cinnamon stick and cloves. Return the pressure cooker to medium heat. Simmer and stir for 5 minutes to thicken the syrup.
5. Serve warm or chilled. To store, allow to cool and refrigerate for up to a week.

PER SERVING | Calories: 221 | Fat: 0.5 g | Protein: 2.5 g | Sodium: 10 mg | Fiber: 4.5 g | Carbohydrates: 57 g

Fresh Figs Poached in Wine

Sticky, sweet figs burst with flavor when paired with crunchy pine nuts! Serve with Greek yogurt or sour cream.

INGREDIENTS | SERVES 6

1 cup sweet red wine

1 pound fresh figs

½ cup sugar or honey

½ cup pine nuts

1. Add wine to the base of the pressure cooker. Stand the figs in the cooker. Close and lock the lid.
2. Turn heat to high. When the cooker reaches pressure, lower the heat to the minimum needed to maintain pressure. Cook for 3 minutes at low pressure (1 minute at high pressure).
3. Open the pressure cooker by releasing pressure.
4. Move figs to individual dessert dishes.
5. Add sugar to the liquid and cook on high heat, uncovered, to reduce the contents by half. Drizzle figs with syrup and sprinkle with pine nuts. Serve warm or chilled.

PER SERVING | Calories: 271 | Fat: 11 g | Protein: 3 g | Sodium: 16 mg | Fiber: 4.5 g | Carbohydrates: 35 g

Spiced Peaches

This is a deliciously tangy peach equivalent of applesauce. Serve with a dollop of plain yogurt.

INGREDIENTS | SERVES 6

2 pounds peaches, peeled, pitted, and sliced

½ cup water

½ cup honey

1 tablespoon white wine vinegar

⅛ teaspoon ground allspice

1 cinnamon stick

4 whole cloves

½ teaspoon ground ginger

⅛ teaspoon cayenne pepper

1 tablespoon minced candied ginger

3 whole black peppercorns

1. Add all ingredients to pressure cooker. Close and lock the lid.
2. Turn the heat up to high. When the cooker reaches pressure, lower the heat to the minimum needed to maintain pressure. Cook for 3–5 minutes at high pressure.
3. Open the pressure cooker by releasing pressure. Remove and discard the cinnamon stick, cloves, and peppercorns. Return the pressure cooker to medium heat. Simmer and stir for 5 minutes to thicken the syrup.
4. Serve warm or chilled. To store, allow to cool and refrigerate for up to 1 week.

PER SERVING | Calories: 144 | Fat: 0.5 g | Protein: 1.5 g | Sodium: 1 mg | Fiber: 2.5 g | Carbohydrates: 37 g

Dried Apricots and Plums

The orange zest in this dessert gives all of the dried fruits a fresh, juicy note.

INGREDIENTS | SERVES 8

1 cup water

1 tablespoon orange zest

¾ cup light-colored honey

1½ cups dried apricots

1½ cups dried plums, pitted

1. Add all of the ingredients to the pressure cooker. Close and lock the lid.
2. Turn the heat up to high. When the cooker reaches pressure, lower the heat to the minimum needed to maintain pressure. Cook for 5 minutes at high pressure.
3. Open with the natural release method (see Chapter 1).
4. Serve warm or chilled.

PER SERVING | Calories: 232 | Fat: 0 g | Protein: 2 g | Sodium: 4 mg | Fiber: 4 g | Carbohydrates: 61 g

Brown Betty Apple Dessert

This dessert is a cross between a cobbler and a bread pudding. It's an American classic usually made with apples, but pears or berries are also a great choice.

INGREDIENTS | SERVES 6

2 cups dry bread crumbs

½ cup sugar

1 teaspoon cinnamon

Juice and zest of 1 lemon

1 cup olive oil, divided

8 apples, peeled, cored, and diced

2 cups water

1. Combine crumbs, sugar, cinnamon, lemon juice, lemon zest, and ½ cup oil in a mixing bowl. Set aside.
2. In a greased ovensafe dish that will fit in your cooker loosely, add a thin layer of crumbs, then one of diced apples. Continue filling the container with alternating layers of crumbs and apples until all ingredients are finished. Pour ½ cup olive oil on top.
3. Prepare the pressure cooker by filling it with 2 cups of water and inserting the trivet or steamer basket. Make a foil sling by folding a long piece of foil into three and lower the uncovered container into the pressure cooker. Close and lock the lid.
4. Turn the heat up to high. When the cooker reaches pressure, lower the heat to the minimum needed to maintain pressure. Cook for 15–20 minutes at high pressure.
5. Open with the natural release method (see Chapter 1).
6. Pull dish out carefully and let stand for 5 minutes before serving.

PER SERVING | Calories: 629 | Fat: 38 g | Protein: 5.5 g | Sodium: 264 mg | Fiber: 4.5 g | Carbohydrates: 70 g

Plum Pudding with Brandy Sauce

This traditional steamed Christmas pudding can be made up to 1 month in advance if you refrigerate it in a brandy-soaked cheesecloth in a covered container. If made ahead, steam it or heat it gently in the microwave before serving it with the brandy sauce.

INGREDIENTS | SERVES 10

1 cup pitted and chopped, dried plums

1 cup dried currants

1 cup dried cranberries

1 cup raisins

1 cup minced, candied lemon peel

½ cup dark rum

1 cup butter, divided

1½ cups all-purpose flour

1 cup dried bread crumbs

½ cup chopped pecans

1 tablespoon minced, candied ginger

1 teaspoon baking soda

½ teaspoon salt

1 teaspoon ground cinnamon

¼ teaspoon ground nutmeg

¼ teaspoon ground cloves

3 eggs

2 cups packed light brown sugar, divided

3 cups water

1 cup heavy cream

¼ cup brandy

1. Place the dried plums, currants, cranberries, raisins, candied lemon peel, and rum in a bowl. Stir to mix. Cover and let stand at room temperature for 8 hours.
2. Partially freeze ¾ cup butter.
3. Add the flour, bread crumbs, pecans, ginger, baking soda, salt, cinnamon, nutmeg, and cloves to a large mixing bowl. Stir to mix.
4. Grate the partially frozen butter into the flour mixture. Add the marinated fruit. Toss grated butter and fruit into flour mixture. Add eggs and 1 cup of brown sugar to a separate bowl; whisk to mix. Pour into the flour/butter/fruit mixture and mix well.
5. Wrap the base of a 7- or 8-inch springform pan with heavy-duty aluminum foil. Transfer the batter to the springform pan, pressing down to eliminate any air pockets. Cover tightly with foil.
6. Prepare the pressure cooker by filling it with water and inserting the trivet or steamer basket. Make a foil sling by folding a long piece of foil into three and lower the springform pan into the pressure cooker. Close and lock the lid.
7. Turn the heat up to high. When the cooker reaches pressure, lower the heat to the minimum needed to maintain pressure. Cook for 40–45 minutes at high pressure.
8. Open with the natural release method (see Chapter 1).
9. Remove foil cover and let cool for 15 minutes. Run a knife around the edge of the pudding to loosen it from the sides of the pan. Unmold the pudding and transfer it to a plate.
10. To make the brandy sauce, add remaining cup of brown sugar, cream, and ¼ cup butter to a saucepan placed over medium-high heat. Simmer and stir until sugar dissolves, about 3 minutes. Stir in the brandy. Simmer on very low heat and stir for 10 minutes. Serve over the pudding.

PER SERVING | Calories: 752 | Fat: 33 g | Protein: 7 g | Sodium: 193 mg | Fiber: 4 g | Carbohydrates: 104 g

French Cherry Clafoutis

This French dessert is usually made with unpitted cherries, to keep them from "bleeding" their juice into the batter. You can also make this dessert with raspberries, blackberries, and whole, small alpine strawberries.

INGREDIENTS | SERVES 6

2 eggs

½ cup sugar

1 tablespoon vanilla extract

¾ cup flour

1 cup milk

3 cups (about 1 pound) cherries, pitted

2 cups water

1. Butter a heatproof dish and set aside.
2. In a mixing bowl, add the eggs, sugar, and vanilla and whisk well. Stir in the flour and milk. Pour the mixture into the prepared container, then evenly distribute the cherries into the mixture and cover with foil.
3. Prepare the pressure cooker by filling it with water and inserting the trivet or steamer basket. Make a foil sling by folding a long piece of foil into three and lower the covered container into the pressure cooker. Close and lock the lid.
4. Turn the heat up to high. When the cooker reaches pressure, lower the heat to the minimum needed to maintain pressure. Cook for 15–20 minutes at high pressure.
5. When time is up, open the pressure cooker by releasing pressure.
6. Check to see if the dessert is done by inserting a toothpick into its center. The dessert is done if the toothpick comes out clean. If it still needs more cooking time, close and lock the lid again and let the residual heat of the pan keep cooking. Check to see if it is done after 5 minutes.
7. Remove the dish from the pressure cooker. Serve warm or chilled.

PER SERVING | Calories: 225 | Fat: 3 g | Protein: 6 g | Sodium: 41 mg | Fiber: 2 g | Carbohydrates: 43 g

Date Pudding

This is a rich, decadent dessert in the tradition of an English sticky toffee pudding. You can double the number of servings if you layer the pudding in parfait glasses with caramel sauce, chopped toasted pecans, and whipped cream.

INGREDIENTS | SERVES 8

2½ cups pitted and chopped dates

1½ teaspoons baking soda

1⅔ cups boiling water

2 cups dark brown sugar, packed

½ cup butter, softened

3 large eggs

2 teaspoons vanilla

3½ cups all-purpose or cake flour

4 teaspoons baking powder

⅛ teaspoon salt

Quick Caramel Sauce

Add 1½ cups packed brown sugar, ½ cup butter, and 3 cups heavy cream to a saucepan over medium heat. Bring to a boil, stirring constantly. Reduce heat and maintain a simmer for 6 minutes, continuing to stir. Refrigerate leftovers in a covered container for 2 weeks, or until the expiration date given on the heavy cream container.

1. Add the dates to a mixing bowl and toss them together with the baking soda. Bring water to a boil and pour over the dates. Set aside until cooled.
2. Add the brown sugar and butter to a food processor. Process to cream them together, then continue to process while you add the eggs and vanilla. Use a spatula to scrape the brown sugar mixture into the bowl with the dates and their soaking liquid. Stir to mix.
3. Add the flour, baking powder, and salt to another bowl and stir to mix. Fold into the date and brown sugar mixture.
4. Wrap the base of a 7- or 8-inch springform pan with heavy-duty aluminum foil. Transfer the batter to the springform pan, pressing it down into the pan to eliminate any air pockets. Cover tightly with foil.
5. Prepare the pressure cooker by filling it with water and inserting the trivet or steamer basket. Make a foil sling by folding a long piece of foil into three and lower the springform pan into the pressure cooker. Close and lock the lid.
6. Turn the heat up to high. When the cooker reaches pressure, lower the heat to the minimum needed to maintain pressure. Cook for 45–50 minutes at high pressure.
7. Open with the natural release method (see Chapter 1).
8. Remove foil cover and let cool for 15 minutes. Unmold the pudding and transfer it to a plate to serve.

PER SERVING | Calories: 498 | Fat: 13.5 g | Protein: 4 g | Sodium: 562 mg | Fiber: 4.5 g | Carbohydrates: 96 g

Piña Colada Bread Pudding

This delightful dessert is full of tropical flavors. Whole milk takes the place of heavy cream, and honey is used instead of white sugar for a lighter, but still rich, treat.

INGREDIENTS | SERVES 8

1 (16-ounce) can cream of coconut

1 cup whole milk

3 large eggs

4 tablespoons vegetable oil

¾ cup light-colored honey

1½ teaspoons rum extract

¼ teaspoon ground nutmeg

1 (20-ounce) can pineapple chunks, drained, or 1 fresh pineapple, peeled and diced

1¼ cups coconut flakes

8 cups French bread, torn into 2-inch cubes

1½ cups water

Saucy Syrup

Save the juice drained from the pineapple can (if not using fresh pineapple) and add 1 tablespoon of butter. Simmer over medium-low heat until it thickens and serve the syrup over the bread pudding.

1. Add the cream of coconut, milk, eggs, oil, honey, rum extract, and nutmeg to a large bowl. Whisk to mix thoroughly. Stir in the drained pineapple and coconut flakes. Fold in the bread cubes and stir to coat. Pour into a heat-proof bowl.

2. Prepare the pressure cooker by filling it with water and inserting the trivet or steamer basket. Make a foil sling by folding a long piece of foil into three and lower the uncovered bowl into the pressure cooker. Close and lock the lid.

3. Turn the heat up to high. When the cooker reaches pressure, lower the heat to the minimum needed to maintain pressure. Cook for 10–15 minutes at high pressure.

4. Open with the natural release method (see Chapter 1).

5. Pull container out carefully and let stand for 5 minutes before serving warm or chilled.

PER SERVING | Calories: 716 | Fat: 42 g | Protein: 10 g | Sodium: 256 mg | Fiber: 7.5 g | Carbohydrates: 90 g

Lemon Poppy Seed Cake

Make this cake ahead of time. The flavor improves if you wrap it in plastic wrap and store it for 1–2 days before you serve it.

INGREDIENTS | SERVES 8

½ cup butter, softened
1 cup sugar
2 eggs, separated
1 teaspoon vanilla
2 lemons, juice and zest, divided
1¼ cups all-purpose flour
1 teaspoon baking soda
1 teaspoon baking powder
¼ teaspoon salt
⅔ cup whole milk
⅓ cup poppy seeds
2 cups water
½ cup powdered sugar, sifted

1. Add the butter and sugar to a large mixing bowl and beat until light and fluffy. Beat in the egg yolks, vanilla, and the grated zest and juice from 1 lemon.
2. In a separate bowl, mix together the flour, baking soda, baking powder, and salt. Add the flour mixture and milk in 3 batches to the butter mixture, mixing after each addition. Stir in the poppy seeds.
3. Add the egg whites to a chilled bowl. Whisk or beat until stiff. Fold the egg whites into the poppy seed batter.
4. Butter a 4-cup soufflé dish or Bundt pan. Transfer the batter to the pan and cover well with foil.
5. Prepare the pressure cooker by filling it with water and inserting the trivet or steamer basket. Make a foil sling by folding a long piece of foil into three and lower the covered dish into the pressure cooker. Close and lock the lid.
6. Turn the heat up to high. When the cooker reaches pressure, lower the heat to the minimum needed to maintain pressure. Cook for 35–40 minutes at high pressure.
7. Open with the natural release method (see Chapter 1).
8. Lift the dish from the pressure cooker and place it on a cooling rack. Remove foil cover and let cool.
9. To make the glaze, whisk the juice and grated zest from the remaining lemon together with the powdered sugar. Transfer cake to a serving platter and drizzle glaze over the top.

PER SERVING | Calories: 366 | Fat: 16 g | Protein: 5.5 g | Sodium: 322 mg | Fiber: 2 g | Carbohydrates: 51 g

Maple Dessert Bread

Toast leftovers and have them for breakfast!

INGREDIENTS | SERVES 8

½ cup unbleached all-purpose flour
½ cup stone-ground cornmeal
½ cup whole wheat flour
½ teaspoon baking powder
¼ teaspoon fine salt
¼ teaspoon baking soda
½ cup maple syrup
½ cup buttermilk
1 large egg
2 cups water

1. Add the all-purpose flour, cornmeal, whole wheat flour, baking powder, salt, and baking soda to a mixing bowl. Stir to combine.
2. Add the maple syrup, buttermilk, and egg to another mixing bowl. Whisk to mix, then pour into the flour mixture. Mix until a thick batter is formed.
3. Butter the inside of a 6-cup heatproof pudding mold or baking pan. Pour the batter into the dish and cover tightly with foil.
4. Prepare the pressure cooker by filling it with water and inserting the trivet or steamer basket. Make a foil sling by folding a long piece of foil into three and lower the covered dish into the pressure cooker. Close and lock the lid.
5. Turn the heat up to high. When the cooker reaches pressure, lower the heat to the minimum needed to maintain pressure. Cook for 40–45 minutes at high pressure.
6. Open with the natural release method (see Chapter 1).
7. Remove lid. Lift pan from pressure cooker and place on a cooling rack. Remove foil.
8. Check if the bread is done by inserting a toothpick into its center. It's done if the toothpick comes out clean. If the toothpick comes out wet, place the foil over the pan and return it to the pressure cooker for 5 more minutes at high pressure, repeating if necessary.
9. Use a knife to loosen the bread and invert it onto the cooling rack. Serve the bread warm.

PER SERVING | Calories: 153 | Fat: 1 g | Protein: 4 g | Sodium: 171 mg | Fiber: 1.5 g | Carbohydrates: 32 g

Lemon Pot de Crème

Pot de Crème is the little-known cousin of Crème Caramel and Crème Brûlée. It's the easiest custard to make because it can be served right in the ramekin, or cup, it's made in and does not require you to make caramel or brulée sugar. Garnish with your favorite fruit syrup, candied fruits, or toasted nuts.

INGREDIENTS | SERVES 6

1 cup whole milk
1 cup heavy cream
Zest of 1 lemon, cut into large strips
2 cups water
1 teaspoon vegetable oil
6 egg yolks
⅔ cup white sugar

1. In a heavy-bottomed saucepan, or in base of an additional uncovered pressure cooker, add milk, cream, and lemon zest. Cook over medium heat, stirring occasionally until the mixture begins to bubble. Turn off the heat and let cool (about 20–30 minutes).
2. Prepare the pressure cooker by filling it with water and inserting the trivet or steamer basket.
3. Oil 6 teacups or ramekins.
4. In a mixing bowl, add the egg yolks and sugar and whisk until the sugar is dissolved. Pour the cooled mixture slowly into the yolk mixture. Whisk lightly to combine, but do not whip.
5. Pour mixture into cups, cover them with foil, and arrange in steamer basket so that all are straight. Stack some of the cups on top in a second layer. Close and lock the lid.
6. Turn the heat up to high. When the cooker reaches pressure, lower the heat to the minimum needed to maintain pressure. Cook ramekins or cups for 8–10 minutes at high pressure.
7. Open with the natural release method (see Chapter 1).
8. Open the pressure cooker and carefully lift out the custards. Open the first and jiggle it a bit. It should be nearly solid (they will solidify further when chilled). Remove the custards and leave to cool uncovered for about 30–45 minutes. Then cover with plastic wrap and refrigerate for 3–24 hours before serving.

PER SERVING | Calories: 310 | Fat: 21 g | Protein: 5 g | Sodium: 43 mg | Fiber: 0 g | Carbohydrates: 26 g

Chocolate Berry Pudding

You can cut out some of the fat in this Chocolate Berry Pudding by replacing the milk and cream with skim or 2% milk, but add one more egg to the batter if you do.

INGREDIENTS | SERVES 6

6 slices day-old challah or brioche, torn into chunks

½ cup raspberry preserves

1 tablespoon butter

½ cup diced, dried strawberries

½ cup chopped hazelnuts

½ cup bitter cocoa powder

½ cup sugar

⅛ teaspoon salt

2 tablespoons butter, melted

3 large eggs

2 cups whole milk

2 cups heavy cream

1 tablespoon vanilla

2 cups water

Challah and Brioche

Challah is a slightly sweet, yeast-leavened Jewish egg bread. Brioche is a similar sweetened French bread. The dough can be used as the base for myriad pastries. This dessert won't be as sweet if you use white or French bread, but it will still be very good.

1. Remove dark crusts from bread. Lightly toast fresh bread. Spread raspberry preserves over the bread.
2. Butter a 5-cup heatproof soufflé dish. Layer half the bread in the bottom of the soufflé dish. Sprinkle with dried fruit and chopped hazelnuts. Add remaining bread, preserves-side down.
3. Whisk the cocoa, sugar, and salt together in a mixing bowl. Add butter and eggs, and whisk to mix. Whisk in milk, cream, and vanilla.
4. Pour half the cocoa mixture over the bread. Tap down the dish and wait several minutes for the bread to absorb the liquid. Pour in remaining cocoa mixture.
5. Prepare the pressure cooker by filling it with water and inserting the trivet or steamer basket. Make a foil sling by folding a long piece of foil into three and lower the uncovered dish into the pressure cooker. Close and lock the lid.
6. Turn the heat up to high. When the cooker reaches pressure, lower the heat to the minimum needed to maintain pressure. Cook for 15 minutes at high pressure.
7. Open with the natural release method (see Chapter 1).
8. Remove the dish from the pressure cooker and serve warm or chilled.

PER SERVING | Calories: 687 | Fat: 47 g | Protein: 12 g | Sodium: 160 mg | Fiber: 4 g | Carbohydrates: 59 g

Molten Chocolate Mug Cake

This recipe is just for one, but you can easily double it and make two mugs without increasing the pressure cooking time. You can also substitute the orange zest with vanilla, almond extract, or lemon zest.

INGREDIENTS | SERVES 1

4 tablespoons flour

¼ teaspoon orange zest

4 tablespoons sugar

⅛ teaspoon salt

1 tablespoon unsweetened cocoa powder

½ teaspoon baking powder

1 medium egg

4 tablespoons milk

2 tablespoons extra-virgin olive oil

2 cups water

1. In a medium-sized mug, add the flour, orange zest, sugar, salt, cocoa powder, and baking powder and mix with a fork.
2. In a small bowl, beat the egg, milk, and olive oil. Pour egg mixture into mug and mix vigorously until smooth.
3. Prepare the pressure cooker by filling it with water and inserting the trivet or steamer basket. Lower the uncovered mug into the pressure cooker. Close and lock the lid.
4. Turn the heat up to high. When the cooker reaches pressure, lower the heat to the minimum needed to maintain pressure. Cook for 5–8 minutes at high pressure.
5. When time is up, open the pressure cooker by releasing pressure.
6. Carefully remove mug and serve immediately. Poke the top of the cake to release steam and stop the molten center from cooking further.

PER SERVING | Calories: 661 | Fat: 34 g | Protein: 12 g | Sodium: 629 mg | Fiber: 2.5 g | Carbohydrates: 81 g

Tapioca Pudding

Add another dimension to this dish by combining it with other flavors. You can stir in some toasted pecans, chocolate chips, or coconut. Top it off by serving with a dollop of whipped cream.

INGREDIENTS | SERVES 4

½ cup small pearl tapioca

2 cups water, divided

⅓ cup sugar

1 tablespoon butter

2 large eggs

⅛ teaspoon salt

1½ cups whole milk

1 cup heavy cream

1 teaspoon vanilla

1. Combine the tapioca and 1 cup water in a small bowl. Cover and let soak overnight.
2. In a separate bowl, add the sugar, butter, eggs, and salt and beat with a whisk until smooth. Stir in the milk, cream, and vanilla.
3. Drain the tapioca and stir into the milk mixture. Pour into a heatproof bowl or casserole dish and cover tightly with foil.
4. Prepare the pressure cooker by filling it with 1 cup of water and inserting the trivet or steamer basket. Make a foil sling by folding a long piece of foil into three and lower the covered dish into the pressure cooker. Close and lock the lid.
5. Turn the heat up to high. When the cooker reaches pressure, lower the heat to the minimum needed to maintain pressure. Cook for 8–10 minutes at high pressure.
6. When time is up, open the pressure cooker by releasing pressure.
7. Transfer the bowl or casserole dish to a cooling rack and remove the foil. Stir. Taste for flavor and add more vanilla if desired. Chill until ready to serve.

PER SERVING | Calories: 457 | Fat: 30 g | Protein: 7 g | Sodium: 175 mg | Fiber: 0 g | Carbohydrates: 39 g

Cinnamon Brown Rice Pudding with Raisins

This pudding is a perfect dessert, but it's even better for breakfast!

INGREDIENTS | SERVES 2

1 cup short-grain brown rice

1⅓ cups water

1 tablespoon vanilla extract

1 cinnamon stick

1 tablespoon butter

1 cup raisins

3 tablespoons honey

½ cup heavy cream

1. Add rice, water, vanilla, cinnamon stick, and butter to the pressure cooker. Close and lock the lid.
2. Turn the heat up to high. When the cooker reaches pressure, lower the heat to the minimum needed to maintain pressure. Cook for 20–22 minutes at high pressure.
3. Open with the natural release method (see Chapter 1).
4. Remove the cinnamon stick and stir in the raisins, honey, and cream.
5. Let stand 5 minutes, then serve warm.

PER SERVING | Calories: 699 | Fat: 29 g | Protein: 6 g | Sodium: 39 mg | Fiber: 4.5 g | Carbohydrates: 109 g

Creamy Coconut Rice Pudding

Garnish this pudding with a sprinkling of ground cinnamon and serve with a dollop of whipped cream.

INGREDIENTS | SERVES 6

1½ cups arborio rice

2 cups nonfat milk

1 (14-ounce) can coconut milk

1 cup water

½ cup sugar

2 teaspoons ground cinnamon

½ teaspoon salt

1½ teaspoons vanilla extract

1 cup dried cherries, dried strawberries, or golden raisins

1. Add the rice, milk, coconut milk, water, sugar, cinnamon, and salt to the pressure cooker. Cook and stir to dissolve the sugar over medium-high heat and bring to a boil. Close and lock the lid.
2. Turn the heat up to high. When the cooker reaches pressure, lower the heat to the minimum needed to maintain pressure. Cook for 10–13 minutes at high pressure.
3. Open the pressure cooker by releasing pressure. Stir in the vanilla extract and dried fruit. Add cover, but do not lock. Let stand for 15 minutes. Stir and serve.

PER SERVING | Calories: 421 | Fat: 14 g | Protein: 7.5 g | Sodium: 241 mg | Fiber: 2.5 g | Carbohydrates: 67 g

Jennadene's Ricotta Cake

Some readers of www.hippressurecooking.com are also talented cooks. One reader, Jen Smith from River Murray, Australia, submitted a stunning recipe that she agreed to let me share with you. Serve the cake dusted with powdered sugar or chocolate.

INGREDIENTS | SERVES 6

1 pound ricotta cheese
2 eggs
2 tablespoons granulated sugar
¼ cup honey
Zest and juice of ½ orange
¼ teaspoon vanilla extract
½ cup dates, soaked for 20 minutes, drained, and finely chopped
2 cups water

Want to Submit Your Recipe?

The *www.hippressurecooking.com* website is always happy to feature great recipes from readers of the website (and this book)!

1. Beat ricotta until smooth, then set aside.
2. In a separate bowl or food processor, beat the eggs and sugar for 3 minutes. Combine the egg mixture with the ricotta.
3. In a small saucepan, warm the honey and whisk in orange juice, orange zest, and vanilla.
4. Stir the honey mixture into the ricotta mixture and add the chopped dates. Mix well for at least a few minutes to distribute the dates and create a smooth batter.
5. Pour into a buttered heatproof dish and cover with foil.
6. Prepare the pressure cooker by filling it with water and inserting the trivet or steamer basket. Make a foil sling by folding a long piece of foil into three and lower the covered dish into the pressure cooker. Close and lock the lid.
7. Turn the heat up to high. When the cooker reaches pressure, lower the heat to the minimum needed to maintain pressure. Cook for 22–25 minutes at high pressure.
8. When time is up, open the pressure cooker by releasing pressure.
9. Serve warm or well chilled.

PER SERVING | Calories: 233 | Fat: 7.5 g | Protein: 11 g | Sodium: 117 mg | Fiber: 1.5 g | Carbohydrates: 32 g

Banana Cream Custard

Dark rum bumps up the flavor of this recipe, making it a rich, delicious way to use up ripe bananas. Think of this dessert as a banana eggnog pudding.

INGREDIENTS | SERVES 6

1 tablespoon butter
2 slices bread, crusts removed
2 ripe bananas
2 tablespoons fresh lemon juice
1 cup heavy cream
2 large eggs
½ cup dark brown sugar, packed
1 teaspoon ground nutmeg
2 tablespoons dark rum
1 tablespoon vanilla
2 cups water

1. Butter the inside of a 5-cup casserole dish that will fit inside the pressure cooker on the rack. Set aside.
2. Add the bread to a blender or food processor and pulse to create soft bread crumbs. Remove and set aside.
3. To the empty processor, add the bananas and lemon juice. Purée while gradually adding in the cream. Add the eggs and pulse to mix. Then add the brown sugar, nutmeg, rum, and vanilla. Pulse until mixed. Stir in the reserved bread crumbs.
4. Pour the banana mixture into the prepared casserole dish and cover tightly with foil.
5. Prepare the pressure cooker by filling it with water and inserting the trivet or steamer basket. Make a foil sling by folding a long piece of foil into three and lower the covered casserole into the pressure cooker. Close and lock the lid.
6. Turn the heat up to high. When the cooker reaches pressure, lower the heat to the minimum needed to maintain pressure. Cook for 18–20 minutes at high pressure.
7. Open with the natural release method (see Chapter 1).
8. Transfer the casserole dish to a cooling rack and remove the foil. Serve warm or chilled.

PER SERVING | Calories: 328 | Fat: 18 g | Protein: 5 g | Sodium: 114 mg | Fiber: 1.5 g | Carbohydrates: 35 g

Crema Catalana

Crema Catalana is Spain's Crème Brûlée—with a little less fat!
This recipe replaces half of the cream with milk, for a still very rich, but lighter fare.

INGREDIENTS | SERVES 6

1 cup whole milk

1 cup heavy cream

Zest of 1 orange, cut into large strips

1 cinnamon stick, or ½ teaspoon ground cinnamon

2 cups water

1 teaspoon vegetable oil

6 egg yolks

⅔ cup granulated sugar

⅛ teaspoon nutmeg

2 tablespoons demerara or raw sugar

1. In a heavy-bottomed saucepan, heat milk, cream, orange zest, and cinnamon over medium heat. Stir occasionally until the mixture begins to bubble. Turn off the heat and let cool (about 20–30 minutes). Remove the cinnamon stick (if used).
2. In the meantime, prepare the pressure cooker by filling it with water and inserting the trivet or steamer basket. Oil 6 teacups or ramekins.
3. In a mixing bowl, whisk the egg yolks and granulated sugar until the sugar is dissolved. Slowly pour in the cooled milk mixture and incorporate it into the yolks. Whisk lightly, but do not whip the mixture.
4. Pour mixture into cups, cover with foil, and arrange in steamer basket so that all are sitting straight. You can stack some of the cups on top in a second layer. Close and lock the lid.
5. Turn the heat up to high. When the cooker reaches pressure, lower the heat to the minimum needed to maintain pressure. Cook for 5–8 minutes at high pressure.
6. Open with the natural release method (see Chapter 1).
7. Carefully lift out the custards. Open the first and jiggle it a bit. It should be nearly solid (they will solidify further when chilled). Remove the custards and leave to cool uncovered for about 30–45 minutes. Then, cover with plastic wrap and refrigerate for 3–24 hours.
8. Immediately before serving, sprinkle the top of the custards with nutmeg and demerara sugar. Caramelize the sugar by sliding custards under the broiler or by scorching the top with a culinary torch.

PER SERVING | Calories: 326 | Fat: 21 g | Protein: 5 g | Sodium: 43 mg | Fiber: 0 g | Carbohydrates: 30 g

Crème Caramel

Caramelized sugar is very, very hot—and it will stick to your skin and keep burning. ALWAYS wear protection on your hands and keep children and pets out of the kitchen when working with hot caramel.

INGREDIENTS | SERVES 6

2⅔ cups granulated sugar, divided
2 cups whole milk
1 vanilla bean, sliced in half
2 cups water
5 eggs, 4 whole plus 1 yolk

PER SERVING | Calories: 542 | Fat: 6.5 g | Protein: 8 g | Sodium: 96 mg | Fiber: 0 g | Carbohydrates: 116 g

1. Pour 2 cups sugar in a sauté pan and place over low heat for about 10 minutes, without stirring. As soon as almost all the sugar has turned to caramel, turn off the heat.
2. Working with one ramekin at a time, pour some caramel into the bottom and, with an oven glove–covered hand, swirl the ramekin so that the caramel coats about half of the inside. Repeat with 5 other ramekins. Work quickly as the caramel in the pan will also be cooling. Set aside.
3. In a heavy saucepan, heat milk and vanilla bean over medium heat. Stir occasionally until mixture begins to bubble. Turn off the heat and let cool (30 minutes). Remove vanilla bean and scrape the seeds into the mixture.
4. Fill pressure cooker with water and insert the trivet or steamer basket.
5. In a mixing bowl, whisk the eggs and yolk and ⅔ cup granulated sugar until the sugar is dissolved. Slowly pour in the cooled milk mixture and incorporate it into the yolks. Whisk lightly, but do not whip the mixture.
6. Pour mixture into the prepared ramekins, cover with foil and arrange in steamer basket so that all are sitting straight. You can stack some of the cups on top in a second layer. Close and lock the lid.
7. Turn the heat up to high. When the cooker reaches pressure, lower the heat to the minimum needed to maintain pressure. Cook for 5–8 minutes at high pressure .
8. Open with the natural release method (see Chapter 1).
9. Carefully lift out the custards. Open the first and jiggle it a bit. It should be nearly solid (they will solidify further when chilled). Remove the custards and leave to cool uncovered for about 30–45 minutes. Then, cover with plastic wrap and refrigerate for 3–24 hours.
10. To serve, run a skewer around the edge of each ramekin and flip upside down on a dessert plate.

Crème Brûlée

This is usually made with 2 cups of cream (36 percent fat), but we're going to replace it with milk Δ(4 percent fat). The eggs will make this recipe lighter, but still creamy.

INGREDIENTS | SERVES 6

1 cup whole milk

1 cup heavy cream

1 vanilla bean, sliced in half

2 cups water

1 teaspoon vegetable oil

6 egg yolks

⅔ cup granulated sugar

2 tablespoons demerara or raw sugar

1. In a heavy-bottomed saucepan, heat milk, cream, and vanilla bean over medium heat. Stir occasionally until the mixture begins to bubble. Turn off the heat and let cool (about 20–30 minutes). Remove the vanilla bean and scrape the seeds into the mixture.
2. In the meantime, prepare the pressure cooker by filling it with water and inserting the trivet or steamer basket. Oil 6 teacups or ramekins.
3. In a mixing bowl, whisk the egg yolks and granulated sugar until the sugar is dissolved. Slowly pour in the cooled milk mixture and incorporate it into the yolks. Whisk lightly, but do not whip the mixture.
4. Pour mixture into cups, cover with foil, and arrange in steamer basket so that all are sitting straight. You can stack some of the cups on top in a second layer. Close and lock the lid.
5. Turn the heat up to high. When the cooker reaches pressure, lower the heat to the minimum needed to maintain pressure. Cook for 5–8 minutes at high pressure.
6. Open with the natural release method (see Chapter 1).
7. Carefully lift out the custards. Open the first and jiggle it a bit. It should be nearly solid (they will solidify further when chilled). Remove the custards and leave to cool uncovered for about 30–45 minutes. Then, cover with plastic wrap and refrigerate for 3–24 hours.
8. Immediately before serving, sprinkle the top of the custards with demerara sugar. Caramelize the sugar by sliding custards under the broiler or by scorching the top with a culinary torch.

PER SERVING | Calories: 326 | Fat: 21 g | Protein: 5 g | Sodium: 43 mg | Fiber: 0 g | Carbohydrates: 30 g

Vanilla Pot de Crème

Garnish with your favorite fruit syrup, candied fruits, or toasted nuts and serve warm or chilled.

INGREDIENTS | SERVES 6

1 cup whole milk

1 cup heavy cream

1 vanilla bean, halved

2 cups water

1 teaspoon vegetable oil

6 egg yolks

⅔ cup granulated sugar

1. In a heavy-bottomed saucepan, heat milk, cream, and vanilla bean over medium heat. Stir occasionally until the mixture begins to bubble. Turn off the heat and let cool (about 20–30 minutes). Remove the vanilla bean and scrape the seeds into the mixture.
2. In the meantime, prepare the pressure cooker by filling it with water and inserting the trivet or steamer basket. Oil 6 teacups or ramekins.
3. In a mixing bowl, whisk the egg yolks and granulated sugar until the sugar is dissolved. Slowly pour in the cooled milk mixture and incorporate it into the yolks. Whisk lightly, but do not whip the mixture.
4. Pour mixture into cups, cover with foil and arrange in steamer basket so that all are sitting straight. You can stack some of the cups on top in a second layer. Close and lock the lid.
5. Turn the heat up to high. When the cooker reaches pressure, lower the heat to the minimum needed to maintain pressure. Cook for 8–10 minutes at high pressure.
6. Open with the natural release method (see Chapter 1).
7. Open the pressure cooker and carefully lift out the custards. Open the first and jiggle it a bit. It should be nearly solid (they will solidify further when chilled). Remove the custards and leave to cool uncovered for about 30–45 minutes. Then, cover with plastic wrap and refrigerate for 3–24 hours before serving.

PER SERVING | Calories: 310 | Fat: 21 g | Protein: 5 g | Sodium: 43 mg | Fiber: 0 g | Carbohydrates: 26 g

Pressure Cooker Buying Tips

If you don't know what to look for, all pressure cookers can start to look the same. There are few areas where you should not compromise, though.

Pressure Cooker Size

Beginners should start with a 6-quart (or 6-liter) pressure cooker. The recipes in this book, and most of the recipes you will find in other cookbooks, are designed for this pressure cooker. If you can afford it, buy a set with two pressure cooker bases that share a lid. You can use the small one for vegetables, sauces, and sides, and the big one for meats, beans, grains, and main dishes.

A family of four can comfortably use a 6-quart pressure cooker and double most recipes to accommodate guests. The 3-quart and 4-quart sizes are good for couples. Larger groups or families should look into 8-quart or larger cookers. Here are the sizes you're most likely to find and how they can be used:

- 1- to 2-quart—"small frypan" sized. These small, shallow pressure cookers are good for making sauces because of their small size. They will reach pressure faster, but they also cook less food. This size is great for one or two persons. It can pressure cook 1 cup of dry rice (2 servings) or 1 cup of soaked dry beans. Sometimes this small pressure cooker is included as part of a set.
- 3- to 4-quart—"large frypan" sized. This low and wide pressure cooker is great for browning meat because of the larger surface area that remains in direct contact with the heat from the stovetop. You can pressure cook 1½ cups of dry rice (3 servings) or 1½ cups soaked dry beans in a 3- to 4-quart cooker. This size works well for two people or as a second pressure cooker for cooks who do the majority of their cooking using pressure cookers.
- 5- to 8-quart—"stockpot" sized. This size is most recommended for beginners. It's great for stews, soups, and chilis. If you can only afford

one pressure cooker, this is the one you should start with (the small and large ones can come later). This size is good for a family of 4–6 people.

- 10-quart or larger—"pressure cooker or canner" size. Because of their size, these pressure cookers can also be used as canners. These are the pressure cookers you see on all the cooking shows, like *Top Chef* or *Next Iron Chef*. They can feed a crowd, but they require more time and liquid to reach pressure. These pots are very heavy even when they're empty, and they can be tricky to fit in the average sink under the spout for a cold-water quick release or wash.

Pressure Cooker Features

Whatever size pressure cooker you consider buying, be sure not to skimp on these features:

- **Spring Valve:** This is the latest technology in pressure cookers. Spring-valve pressure cookers won't fill your kitchen with steam and the sound of steam engine pistons firing once every minute or two. It also has almost no evaporation and requires less energy to operate.
- **Stainless Steel:** If you are going to invest in a quality cooker, opt for the stainless steel models, not the less expensive aluminum pressure cookers. Aluminum cookware is "reactive," which means that it reacts to and changes the flavor of acidic ingredients (tomatoes, lemon, wine, etc.).
- **Two Pressure Settings:** A two-setting pressure cooker has a "high" setting, which allows you to cook foods like meats, legumes, or anything dense that needs a long time to cook, and a "low" setting for cooking vegetables, fish, eggs, and other delicate foods. Some pressure cookers have a switch to select the pressure setting, while others will show you one or two rings to let you know it has reached high or low pressure.
- **Safety Features:** Do not purchase a pressure cooker unless it has a lock that will keep you from accidentally opening the cooker while it is under pressure. There should also be a secondary safety pressure release valve that will kick in should the first one fail, and either metal cut-outs on the lip of the lid or a collapsing gasket that will kick in should the first two safety mechanisms fail.

In addition, don't buy a used pressure cooker unless it is a recent model manufactured within the last ten years. Make sure the rubber or silicone gaskets and valves are in good condition, and don't buy it if the instruction manual is not included.

Stovetop Versus Electric Pressure Cookers

There are both advantages and disadvantages to using an electric pressure cooker versus a stovetop pressure cooker. Stovetop pressure cookers offer more control over opening the cooker quickly while cooking delicate foods and vegetables, and are generally calibrated to operate at the standard operating pressure (13–15 PSI), which means faster cooking times compared to an electric cooker which may not meet the standard. On the other hand, electric pressure cookers can be slow to reach and release pressure, which is better suited for foods that need a long cooking time like meats and stews.

Stovetop Pressure Cookers

The advantages of a stovetop pressure cookers include:

- Its ability to operate under the standard 13–15 PSI.
- You can operate the cooker on any heat source (gas, electric, induction, and even fire).
- It will reach pressure quickly.
- It can be opened immediately using the cold-water quick release method. Natural release method takes about 10 minutes.
- It has a stainless steel interior.
- It can be put away with other pots and pans, and the base can be used as a normal pan for cooking (without the pressure cooking lid).

Some disadvantages of the stovetop pressure cookers include:

- Usually it does not have a built-in timer (though these models are just starting to be introduced in Europe).
- It will take a little bit of time (maybe 3–4 recipes) to learn the right heat setting for the cooker to maintain pressure.

Electric Pressure Cookers

The advantages of electric pressure cookers include:

- It will automatically regulate the heat, so you can set it and forget it.
- It has a built-in timer that starts counting the pressure cooking time automatically once the cooker has reached pressure. Some also include delay and scheduling functions to begin pressure cooking at specific times.

Some disadvantages of using an electric pressure cooker are:

- Some operate at 15 PSI, others 13, 11, 9, 8, and even 6 PSI, prolonging the required pressure cooking times (see Appendix B).
- It only works with electricity.
- It takes longer to reach pressure because the heating element needs to heat up.
- It cannot be opened until the cooker *wants* to be opened (controlled by temperature and fuzzy logic). Natural release method can take 20–30 minutes as the integrated heating element cannot be removed for it to open faster.
- It comes with a removable insert, which is usually covered with non-stick coating. As of the writing of this book, only one electric pressure cooker manufacturer, Instant Pot, makes an electric pressure cooker with a stainless steel insert.
- It requires valuable counter space and proximity to an electrical outlet. It cannot be easily stowed away (they are usually quite tall).

Visit *www.hippressurecooking.com* for detailed pressure cooker reviews with photographs and comparative scores.

Pressure Cooking Times

The cooking times listed in recipes are sometimes shown for both high and low pressures. Each manufacturer defines high and low pressure differently, so consult your pressure cooker manual to be sure you have the correct pressure. The following tables show pressure ranges in Pounds per Square Inch (PSI), but your instruction manual might denote the pressure by kilo Pascal (kPa) or Bar (unit of measure to define pressure. You can use the table below to determine whether your pressure cooker fits into the standard definitions of High and Low pressures.

Pressure	Low	High
PSI	6–8	12–15
kPa	40–55	80–100
Bar	0.4–0.55	0.8–1

If the pressure in your electric pressure cooker does not fall within the ranges listed in the table above, for high and low pressure the pressure cooking time of each item and recipe will need to be adjusted. But don't worry, this book is written with this in mind and provides most cooking times in ranges. For example, "5–7 minutes." If your electric pressure cooker only reaches 11 PSI, or less, always use the higher number in the suggested pressure cooking time range (7 minutes in the example).

The pressure inside all pressure cookers is affected by external pressure. For example, if you live a high-altitude area, the cooking times for pressure-cooked foods will need to be adjusted. The general rule is to increase cooking time by 5 percent for every 1,000 feet above 2,000-foot elevation. This could mean just adding a minute or two to your cooking time or, at higher elevations, increasing the pressure cooking time by up to a third.

In addition, if you're using a stovetop pressure cooker, you may need to make adjustments to your cooking time depending upon your heat source. Some heat sources may include:

- **Electric or Halogen Cooktop:** These cooktops do not change temperature as quickly as the pressure cooker expects them to, which could scorch the food. To avoid this, start the pressure cooker on a high-heat burner while preheating a second burner at low heat. When the cooker reaches pressure, turn off the high-heat burner and carefully move the cooker to the low-heat burner while cooking under pressure.
- **Induction Cooktop:** Pressure cookers heated on induction cooktops reach pressure quickly (60 percent faster than gas or electric). This could result in undercooked food. Add 2 to 3 minutes of additional cooking time under pressure to compensate for the shorter time the cooker is heating before reaching pressure.
- **Gas Cooktop:** Follow directions and cooking times as given for standard pressure cookers in the recipes.

Pressure Cooking Times, in Minutes

Legumes	Nonsoaked	Soaked*	Pressure	Open Method
Adzuki	14–20	5–9	High	Natural
Anasazi	20–22	4–7	High	Natural
Black	22–24	4–6	High	Natural
Black-eyed peas	6–7	3	High	Natural
Borlotti	20–25	7–10	High	Natural
Cannellini	25–30	6–8	High	Natural
Chickpeas	35–40	13–15	High	Natural
Chickpeas, split	5–7	--	High	Natural
Corona	25–30	8–10	High	Natural
Cranberry (see Borlotti)				
Fava, dried	25–30	10–12	High	Natural
Fava, fresh	10	--	High	Normal
Garbanzo (see Chickpeas)				
Giant white(see Corona)				
Great northern	25–30	6–8	High	Natural
Haricots (see Cannellini)				
Kidney, white (see Great northern)				
Lentils, French green, green, or mini	8–10	--	High	Natural
Lentils, red or yellow (split)	4–6	–	High	Natural
Lentils, regular	10–12	–	High	Natural
Lima, baby or large	12–15	5–7	High	Natural
Mung	6–8	--	High	Natural
Navy, pea or white (haricot)	18–20	6–8	High	Natural
Peanuts, fresh	--	45–50	High	Natural
Peas, dried, whole	16–18	8–10	High	Natural
Peas, split, green or yellow	6–10	–	High	Natural
Pinto	22–24	4–6	High	Natural
Red kidney	22–24	5–8	High	Natural
Romano (see Borlotti)				
Scarlet runner	18–20	5–8	High	Natural
Soy, black	35–40	20–22	High	Natural
Soy, red (see Adzuki)				
Soy, yellow or beige	35–40	20–22	High	Natural
White (see Navy)				

*Soaked at least 8 hours, or overnight

Fish and Seafood	Minutes	Pressure
Calamari	15–20	High
Carp	4–6	High
Clams, fresh	4–6	High
Cod	3	Low
Crab	2–3	Low
Eel	8–10	High
Fish fillet	2–3	Low
Fish soup or stock	5–6	High
Fish steak	3–4	High
Fish, in packet (al Cartoccio)	12–15	High
Fish, mixed pieces (for fish soup)	6–8	Low
Fish, whole, gutted	5–6	Low
Frog legs	8	High
Haddock	6–7	Low
Halibut	6–7	Low
Lobster	8–12	Low
Lobster, 2 lb.	2–3	Low
Mussels	3–4	Low
Ocean perch	6–7	Low
Octopus	15–20	High
Oysters	4–6	Low
Perch	4–6	Low
Prawns (shrimp)	1–2	Low
Salmon	5–6	Low
Scallop	1	High
Squid	2–4	High
Trout	8–12	Low

Fruit	Fresh	Dried	Pressure
Apples	2–3	3	High
Apricot	2–4	4	High
Blackberries	8–10	–	High
Blueberries	8–10	–	High
Cherries	2	–	High
Coconut milk	5	–	Low
Cranberries	4–5	5	High
Figs	3	6–8	High
Grapes/raisins	2	5–7	High
Kumquat, slices	10–13	--	High
Lemon, wedges	15–18	--	High
Orange, wedges	15–18	--	High
Peaches	2–3	4–6	High
Pears, sliced	3–4	--	High
Pears, whole	5	4	High
Plums/prunes	4–5	8–10	High
Quince	10	–	High
Raspberries	1	–	High
Strawberries	1	–	High

Pressure Cooking Times, in Minutes *(continued)*

Grains, Rice, and Pasta	Liquid per Cup	Minutes	Pressure	Open Method
Amaranth	2 cups	8	High	Normal
Barley, flakes	4½ cups	9	High	Normal
Barley, pearl	2 cups	18–20	High	Natural
Barley, whole	2¼ cups	30–35	High	Natural
Buckwheat	2 cups	3	High	Natural
Bulgur	3 cups	8–10	High	Normal
Cornmeal (see Polenta or Hominy)				
Farro, semi-pearled	2½ cups	15	High	Normal
Hominy	4 cups	10	High	Normal
Kamut, whole	3 cups	10–12	High	Natural
Millet	2 cups	10	High	Natural
Oats, rolled	4 cups	10	High	Normal
Oats, steel-cut	3 cups	5	High	Normal
Polenta, coarse	4 cups	8	High	Quick
Polenta, fine (not instant)	3 cups	5	Low	Quick
Quinoa	1½ cup	1	High	Natural
Rice, arborio	2 cups	7	High	Quick
Rice, basmati	1½ cup	4	High	Natural
Rice, basmati (soaked)	1	1	High	Natural (10 min)
Rice, brown	1½ cups	20–25	High	Natural
Rice, brown (soaked)	1 cup	12	High	Natural (10 min)
Rice, jasmine (rinsed)	1 cup	1	High	Natural
Rice, parboiled	1½ cup	6	Low	Normal
Rice, pudding	3 cups	10	High	Normal
Rice, white long-grain	1½ cup	4	High	Normal
Rice, white short-grain	1½ cup	8	High	Normal
Rice, wild	3 cups	25	Low	Natural
Semolina	3 cups	4–6	Low	Quick
Spelt berries (see Farro)				
Wheat berries	3 cups	30–40	High	Natural

Meat and Poultry	Minutes	Pressure
Beef, brisket	50–70	High
Beef, cubed	10–15	High
Beef, ground	6	High
Beef, osso buco	20–25	High
Beef, oxtail	30–45	High
Beef, ribs	25	High
Beef, roast	25–30	High
Beef, round	50–60	High
Beef stock (bones, etc.)	45–60	High
Beef, tongue	50	High
Boar, cubed	15–20	High
Boar, roast	30–45	High
Chicken, breasts (boneless)	4–5	High
Chicken liver	3	High
Chicken, pieces (bone-in)	8–10	High
Chicken stock (bones, etc.)	30–35	High
Chicken, whole (up to 4 lbs/2k)	15–20	High
Cornish hen, whole	8–10	High
Deer, saddle	15	High
Deer, roast	20–30	High
Duck, pieces	8	High
Duck, whole	25–30	High
Elk, roast	25	High
Elk stew	15–20	High
Goat	15–20	High
Goose, pieces	15–20	High
Ham (see Pork)		
Hare	30	High
Lamb, chops	3–7	High
Lamb, ground	8–15	High
Lamb, leg/shank	35–45	High
Lamb, roast	15–20	High
Lamb, shoulder	20–25	High
Lamb stew	10–15	High

Meat and Poultry	Minutes	Pressure
Mutton (see Lamb)		
Pheasant	15–20	High
Pigeon	20–25	High
Pork, belly	35–40	High
Pork, chops or steaks	8–10	High
Pork, cubes	10	High
Pork, ground	5	High
Pork, ribs (steamed)	15–20	High
Pork, ribs (boiled)	10–15	High
Pork, roast	25–30	High
Pork, root/ham hock	35–40	High
Pork sausage (boiled)	5–8	High
Pork sausage (steamed)	8–10	High
Pork, shank	30–35	High
Pork, shoulder	45–50	High
Pork stew	15–20	High
Pork stock (bones, etc.)	45–60	High
Quail	7–9	High
Rabbit	15–18	High
Roast beef, medium	8–10	High
Roast beef, rare	6–8	High
Roast beef, well done	10–12	High
Squab (see Pigeon)		
Tripe	15	High
Turkey, breast (sliced)	7–9	High
Turkey, breast (stuffed or rolled)	20	High
Turkey, legs	25–30	High
Turkey, wings	15	High
Veal, chop or steak	5–8	High
Veal, ground	5–6	High
Veal, osso buco	15–20	High
Veal, roast	15–20	High
Veal stock (bones, etc.)	45–60	High
Veal, tongue	40	High
Venison (see Deer)		

Pressure Cooking Times, in Minutes *(continued)*

Vegetables	High Pressure	Low Pressure
Artichoke, hearts	2–3	5–7
Artichoke, pieces or baby	4–6	8–10
Artichoke, whole large	9–11	15–20
Artichokes, whole medium	6–8	10–12
Asparagus	1–2	4–6
Beans, fresh	--	15–18
Beet, cubed	4	6–8
Beet, whole (small, medium, large)	10, 15, 20	25–30
Beet greens	2	4
Bok choy	--	1
Broccoli	2–3	5–8
Brussels sprouts	4	6–8
Cabbage (red, green, savoy)	2–4	7 to 10
Carrots, sliced	1–2	3–4
Carrots, whole	3–4	5–6
Cauliflower, florets	2–3	5–8
Cauliflower, whole	6	8–10
Celeriac	3–4	6–8
Celery, sliced	2–3	6–8
Chard, Swiss	2	4
Collards	3–4	8–10
Corn, kernels	2–3	5–8
Corn on the cob	5	8–10
Eggplant	2–3	4–6
Endive	1–2	–
Fennel	2–3	5–6
Green beans	2–3	5–7
Greens, chopped	2–3	5–6
Kale, curly	2–3	5
Kohlrabi, pieces	2–3	5–8

Vegetables	High Pressure	Low Pressure
Leeks	3	5–8
Okra	2–3	–
Onions	3	5–8
Onions, baby	2–3	5–8
Parsnips	2–3	5–8
Peas	2–3	5
Peppers, bell	3–4	6–7
Peppers, small	–	1–2
Potatoes, baby or fingerling	5–6	8–10
Potatoes, quartered	5	8–10
Potatoes, small, new, or red	5	8–10
Potatoes, sweet	5	8–10
Potatoes, whole	12–15	18–20
Pumpkin, sliced	3–4	5–8
Rutabagas	3	5
Spinach, fresh	2	3–4
Squash, acorn, halved	8	–
Squash, banana, cubed	3–4	–
Squash, butternut, halves	6	–
Squash, butternut, large chunks	4	–
Squash, spaghetti, halved	9	–
Squash, summer (see Zucchini)		
Tomato, sauce	6	–
Tomato, slices	3	3–5
Turnips, sliced	3	8–10
Turnips, whole	5	10–15
Yams (see Potatoes, sweet)		
Zucchini	2–3	5–7

Standard U.S./Metric Measurement Conversions

VOLUME CONVERSIONS

U.S. Volume Measure	Metric Equivalent
⅛ teaspoon	0.5 milliliters
¼ teaspoon	1 milliliters
½ teaspoon	2 milliliters
1 teaspoon	5 milliliters
½ tablespoon	7 milliliters
1 tablespoon (3 teaspoons)	15 milliliters
2 tablespoons (1 fluid ounce)	30 milliliters
¼ cup (4 tablespoons)	60 milliliters
⅓ cup	90 milliliters
½ cup (4 fluid ounces)	125 milliliters
⅔ cup	160 milliliters
¾ cup (6 fluid ounces)	180 milliliters
1 cup (16 tablespoons)	250 milliliters
1 pint (2 cups)	500 milliliters
1 quart (4 cups)	1 liter (about)

WEIGHT CONVERSIONS

U.S. Weight Measure	Metric Equivalent
½ ounce	15 grams
1 ounce	30 grams
2 ounces	60 grams
3 ounces	85 grams
¼ pound (4 ounces)	115 grams
½ pound (8 ounces)	225 grams
¾ pound (12 ounces)	340 grams
1 pound (16 ounces)	454 grams

OVEN TEMPERATURE CONVERSIONS

Degrees Fahrenheit	Degrees Celsius
200 degrees F	95 degrees C
250 degrees F	120 degrees C
275 degrees F	135 degrees C
300 degrees F	150 degrees C
325 degrees F	160 degrees C
350 degrees F	180 degrees C
375 degrees F	190 degrees C
400 degrees F	205 degrees C
425 degrees F	220 degrees C
450 degrees F	230 degrees C

BAKING PAN SIZES

American	Metric
8 x 1½ inch round baking pan	20 x 4 cm cake tin
9 x 1½ inch round baking pan	23 x 3.5 cm cake tin
11 x 7 x 1½ inch baking pan	28 x 18 x 4 cm baking tin
13 x 9 x 2 inch baking pan	30 x 20 x 5 cm baking tin
2 quart rectangular baking dish	30 x 20 x 3 cm baking tin
15 x 10 x 2 inch baking pan	30 x 25 x 2 cm baking tin (Swiss roll tin)
9 inch pie plate	22 x 4 or 23 x 4 cm pie plate
7 or 8 inch springform pan	18 or 20 cm springform or loose bottom cake tin
9 x 5 x 3 inch loaf pan	23 x 13 x 7 cm or 2 lb narrow loaf or pate tin
1½ quart casserole	1.5 liter casserole
2 quart casserole	2 liter casserole

Index

Note: Page numbers in **bold** indicate recipe category lists.

Accessories, 18
Acidulated bath, 34
Adzuki Beans, 94
African Lamb Stew and Couscous, 183
All-American Mac & Cheese, 205
Aloo Gobi, 174
Amaranth, 223, 290
Amaretti-Stuffed Apricots, 259
Anise, 107
Appetizers, **19–30**
   Asparagus with Yogurt Crème, 22
   Baba Ganoush, 20
   Boiled Peanuts, 27
   Cipolline Agrodolce (Sweet and Sour Pearl Onions), 21
   Hummus, 23
   Lemon and Rosemary Cannellini Cream, 24
   Mini Cabbage Rolls, 30
   Spicy Black Bean Dip, 25
   Steamed Artichokes, 26
   Steamed Spring Rolls, 29
   Steamy Carrot Coins, 27
   Tomatillo Salsa, 28
Apples
   about: dicing, 257; nutritional value of skin, 256; slicing before cooking, 149, 257
   Brown Betty Apple Dessert, 264
   Cinnamon Apple Butter, 253
   Cranberry Applesauce, 257
   Only-Apples Sauce, 256
   pork with, 146, 149

Red Cabbage and Apples, 44
Stuffed Apples, 258
Apricots
   Amaretti-Stuffed Apricots, 259
   Dried Apricot Preserves, 242
   Dried Apricots and Plums, 263
   Dried Fruit Compote, 256
   Fresh Apricot Jam, 245
   Golden Fruit Compote, 262
   Peach-Apricot Preserves with Toasted Almonds, 251
Arborio Rice, 215
Artichokes
   about: cooking times, 292; eating stems, 26; preventing oxidation of, 34
   Garlic Braised Artichokes, 34
   Quinoa and Artichoke Hearts Salad, 232
   Steamed Artichokes, 26
Asparagus
   about: cooking time, 292; peak season for, 83
   Asparagus with Yogurt Crème, 22
   Creamy Asparagus Soup, 83
   Lemon Zest Asparagus, 33
Automatic release, 17

Baba Ganoush, 20
Balsamic and Fig Pork Chops, 145
Bamboo shoots, in Steamed Spring Rolls, 29
Banana Cream Custard, 277
Barbecue Pork Ribs, 147
Barbecue Sauce with Smoked Paprika and Molasses, 236
Barley. *See* Grains

about: cooking times, 290; soaking, 223
Barley and Gorgonzola Risotto, 224
Barley and Tuna Salad, 225
Pearl Barley, 224
Summer Barley Caprese Salad, 225
Whole Barley, 223
Basic Pasta, 209
Basic Tomato Sauce, 196
Basic White Risotto, 216
Basmati Rice, 210
Bavarian Kale, 51
Bay leaves, 186
Beans. *See* Green beans; Legumes
Beef and veal, **129–42**
   about: cooking times, 291; leaner cuts, 133; sliders, 146; tagine with, 155
   Beef and Guinness Stew, 133
   Beef Biryani, 134
   Beef Pot Roast, 180
   Beef Rogan Josh, 140
   Beef Stock, 72
   Bolognese Meat Sauce, 201
   Cincinnati Chili, 138
   Citrus Corned Beef and Cabbage, 136
   Easy Beef Stew, 182
   Greek Meatball Soup, 87
   Hearty Stuffed Peppers, 177
   Italian Boiled Beef Roast, 131
   Italian Summer Veal Roast, 141
   Mushroom-Stuffed Veal Roll, 139
   Pam's Osso Buco, 142
   Penne in Ragu, 204

Pot Roast, 135
Ropa Vieja, 137
Sloppy Joes, 132
South African Ground Beef
    Casserole (Babotie), 130
Texas Firehouse Chili, 137
Turkish Stuffed Eggplant
    Boats, 178
Vietnamese Beef Noodle
    Soup, 85
Beer BBQ Pork Sliders with
    Apple, 146
Beer-Braised Savoy Cabbage, 43
Beets
    about: cooking times, 292; heal-
        ing powers of, 35
    Beet and Carrot Salad, 45
    Braised Beet Greens, 36
    Golden Beets, 35
    White Beets and Greens, 37
Benefits, of pressure cooking, 12
Berries
    about: cooking times, 289; fresh
        and canned cranberries, 126
    Blackberry Jam, 246
    Blueberry Jam, 243
    Chocolate Berry Pudding, 272
    Cranberry and Walnut Braised
        Turkey Wings, 126
    Cranberry Applesauce, 257
    Cranberry Pecan Rice, 212
    Fresh Cranberry Sauce, 235
    Strawberry Jam, 244
    Wild Berry Black Currant Jam,
        248
Black beans. See Legumes
Black-eyed peas. See Legumes
Boiled Peanuts, 27
Bok choy, 38, 292
Bolognese Meat Sauce, 201
Boozy Taters, 56
Braised Beet Greens, 36
Braised Quail, 156

Broccoli
    about: cooking time, 292
    Broccoli and Citrus Salad, 33
    Broccoli in Lemon Sauce, 39
    Ginger Soy Pork Chops with
        Broccoli and Rice, 192
    Spicy Braised Broccoli, 39
Broccoli rabe, spicy, 40
Brown Betty Apple Dessert, 264
Brown rice. See Rice
Brussels sprouts
    about: cooking time, 292; his-
        tory of, 41
    Pan-Seared Brussels
        Sprouts, 42
    Red, White, and Green Brussels
        Sprout Salad, 41
Bulgur
    about: cooking time, 290
    Bulgur recipe, 226
    Bulgur Stuffing, 227
    Cracked Wheat and Chickpea
        Pilaf with Lemon, 227
Burritos
    Fish Burritos, 167
    Mexican Burrito Rice, 213
Butternut squash. See Squash

Cabbage
    about: buying, 43; cooking
        time, 292
    Beer-Braised Savoy
        Cabbage, 43
    Citrus Corned Beef and
        Cabbage, 136
    Mini Cabbage Rolls, 30
    Red Cabbage and Apples, 44
    Steamed Spring Rolls, 29
Calamari, tomato-braised, 171
Cannellini and Mint Bean
    Salad, 104
Caramel, 267, 279
Carnitas in Lettuce Cups, 151

Carrots
    about: cooking times, 292
    Beet and Carrot Salad, 45
    Carrots in Milk, 46
    Gingered Carrots, 46
    Steamy Carrot Coins, 27
    Thai Carrot Soup, 84
    Tie-Dyed Baby Carrots, 45
    Winter Vegetable Medley, 68
Catfish. See Fish and seafood
Cauliflower
    about: cooking times, 292
    Aloo Gobi, 174
    Cauliflower and Fennel Velouté,
        92
    Indian-Style Cauliflower and
        Potatoes, 63
Celeriac, cooking time, 292
Celery, cooking time, 292
Chana Masala, 105
Cheese
    All-American Mac & Cheese,
        205
    Barley and Gorgonzola Risotto,
        224
    Cheesy Penne Casserole, 204
    Italian Mac & Cheese, 206
    Jennadene's Ricotta Cake, 276
    Ricotta-Stuffed Zucchini, 176
    Three Cheese Polenta, 231
Cherries
    Dried Fruit Compote, 256
    French Cherry Clafoutis, 266
Chicken, **113**
    about: cooking times, 291; posi-
        tioning in pressure cooker,
        120; tagine with, 155
    Cajun-Style Chicken with Rice,
        193
    Chicken Bordeaux, 114
    Chicken Masala, 115
    Chicken Paprika, 119
    Chicken Stock, 70

Chicken—*continued*
    Chicken with Mushrooms in White Wine, 114
    Citrus Spice Chicken, 118
    Curry Yogurt Chicken, 121
    Herbed Chicken Stew with Dumplings, 191
    Italian Herb and Lemon Chicken, 116
    Jambalaya with Chicken, Sausage, and Shrimp, 179
    Mushroom Chicken with Potatoes, 189
    Quick "Paella," 194
    Satay-Flavored Chicken, 121
    Spanish Chicken and Rice, 185
    Spicy Ginger Chicken, 117
    Whole Beer-Can-Chicken, 120
Chickpeas. *See* Legumes
Chiffonade, 84
Chilis and stews
    about: "two-, three-, four-, and five-way" chili, 138
    African Lamb Stew and Couscous, 183
    Beef and Guinness Stew, 133
    Chickpea, Cannellini, and Barley Stew, 112
    Cincinnati Chili, 138
    Fast African Peanut Stew, 184
    Five Pepper Chili, 110
    Herbed Chicken Stew with Dumplings, 191
    Italian Chickpea and Barley Stew, 187
    Lentil and Black Bean Chili, 99
    Red Bean Chili, 105
    Texas Firehouse Chili, 137
    Turkey and Vegetable Stew, 181
    Veggie Chili, 111
Chipotle-Cilantro Black Beans, 99
Chocolate
    Chocolate Berry Pudding, 272

    Molten Chocolate Mug Cake, 273
Cincinnati Chili, 138
Cinnamon Apple Butter, 253
Cinnamon Brown Rice Pudding with Raisins, 275
Cipolline Agrodolce (Sweet and Sour Pearl Onions), 21
Citrus
    Broccoli and Citrus Salad, 33
    Broccoli in Lemon Sauce, 39
    Citrus Corned Beef and Cabbage, 136
    Citrus Spice Chicken, 118
    Lemon and Rosemary Cannellini Cream, 24
    Lemon Brown and Wild Rice, 222
    Lemon Curd, 254
    Lemon Marmalade, 250
    Lemon Poppy Seed Cake, 269
    Lemon Pot de Crème, 271
    Lemon Zest Asparagus, 33
    Mixed-Citrus Marmalade, 249
Coconut
    Coconut Fish Curry, 168
    Coconut Rice, 212
    Creamy Coconut Rice Pudding, 275
    Piña Colada Bread Pudding, 268
Cold-water quick release, 17
Collards
    about: cooking time, 292
    JL's Farro, Bean, and Collard Green Wraps, 174
    Southern-Style Collards, 47
Condiments and preserves, **234**–54
    about: determining gel point, 242; half full rule, 243
    Barbecue Sauce with Smoked Paprika and Molasses, 236
    Blackberry Jam, 246

    Blueberry Jam, 243
    Cinnamon Apple Butter, 253
    Dried Apricot Preserves, 242
    Dried Plum Sauce, 240
    Fresh Apricot Jam, 245
    Fresh Cranberry Sauce, 235
    Green Tomato Chutney, 240
    Lemon Curd, 254
    Lemon Marmalade, 250
    Mango Chutney, 238
    Mixed-Citrus Marmalade, 249
    Peach-Apricot Preserves with Toasted Almonds, 251
    Peach Jam, 247
    Rainbow Bell Pepper Marmalade, 241
    Strawberry Jam, 244
    Sweet Onion Relish, 237
    Tomato Chutney with Fresh Ginger Root, 239
    Vanilla-Spice Pear Butter, 252
    Wild Berry Black Currant Jam, 248
Cooktops, cooking with, 287
Corn. *See also* Polenta
    about: cooking times, 292
    Corn Chowder, 82
    Corn on the Cob, 48
    Creamed Corn, 49
    Roasted Corn and Brown Rice, 221
    Succotash, 112
Couscous, African lamb stew and, 183
Creamed Corn, 49
Cream of Chestnut Soup, 78
Cream substitute, 205
Creamy Asparagus Soup, 83
Creamy Coconut Rice Pudding, 275
Creamy Lima Bean Soup, 81
Crema Catalana, 278
Crème Brûlée, 280

Crème Caramel, 279
Cuban Black Beans and Rice, 186
Cuban Black Bean Soup, 86
Curry Yogurt Chicken, 121

Date Pudding, 267
Desserts. *See* Fruits and desserts
Dishes, for use in pressure
   cookers, 18, 61, 165
Dos and don'ts, 14–15
Dried Apricot Preserves, 242
Dried Apricots and Plums, 263
Dried Fruit Compote, 256
Dried Plum Sauce, 240

Easy Beef Stew, 182
Egg Drop Soup, 77
Eggplant
   about: cooking time, 292
   Baba Ganoush, 20
   Eggplant Caponata, 48
   Lighter Ratatouille, 67
   Spicy Eggplant Sauce, 198
   Turkish Stuffed Eggplant
     Boats, 178
Endive, cooking time, 292
Energy savings, 12

Farro
   Farro and Dried Porcini
     Mushroom Pilaf, 228
   JL's Farro, Bean, and Collard
     Green Wraps, 174
   Pearled Farro, 228
Fast African Peanut Stew, 184
Fennel
   about: cooking time, 292;
     edibility of, 50
   Cauliflower and Fennel
     Velouté, 92
   Milk-Braised Fennel, 50

Figs
   Balsamic and Fig Pork Chops,
     145
   Dried Fruit Compote, 256
   Fresh Figs Poached in Wine,
     262
   Turkey Thighs in Fig Sauce, 122
Fish and seafood, **158**–71
   about: clams not opening, 160;
     cleaning mussels, 159; cook-
     ing times, 289; tenderizing
     octopus, 170
   Barley and Tuna Salad, 225
   Catfish in Creole Sauce, 161
   Coconut Fish Curry, 168
   Fish Burritos, 167
   Fish en Papillote, 163
   Fish Stock, 71
   Gulf Grouper with Peppers and
     Tomatoes, 169
   Jambalaya with Chicken,
     Sausage, and Shrimp, 179
   Louisiana Grouper, 171
   Manhattan Clam Chowder, 90
   Mediterranean Steamed Fish
     Fillet, 165
   New England Clam Chowder,
     89
   Paprika Catfish with Fresh Tar-
     ragon, 169
   Poached Octopus, 170
   Red Snapper in Rice Wine and
     Miso, 166
   Steamed Clams, 160
   Steamed Mussels, 159
   Tomato-Braised Calamari, 171
   Trout in Parsley Sauce, 164
   Whitefish Fillet with
     Veggies, 162
Five Pepper Chili, 110
Foil slings, 61

French Cherry Clafoutis, 266
French Onion Soup, 80
Fresh Apricot Jam, 245
Fresh Cranberry Sauce, 235
Fresh Figs Poached in Wine, 262
Fresh Herb Polenta, 231
Fresh Tomato Sauce, 74, 196
Fruits and desserts, **255**–81. *See
   also specific fruits*
   about: fruit cooking times, 289
   Amaretti-Stuffed Apricots, 259
   Banana Cream Custard, 277
   Brown Betty Apple
     Dessert, 264
   Chocolate Berry Pudding, 272
   Cinnamon Brown Rice
     Pudding with Raisins, 275
   Cranberry Applesauce, 257
   Creamy Coconut Rice
     Pudding, 275
   Crema Catalana, 278
   Crème Brûlée, 280
   Crème Caramel, 279
   Date Pudding, 267
   Dried Apricots and Plums, 263
   Dried Fruit Compote, 256
   French Cherry Clafoutis, 266
   Fresh Figs Poached in
     Wine, 262
   Golden Fruit Compote, 262
   Jennadene's Ricotta Cake, 276
   Lemon Poppy Seed Cake, 269
   Lemon Pot de Crème, 271
   Maple Dessert Bread, 270
   Molten Chocolate Mug Cake,
     273
   Only-Apples Sauce, 256
   Pear Clafoutis, 261
   Pears Poached in Wine, 260
   Piña Colada Bread
     Pudding, 268

Fruits and desserts—*continued*
  Plum Pudding with Brandy
    Sauce, 265
  Quick Caramel Sauce, 267
  Spiced Peaches, 263
  Stuffed Apples, 258
  Tapioca Pudding, 274
  Vanilla Pot de Crème, 281
Fusilli in Spinach Pesto, 207

Game
  about: cooking time, 291
  Braised Quail, 156
  Rabbit Cacciatore, 157
Garam masala, 115
Garlic Braised Artichokes, 34
Gas cooktops, cooking with, 287
Gel point, determining, 242
Ginger
  about: fresh vs. ground, 46
  Butternut Squash and Ginger
    Soup, 79
  Gingered Carrots, 46
  Ginger Soy Pork Chops with
    Broccoli and Rice, 192
Golden Beets, 35
Golden Fruit Compote, 262
Grains, **202**–3. *See also* Barley;
  Corn; Rice; Wild rice
  about: cooking times, 290;
    pearl barley, 76; rinsing
    quinoa, 232; scorching
    polenta, 230
  African Lamb Stew and
    Couscous, 183
  Amaranth, 223
  Buckwheat, 226
  Bulgur, 226
  Bulgur Stuffing, 227
  Cracked Wheat and Chickpea
    Pilaf with Lemon, 227
  Farro and Dried Porcini
    Mushroom Pilaf, 228

Fresh Herb Polenta, 231
Herb and Quinoa Stuffed Toma-
    toes, 175
Irish Oatmeal and Fruit, 229
Italian Chickpea and Barley
    Stew, 187
JL's Farro, Bean, and Collard
    Green Wraps, 174
Mushroom-Barley Soup, 76
Pearled Farro, 228
Polenta, 230
Quinoa, 232
Quinoa and Artichoke Hearts
    Salad, 232
Steel-Cut Oats, 229
Three Cheese Polenta, 231
Three-Grain Rice Pilaf, 214
Wheat Berries, 233
Wheat Berry Salad, 233
Greek Meatball Soup, 87
Green beans
  about: cooking time, 292
  Green Bean and Pine Nut
    Salad, 56
  Green Bean and Potato
    Salad, 57
  Southern Italian Green Beans
    and Tomatoes, 55
Greens
  about: cooking times, 292
  Braised Beet Greens, 36
  JL's Farro, Bean, and Collard
    Green Wraps, 174
  Southern-Style Collards, 47
  White Beets and Greens, 37
Green Tomato Chutney, 240
Grouper. *See* Fish and seafood
Gulf Grouper with Peppers and
    Tomatoes, 169

Hearty Stuffed Peppers, 177
Heatproof dishes, 18, 61, 165
Heat sources, 15, 286–87

Herb and Quinoa Stuffed
    Tomatoes, 175
Herbed Chicken Stew with
    Dumplings, 191
Hummus, 23

Indian-Style Cauliflower and
    Potatoes, 63
Induction cooktops, cooking
    with, 287
Insert dishes, 18, 61, 165
Irish Oatmeal and Fruit, 229
Italian Boiled Beef Roast, 131
Italian Chickpea and Barley
    Stew, 187
Italian Herb and Lemon
    Chicken, 116
Italian Lentils in Tomato
    Sauce, 100
Italian Mac & Cheese, 206
Italian Rice Salad, 215
Italian Summer Veal Roast, 141

Jambalaya with Chicken, Sausage,
    and Shrimp, 179
Jasmine Rice, 210
Jennadene's Ricotta Cake, 276
JL's Farro, Bean, and Collard
    Green Wraps, 174

Kale
  about: cooking time, 292;
    nutritional value, 75
  Bavarian Kale, 51
  Portuguese Kale Soup, 91
  White Bean with Garlic and
    Kale Soup, 75
Kohlrabi, cooking time, 292

Lamb, **143**
  about: cooking times, 291
  African Lamb Stew and
    Couscous, 183

Mediterranean Braised Lamb Shanks, 154

Moroccan Lamb Tagine, 155

Leeks, cooking time, 292

Legumes, **93**–112. *See also* Peas

about: cooking times, 288; lentil varieties, 96; pressure cooking, 23; preventing gas, 88; red beans, 188; soaking, 88; Tex-Mex, 150; using dried, 94

Adzuki Beans, 94

Black Beans, 94

Black Bean Salad, 104

Black-Eyed Peas, 95

Cannellini and Mint Bean Salad, 104

Chana Masala, 105

Chickpea, Cannellini, and Barley Stew, 112

Chickpea Caprese Salad, 106

Chickpeas, 95

Chipotle-Cilantro Black Beans, 99

Cracked Wheat and Chickpea Pilaf with Lemon, 227

Creamy Lima Bean Soup, 81

Cuban Black Beans and Rice, 186

Cuban Black Bean Soup, 86

Five Pepper Chili, 110

Hummus, 23

Italian Chickpea and Barley Stew, 187

Italian Lentils in Tomato Sauce, 100

JL's Farro, Bean, and Collard Green Wraps, 174

Lemon and Rosemary Cannellini Cream, 24

Lentil and Black Bean Chili, 99

Lentils, 96

Lentil Soup, 74

Lima Beans, 96

New Orleans–Style Black Beans and Rice, 187

Not Refried Beans, 102

Pasta and Chickpea Minestrone, 88

Pinto Beans, 97

Pork with Black Beans, 150

Red Bean Chili, 105

Red Beans and Rice, 188

Red Lentil Curry, 101

Southern Black-Eyed Peas, 109

Soybeans, 98

Spicy Black Bean Dip, 25

Spicy Black Beans and Rice, 108

Split Peas, 97

Succotash, 112

Three Bean Salad, 103

Veggie Chili, 111

White Beans, 98

White Beans and Brown Rice, 107

White Bean with Garlic and Kale Soup, 75

Wild Rice and Black Soybeans, 106

Yellow Lentil and Spinach Curry, 101

Lemon. *See* Citrus

Lentils. *See* Legumes

Lettuce cups, carnitas in, 151

Lighter Ratatouille, 67

Light Mushroom Cream Sauce, 199

Light Scalloped Potatoes, 61

Lima beans. *See* Legumes

Louisiana Grouper, 171

Mac & cheese, 205, 206

Mango Chutney, 238

Manhattan Clam Chowder, 90

Maple Dessert Bread, 270

Maple-Glazed Ham with Raisins, 152

Mashed Potatoes, 62

Measurement conversion charts, 293

Meat, cooking times, 291. *See also specific meats*

Mediterranean Braised Lamb Shanks, 154

Mediterranean Steamed Fish Fillet, 165

Mexican Burrito Rice, 213

Milk-Braised Fennel, 50

Milk-Braised Pork Loin, 148

Mini Cabbage Rolls, 30

Mint, using, 52

Mixed-Citrus Marmalade, 249

Mixed Pepper Sauce, 197

Molten Chocolate Mug Cake, 273

Money, saving, 12

Moroccan Lamb Tagine, 155

Mushrooms

about: varieties of, 73

Farro and Dried Porcini Mushroom Pilaf, 228

Light Mushroom Cream Sauce, 199

Mushroom-Barley Soup, 76

Mushroom Broth, 73

Mushroom Chicken with Potatoes, 189

Mushroom-Stuffed Veal Roll, 139

Steamed Spring Rolls, 29

Turkey Breast with Mushrooms, 125

Mushy Peas, 52

Natural pressure release, 17

New England Clam Chowder, 89

New Orleans–Style Black Beans and Rice, 187
Normal pressure release, 17
Not Refried Beans, 102
Nuts and seeds. *See also* Peanuts
    about: fresh chestnuts, 78; toasting, 251
    Cranberry Pecan Rice, 212
    Cream of Chestnut Soup, 78
    Green Bean and Pine Nut Salad, 56
    Peach-Apricot Preserves with Toasted Almonds, 251

Oats
    about: cooking times, 290
    Irish Oatmeal and Fruit, 229
    Steel-Cut Oats, 229
Octopus, poached, 170
Okra, 193, 292
One-pot meals, **172**–94
    African Lamb Stew and Couscous, 183
    Aloo Gobi, 174
    Beef Pot Roast, 180
    Cajun-Style Chicken with Rice, 193
    Cuban Black Beans and Rice, 186
    Easy Beef Stew, 182
    Fast African Peanut Stew, 184
    Ginger Soy Pork Chops with Broccoli and Rice, 192
    Hearty Stuffed Peppers, 177
    Herb and Quinoa Stuffed Tomatoes, 175
    Herbed Chicken Stew with Dumplings, 191
    Italian Chickpea and Barley Stew, 187
    Jambalaya with Chicken, Sausage, and Shrimp, 179

JL's Farro, Bean, and Collard Green Wraps, 174
    Mushroom Chicken with Potatoes, 189
    New Orleans–Style Black Beans and Rice, 187
    Quick "Paella," 194
    Red Beans and Rice, 188
    Ricotta-Stuffed Zucchini, 176
    Spanish Chicken and Rice, 185
    Turkey and Vegetable Stew, 181
    Turkey with Mixed Vegetables and Potatoes, 190
    Turkish Stuffed Eggplant Boats, 178
    Veggie Biryani, 173
Onions
    about: cooking time, 292
    Cipolline Agrodolce (Sweet and Sour Pearl Onions), 21
    French Onion Soup, 80
    Potato Stuffed Onions, 54
    Sweet Onion Relish, 237
Only-Apples Sauce, 256
Opening pressure cookers, 17
Osso Buco, 142

Pam's Osso Buco, 142
Pan-Seared Brussels Sprouts, 42
Paprika Catfish with Fresh Tarragon, 169
Parsnips, cooking time, 292
Pasta, **202**
    about: cooking times, 290; pressure cooking, 208, 209; shapes of, 209
    All-American Mac & Cheese, 205
    Basic Pasta, 209
    Cheesy Penne Casserole, 204
    Fusilli in Spinach Pesto, 207
    Italian Mac & Cheese, 206

Penne in Ragu, 204
    Spicy Tomato Pasta, 208
Pasta and Chickpea Minestrone, 88
Pasta sauces, **195**–201
    about: cooking time, 292; distributing heat of pepper, 198; ragu don'ts, 100
    Basic Tomato Sauce, 196
    Bolognese Meat Sauce, 201
    Fresh Tomato Sauce, 196
    Light Mushroom Cream Sauce, 199
    Mixed Pepper Sauce, 197
    Quick Sausage Ragu, 200
    Spicy Eggplant Sauce, 198
    Spinach Pesto, 207
Peaches
    Golden Fruit Compote, 262
    Peach-Apricot Preserves with Toasted Almonds, 251
    Peach Jam, 247
    Spiced Peaches, 263
Peanuts
    about: Cajun seasoning with, 27
    Boiled Peanuts, 27
    Brown Rice with Peanuts, 220
    Fast African Peanut Stew, 184
Pearl Barley, 224
Pearled Farro, 228
Pears
    about: cooking, 260
    Pear Clafoutis, 261
    Pears Poached in Wine, 260
    Vanilla-Spice Pear Butter, 252
Peas
    about: cooking time, 292; ham and, 91
    Mushy Peas, 52
    Split Peas, 97
    Split-Pea Soup, 90

Veggie Rice Pilaf, 214
Penne in Ragu, 204
Peperonata (Faux Roasted
    Peppers), 53
Pepper, heat of, 25, 198
Peppers
    about: cooking times, 292
    Five Pepper Chili, 110
    Hearty Stuffed Peppers, 177
    Mixed Pepper Sauce, 197
    Peperonata (Faux Roasted
        Peppers), 53
    Rainbow Bell Pepper
        Marmalade, 241
Peppery Brown Rice Risotto, 219
Petit Turkey Meatloaf, 128
Piña Colada Bread Pudding, 268
Pinto Beans, 97
Plums
    Dried Apricots and Plums, 263
    Dried Fruit Compote, 256
    Dried Plum Sauce, 240
    Plum Pudding with Brandy
        Sauce, 265
Polenta
    about: cooking times, 290;
        scorching, 230
    Fresh Herb Polenta, 231
    Polenta recipe, 230
    Three Cheese Polenta, 231
Pork, **143**
    about: cooking times, 291; peas
        and ham, 91
    Balsamic and Fig Pork
        Chops, 145
    Barbecue Pork Ribs, 147
    Beer BBQ Pork Sliders with
        Apple, 146
    Bolognese Meat Sauce, 201
    Carnitas in Lettuce Cups, 151
    Ginger Soy Pork Chops with
        Broccoli and Rice, 192

Jambalaya with Chicken,
    Sausage, and Shrimp, 179
    Maple-Glazed Ham with
        Raisins, 152
    Milk-Braised Pork Loin, 148
    Pork Roast with Apples, 149
    Pork Sausage Hoagies, 144
    Pork Sausage with Bell Peppers
        and Onions, 144
    Pork with Black Beans, 150
    Quick Sausage Ragu, 200
    Sesame Pork with
        Pineapple, 153
Portuguese Kale Soup, 91
Potatoes
    about: cooking times, 292
    Aloo Gobi, 174
    Boozy Taters, 56
    Curried Yams and Potatoes, 59
    Green Bean and Potato
        Salad, 57
    Herb-Roasted Potatoes, 60
    Indian-Style Cauliflower and
        Potatoes, 63
    Light Scalloped Potatoes, 61
    Mashed Potatoes, 62
    Mushroom Chicken with
        Potatoes, 189
    Potato and Parsley Salad, 58
    Potato Stuffed Onions, 54
    Re-Fashioned Potato Soup, 77
    Turkey with Mixed Vegetables
        and Potatoes, 190
    Winter Vegetable Medley, 68
Pot Roast, 135
Poultry. See Chicken; Game;
    Turkey
Preserves. See Condiments and
    preserves
Pressure
    high and low, 17
    for recipes in this book, 18

releasing, 17
Pressure cookers
    accessories for, 18
    dos and don'ts, 14–15
    features and buying tips,
        282–85
    first generation, 13
    heatproof dishes for, 18, 61, 165
    heat sources for, 15, 286–87
    history of, 9–10
    opening methods, 17
    PSI of pressure, 17
    second generation, 13
    steamer baskets for, 18
    stovetop vs. electric, 284–85
    third generation, 14
    trivets for, 18
    types of, 13–14, 284–85
Pressure cooking, 11–18
    benefits of, 12
    heat sources types and, 15,
        286–87
    pressure ranges, 17, 18
    recipes in this book and, 18
    saving time and money, 12
    saving vitamins and energy, 12
    size/density of food and, 180
    step-by-step instructions, 16
    what it is, 12–13
Pressure cooking times, 286–92
    heat source adjustments for,
        286–87
    pressure levels and, 17, 18, 286
Pressure pans (braisers), 60
Pumpkin
    about: cooking time, 292
    Steamed Pumpkin, 64

Quail, braised, 156
Quick "Paella," 194
Quick release, 17
Quick Sausage Ragu, 200

Quinoa
about: rinsing, 232
Herb and Quinoa Stuffed
Tomatoes, 175
Quinoa and Artichoke Hearts
Salad, 232
Quinoa recipe, 232
Three-Grain Rice Pilaf, 214

Rabbit Cacciatore, 157
Rainbow Bell Pepper
Marmalade, 241
Ratatouille, lighter, 67
Red, White, and Green Brussels
Sprout Salad, 41
Red Beans and Rice, 188
Red Cabbage and Apples, 44
Red Lentil Curry, 101
Red Snapper in Rice Wine and
Miso, 166
Re-Fashioned Potato Soup, 77
Releasing pressure, 17
Rhubarb, 248
Rice, **202**. *See also* Wild rice
about: cooking times, 290; no-
rinse, 215; not rinsing brown
rice, 220; rinsing, 210, 211,
220; soaking, 210, 219; spring
roll wrappers, 29
Arborio Rice, 215
Basic White Risotto, 216
Basmati Rice, 210
Beef Biryani, 134
Brown Rice, 219
Brown Rice with Peanuts, 220
Cajun-Style Chicken with Rice,
193
Cinnamon Brown Rice Pudding
with Raisins, 275
Coconut Rice, 212
Cranberry Pecan Rice, 212
Cuban Black Beans and
Rice, 186

Ginger Soy Pork Chops with
Broccoli and Rice, 192
Italian Rice Salad, 215
Jambalaya with Chicken,
Sausage, and Shrimp, 179
Jasmine Rice, 210
Lemon Brown and Wild
Rice, 222
Mexican Burrito Rice, 213
New Orleans–Style Black
Beans and Rice, 187
Peppery Brown Rice
Risotto, 219
Quick "Paella," 194
Red Beans and Rice, 188
Roasted Corn and Brown
Rice, 221
South African Yellow Rice, 211
Spanish Chicken and Rice, 185
Spicy Black Beans and
Rice, 108
Three-Grain Rice Pilaf, 214
Tomato Risotto, 218
Veggie Biryani, 173
Veggie Rice Pilaf, 214
White Beans and Brown
Rice, 107
White Long-Grain Rice, 211
Zucchini Risotto, 217
Ricotta-Stuffed Zucchini, 176
Roasted Corn and Brown Rice, 221
Roasting veggies, 221
Ropa Vieja, 137
Rutabagas, cooking time, 292

Salads
Barley and Tuna Salad, 225
Beet and Carrot Salad, 45
Black Bean Salad, 104
Broccoli and Citrus Salad, 33
Cannellini and Mint Bean
Salad, 104
Chickpea Caprese Salad, 106

Green Bean and Pine Nut
Salad, 56
Italian Rice Salad, 215
Quinoa and Artichoke Hearts
Salad, 232
Red, White, and Green Brussels
Sprout Salad, 41
Summer Barley Caprese
Salad, 225
Three Bean Salad, 103
Wheat Berry Salad, 233
Satay-Flavored Chicken, 121
Sauces. *See also* Condiments and
preserves; Pasta sauces
Italian Salsa Verde, 131
Quick Vinaigrette, 162
Tomatillo Salsa, 28
Yogurt Crème, 22
Sauces (sweet). *See also* Condi-
ments and preserves
Quick Caramel Sauce, 267
Saucy Syrup, 268
Seafood. *See* Fish and seafood
Sesame Pork with Pineapple, 153
Slings, foil, 61
Sloppy Joes, 132
Soups. *See* Stocks, soups, and
chowders
South African Ground Beef
Casserole (Babotie), 130
South African Yellow Rice, 211
Southern Black-Eyed Peas, 109
Southern Italian Green Beans and
Tomatoes, 55
Southern-Style Collards, 47
Soybeans, 98
Spaghetti Squash, 64
Spanish Chicken and Rice, 185
Spiced Peaches, 263
Spicy and Minty Zucchini, 66
Spicy Black Bean Dip, 25
Spicy Black Beans and Rice, 108
Spicy Braised Broccoli, 39

Spicy Broccoli Rabe, 40
Spicy Eggplant Sauce, 198
Spicy Ginger Chicken, 117
Spicy Tomato Pasta, 208
Spinach
    about: cooking times, 292
    Fusilli in Spinach Pesto, 207
    Yellow Lentil and Spinach
        Curry, 101
Split Peas, 97
Split-Pea Soup, 90
Spring rolls, steamed, 29
Squash. *See also* Zucchini
    about: cooking times, 292
    Butternut Squash and Ginger
        Soup, 79
    Spaghetti Squash, 64
    Winter Vegetable Medley, 68
Steamed Artichokes, 26
Steamed Clams, 160
Steamed Mussels, 159
Steamed Pumpkin, 64
Steamed Spring Rolls, 29
Steamer baskets, 18
Steamy Carrot Coins, 27
Steel-Cut Oats, 229
Steps, of pressure cooking, 16
Stew. *See* Chilis and stews
Stewed Green Tomatoes, 62
Stocks, soups, and chowders,
    69–92. *See also* Chilis and stews
    about: chowders, 82
    Beef Stock, 72
    Butternut Squash and Ginger
        Soup, 79
    Cauliflower and Fennel
        Velouté, 92
    Chicken Stock, 70
    Corn Chowder, 82
    Cream of Chestnut Soup, 78
    Creamy Asparagus Soup, 83
    Creamy Lima Bean Soup, 81
    Cuban Black Bean Soup, 86

Egg Drop Soup, 77
Fish Stock, 71
French Onion Soup, 80
Fresh Tomato Sauce, 74
Greek Meatball Soup, 87
Lentil Soup, 74
Manhattan Clam Chowder, 90
Mushroom-Barley Soup, 76
Mushroom Broth, 73
New England Clam
    Chowder, 89
Pasta and Chickpea
    Minestrone, 88
Portuguese Kale Soup, 91
Re-Fashioned Potato Soup, 77
Split-Pea Soup, 90
Thai Carrot Soup, 84
Vegetable Stock, 73
Vietnamese Beef Noodle
    Soup, 85
White Bean with Garlic and
    Kale Soup, 75
Stuffed Apples, 258
Summer Barley Caprese
    Salad, 225
Sweet Onion Relish, 237
Sweet potatoes (yams)
    about: cooking time, 292
    Curried Yams and Potatoes, 59
    Winter Vegetable Medley, 68
Swiss chard
    about: cooking time, 292
    Swiss Chard and Vegetables in
        Parmesan Sauce, 65

Tapioca Pudding, 274
Tarragon, 123
Texas Firehouse Chili, 137
Tex-Mex, about, 150
Thai Carrot Soup, 84
Three Bean Salad, 103
Three Cheese Polenta, 231
Three-Grain Rice Pilaf, 214

Tie-Dyed Baby Carrots, 45
Time, saving, 12
Tomatillo Salsa, 28
Tomatoes
    about: cooking times, 292;
        peeling, 239
    Basic Tomato Sauce, 196
    Fresh Tomato Sauce, 74, 196
    Green Tomato Chutney, 240
    Herb and Quinoa Stuffed
        Tomatoes, 175
    Mixed Pepper Sauce, 197
    Southern Italian Green Beans
        and Tomatoes, 55
    Spicy Tomato Pasta, 208
    Stewed Green Tomatoes, 62
    Succotash, 112
    Tomato-Braised Calamari, 171
    Tomato Chutney with Fresh
        Ginger Root, 239
    Tomato Risotto, 218
Trivets, 18
Trout in Parsley Sauce, 164
Turkey, **113**
    about: cooking times, 291;
        protein from, 125
    Cranberry and Walnut Braised
        Turkey Wings, 126
    Petit Turkey Meatloaf, 128
    Turkey and Vegetable Stew, 181
    Turkey Breast in Yogurt
        Sauce, 124
    Turkey Breast with
        Mushrooms, 125
    Turkey Cacciatore, 127
    Turkey in Tarragon Sauce, 123
    Turkey Thighs in Fig Sauce, 122
    Turkey with Mixed Vegetables
        and Potatoes, 190
Turkish Stuffed Eggplant Boats, 178
Turnips, cooking times, 292

Umami, 40, 196

Valve release, 17
Vanilla Pot de Crème, 281
Veal. *See* Beef and veal
Vegetables and sides, **31–68**. *See also specific vegetables*
    about: cooking times, 292; frozen vs. fresh vegetables, 182; roasting vegetables, 221
    Bavarian Kale, 51
    Beer-Braised Savoy Cabbage, 43
    Beet and Carrot Salad, 45
    Boozy Taters, 56
    Braised Beet Greens, 36
    Broccoli and Citrus Salad, 33
    Broccoli in Lemon Sauce, 39
    Carrots in Milk, 46
    Corn on the Cob, 48
    Creamed Corn, 49
    Curried Yams and Potatoes, 59
    Eggplant Caponata, 48
    Garlic Braised Artichokes, 34
    Gingered Carrots, 46
    Golden Beets, 35
    Green Bean and Pine Nut Salad, 56
    Green Bean and Potato Salad, 57
    Herb-Roasted Potatoes, 60
    Indian-Style Cauliflower and Potatoes, 63
    Lemon Zest Asparagus, 33
    Lighter Ratatouille, 67
    Light Scalloped Potatoes, 61
    Mashed Potatoes, 62
    Milk-Braised Fennel, 50
    Mushy Peas, 52
    Pan-Seared Brussels Sprouts, 42
    Peperonata (Faux Roasted Peppers), 53
    Potato and Parsley Salad, 58
    Potato Stuffed Onions, 54
    Red, White, and Green Brussels Sprout Salad, 41
    Red Cabbage and Apples, 44
    Southern Italian Green Beans and Tomatoes, 55
    Southern-Style Collards, 47
    Soy-Glazed Bok Choy, 38
    Spaghetti Squash, 64
    Spicy and Minty Zucchini, 66
    Spicy Braised Broccoli, 39
    Spicy Broccoli Rabe, 40
    Steamed Pumpkin, 64
    Stewed Green Tomatoes, 62
    Swiss Chard and Vegetables in Parmesan Sauce, 65
    Tie-Dyed Baby Carrots, 45
    Turkey with Mixed Vegetables and Potatoes, 190
    Veggie Rice Pilaf, 214
    White Beets and Greens, 37
    Winter Vegetable Medley, 68
Vegetable Stock, 73
Veggie Biryani, 173
Veggie Chili, 111
Vietnamese Beef Noodle Soup, 85
Vitamin A, 38
Vitamin C, 38
Vitamins, saving, 12

Wheat Berries, 233
Wheat Berry Salad, 233
White beans. *See* Legumes
White Beets and Greens, 37
Whitefish Fillet with Veggies, 162
White Long-Grain Rice, 211
Whole Barley, 223
Whole Beer-Can-Chicken, 120
Wild rice
    about: cooking time, 290
    Lemon Brown and Wild Rice, 222
Wild Rice and Black Soybeans, 106
Wild Rice recipe, 222
Winter Vegetable Medley, 68

Yellow Lentil and Spinach Curry, 101
Yogurt
    about: yogurt crème vs. sour cream, 22
    Curry Yogurt Chicken, 121
    Turkey Breast in Yogurt Sauce, 124
    Yogurt Crème, 22

Zucchini
    about: cooking time, 292; cooking without water, 66
    Ricotta-Stuffed Zucchini, 176
    Spicy and Minty Zucchini, 66
    Zucchini Risotto, 217

Made in the USA
Lexington, KY
02 April 2017